International Series in Operations Research & Management Science

Volume 370

The book series **International Series in Operations Research and Management Science** encompasses the various areas of operations research and management science. Both theoretical and applied books are included. It describes current advances anywhere in the world that are at the cutting edge of the field. The series is aimed especially at researchers, advanced graduate students, and sophisticated practitioners.

The series features three types of books:

• Advanced expository books that extend and unify our understanding of particular areas.

• Research monographs that make substantial contributions to knowledge.

• Handbooks that define the new state of the art in particular areas. Each handbook will be edited by a leading authority in the area who will organize a team of experts on various aspects of the topic to write individual chapters. A handbook may emphasize expository surveys or completely new advances (either research or applications) or a combination of both.

The series emphasizes the following four areas:

Mathematical Programming: Including linear programming, integer programming, nonlinear programming, interior point methods, game theory, network optimization models, combinatorics, equilibrium programming, complementarity theory, multiobjective optimization, dynamic programming, stochastic programming, complexity theory, etc.

Applied Probability: Including queuing theory, simulation, renewal theory, Brownian motion and diffusion processes, decision analysis, Markov decision processes, reliability theory, forecasting, other stochastic processes motivated by applications, etc.

Production and Operations Management: Including inventory theory, production scheduling, capacity planning, facility location, supply chain management, distribution systems, materials requirements planning, just-in-time systems, flexible manufacturing systems, design of production lines, logistical planning, strategic issues, etc.

Applications of Operations Research and Management Science: Including telecommunications, health care, capital budgeting and finance, economics, marketing, public policy, military operations research, humanitarian relief and disaster mitigation, service operations, transportation systems, etc.

This book series is indexed in Scopus.

Fausto Pedro García Márquez • Benjamin Lev •
Huchang Liao
Editors

Outsourcing

Cases and Studies in Using Operations Research and Management Science Methods

Springer

Editors
Fausto Pedro García Márquez
Ingenium Research Group
University of Castilla-La Mancha
Ciudad Real, Spain

Benjamin Lev
Drexel University
Philadelphia, USA

Huchang Liao
Sichuan University
Chengdu, China

ISSN 0884-8289 ISSN 2214-7934 (electronic)
International Series in Operations Research & Management Science
ISBN 978-3-031-95392-7 ISBN 978-3-031-95393-4 (eBook)
https://doi.org/10.1007/978-3-031-95393-4

This Springer imprint is published by the registered company Springer Nature Switzerland AG
The registered company address is: Gewerbestrasse 11, 6330 Cham, Switzerland

Preface

This book aims to offer key theoretical frameworks and the latest empirical research findings on outsourcing within the fields of Management Science and Operations Research. It is designed for professionals seeking to deepen their understanding of the strategic role outsourcing plays across various levels of information and knowledge-based organizations. This includes outsourcing at the global economic scale, within networks and organizations, at the level of teams and work groups, in information systems, and at the individual level as participants in networked environments.

The book is targeted at professionals in areas such as energy, engineering, information science, mathematics, and economics, as well as researchers looking to expand their skills in outsourcing or integrating the discipline into their work. The contributors present original research or case studies, showcasing how outsourcing has been effectively applied in both practical situations and theoretical models.

Ciudad Real, Spain — Fausto Pedro Garcia Marquez
Philadelphia, PA, USA — Benjamin Lev
Chengdu, China — Huchang Liao

Introduction

Outsourcing has become a crucial tool for industries, societies, and governments, making it an important area of study within Management Science (MS) and Operations Research (OR). This book introduces the intersection of outsourcing with MS and OR, beginning each chapter with fundamental concepts and exploring the benefits, advantages, disadvantages, real-world examples, applications, theories, and potential future developments. The content spans a broad range of topics, drawing examples from both private and public sectors. The book also delves into future trends and the evolving role of outsourcing.

Outsourcing is commonly employed to achieve faster results, reduce costs, distribute risk, enhance efficiency, and maintain flexibility. This book connects these aspects with MS and OR models, providing a comprehensive interface between engineering/technology and the organizational, economic, administrative, and planning strategies needed for managing outsourcing effectively.

The landscape of paid domestic work in South Africa is transforming, with a surge in professional domestic cleaning service providers. Chapter 1 examines the role of outsourced domestic cleaning service providers in shaping the domestic work sector in South Africa. Through qualitative interviews with clients and domestic workers, the study explores the advantages and disadvantages of outsourced domestic cleaning services. The findings highlight advantages such as access to professionally trained workers and increased flexibility for clients but also reveal potential disadvantages, including concerns about trust and the well-being of domestic workers. For domestic workers, outsourced domestic cleaning services provide access to employment, opportunities for vocational training, and teamwork that makes the job less isolating. However, the added layers of bureaucracy do not improve the working conditions or the well-being of domestic workers. Chapter 1 contributes to understanding the complex and evolving nature of paid domestic work in South Africa and the implications of the growing trend of outsourced domestic cleaning services for both clients and domestic workers.

Chapter 2 delves into the complex relationship between outsourcing and job quality, focusing on time-related dimensions within the increasing facility management (FM) business. By analysing data from Spain, the study addresses the incidence of outsourcing in key FM occupations and explores the association between outsourcing and time-related dimensions of job quality. The findings reveal that while outsourcing can lead to better job security due to regulatory frameworks, it also results in higher instances of part-time work and scheduling flexibility pressures. Chapter 2 contributes to the broader understanding of outsourcing's impact on labour markets, highlighting the need for policies that mitigate negative outcomes while enhancing job quality.

Because solar photovoltaic (SPv) panels have seen such significant cost reductions in recent years, it has proven to be by far the most dynamic forms of renewable power generation. However, the transition from linear to circular is also crucial for building sustainability in SPv supply chains. The circular economy (CE) is appealing in part because of its ability to bring economic and environmental development objectives together to ensure sustainable production and consumption. To aid in the shift to a more circular economy, several circular-based strategies for various functions such as procurement can be developed. In Chap. 3, critical success factors to ensure a circular outsourcing structure in SPv supply chains are identified and scrutinized. To achieve this, a multi-criteria-based methodology is proposed. The findings of Chap. 3 argue that understanding the actual implications of not converting to circular outsourcing (C12) is the most significant cause of CSF. This study also provides several implications.

Many firms have outsourced most of their outsourcing tasks to third parties in recent years. However, traditional outsourcing procedures have challenges like centralization, data security, complex payment systems, time-consuming and costly dispute resolution methods, and the need for more trusted real-time tracking and monitoring systems. Chapter 4 delves into the paradigm shift from traditional outsourcing methods to new trustless and decentralized Blockchain-based outsourcing methods. Blockchain, with its core principles of decentralization, immutability, and transparency, is a primary candidate to solve the challenges of traditional outsourcing methods. The main objective of Chap. 4 is to explore the benefits of integrating Blockchain in outsourcing supply chain operations and management science methods. Moreover, Chap. 4 also investigates some real-time industrial use cases and research works. The chapter discusses the challenges in integrating Blockchain, potential solutions, and future research directions.

As limited evidence exists on the information technology outsourcing (ITO) practices in the South African financial services industry and the causal drivers thereof, the objective of Chapter 5 is to uncover these sourcing practices and their causal drivers using morphogenetic change theory. Morphogenetic change theory, as a specific instance of critical realist theory, was used to map the ITO decisions over the last 15 years at one of the largest banks in Africa. The causal factors of consolidation, Agile, DevOps, large-scale cloud migrations, and social factors, were identified as drivers for outsourcing and insourcing decisions. These findings enforced the usefulness of the morphogenetic framework in uncovering the causal factors and their dynamic interplay, which are unique to ITO contexts in the financial sector and developing countries.

Chapter 6 seeks to establish the consequences of outsourcing for workers and, more specifically, for workers' precarity. Several econometric studies have shown that there are differentials in working and employment conditions between employees of principals (firms that outsource) and employees of subcontractors. Other studies emphasize the precarity of self-employed workers. Taking the example of a sector that employs workers under four different kinds of status, Chapter 6 examines the links between outsourcing and precarity, emphasizing the notion of economic dependence. To do so, it is drawn upon several field studies to measure the level of dependence between firms and to characterize the nature of outsourcing relations. It is then turning our attention to the effects of outsourcing on two types of precarity: employment precarity and work precarity. These two types of precarity vary from one transport sub-sector to another. In long-distance transport, workers are more likely to be salaried and less vulnerable to precarity. In the parcel delivery sector, interfirm dependence is higher, increasing work and employment precarities. As for platform workers, they are the most precarious deliverers, combining various protection deficiencies. Through these examples, it is shown that the link between outsourcing and precarity is not uniform.

Chapter 7 aims to address the issue of the relationship between fiscal condition and local services outsourcing in the context of Italian municipalities, by attempting to answer the following research question: is the outsourcing of public services facilitated by the fiscal condition of the municipalities? Chapter 7 presents the results of an empirical analysis carried out on all the Italian municipalities. The analysis showed that outsourcing has a positive relationship with fiscal autonomy and a negative relationship with municipal debt. Therefore, the findings suggest that in Italian municipalities outsourcing may be seen as a "politics of good times" in line with other studies recently conducted in the European context.

Outsourcing, a prevalent business strategy rooted in cost efficiency, is a widespread practice across various industries. While this approach has proven effective in reducing expenses and enhancing overall efficiency, its application to the critical realms of war and security poses distinct challenges. Unlike profit-driven sectors, the defence landscape operates on a fundamentally different paradigm. Chapter 8 delves into the intricate rationale underpinning the outsourcing of war and security functions. It scrutinizes the economic, professional, and political justifications that drive organizations to externalize these essential functions, while also shedding light on potential pitfalls and far-reaching implications. By exploring the multifaceted dimensions of outsourcing in the context of war and security, this analysis aims to provide a comprehensive understanding of the motivations and consequences inherent in the strategic decision to outsource such pivotal aspects of national and international stability.

Chapter 9 outlines the role of management accountants and the impact of accounting information on decisions related to outsourcing organizational functions. The research study utilizes a combination of interviews, archival records, and documentation to collect and analyse data from a prominent Saudi organization currently having three major outsourcing agreements in its supply chain function: Third-Party Logistics, Offshore Purchasing, and Third-Party Manufacturing. The three cases demonstrate how management accountants have transitioned from merely supporting the decision-making process to actively participating in it. In these outsourcing cases, the role of management accountants is particularly evident in tasks such as risk analysis, supplier selection, cost analysis for projects and proposals, inventory record monitoring, performance measurement, and detailed reporting of key performance indicators (KPIs). Furthermore, management accountants are shown to play significant roles in addressing strategic issues through their involvement in multifunctional teams, which usually look more at operational processes than just functions. This integration indicates the depth of their engagement and underscores their significance in shaping organizational strategies and operational efficiencies in the context of outsourcing.

Maintenance contracts require outsourcing as a key element. However, the quality of the maintenance service providers' actions is crucial. In inspection maintenance, misclassifications are common and may fail to prevent accidents or lead to unnecessary actions. On the other hand, high-quality suppliers require a substantial amount of investment. To deal with this dilemma, Chap. 10 comes up with a hybrid inspection policy model that aids in picking a suitable supplier for maintaining a single-component system. The term "hybrid" is used to describe the combination of opportunistic inspections (i.e., random) and preventive replacement. Short intervals of opportunities could result in frequent and unnecessary replacements. In contrast, opportunities that occur over a long period may not be utilized for timely replacement. Therefore, a component age threshold (MΔ) is set so that only opportunities arising after this point are considered. This ensures that the replacement, originally planned for $K\Delta$, is anticipated to coincide with the opportunity's arrival, provided that the component is still functioning when the opportunity arises (after $M\Delta$). This proposal extends inspection models based on the delay-time concept and opportunistic actions. The cost rate and mean time between operational failures (MTBOF) are used to evaluate the performance of this policy. The effectiveness of it in assessing the quality of third-party inspectors has been proven. In general, the findings show that investing in higher-quality suppliers is worth it.

Crypto trading has become increasingly popular in recent years, as cryptocurrencies have gained wider acceptance and mainstream attention. Many traders are drawn to the potential for high profits, as the value of some cryptocurrencies has risen dramatically in a short period. Crypto trading can be risky and volatile, as the value of cryptocurrencies can fluctuate rapidly and unpredictably. Traders should carefully research and understand the risks involved, and only invest what they can afford to lose. The traditional way of investing in financial assets like Stocks, Commodities, and real estate has proven to be a good source of passive income. Although it is known that the markets tend to recover after every downfall, holding the assets through a financial crisis prevents the investors from the potential buying opportunities they had before the crash. Although cryptocurrency may yield astronomically huge gains overnight, there is also a huge downside. Monitoring of cryptocurrency trading is crucial for several reasons. It helps prevent fraud and scams, ensures compliance with regulations, reduces market manipulation, and protects investors from losses. Due to the lack of regulation in the cryptocurrency market, monitoring is essential for maintaining the integrity of the market and safeguarding investors. To overcome this, Chap. 11 employs automated forms of trading that can generate revenue. Bots are given a set of trading guidelines defined based on timing, value, amount, or mathematical models. In addition to offering profitable trading opportunities, algorithmic trading increases market liquidity and improves trade execution by minimizing the impact of human emotions. This proposed model uses Docker Compose with Python to automate trading and connect to various exchanges (Binance). Telegram is used here as an interface to manage transactions across various devices that support it. The benefits of automated trading go beyond the elimination of human emotions in trading. It can analyse large volumes of data faster than humans can, allowing for more efficient trades. Automated trading can also minimize the risk of losses, as bots can be programmed to sell when prices fall below a certain threshold.

The facilities management sector contributes towards the realization of many sustainable development goals (SDGs). Facilities management organizations must develop initiatives to meet the challenges, demands, and opportunities for sustainable development. With contemporary events, changing focus and needs, business process reengineering and uncertainties and reforms, ideas and strategies need to be carefully integrated to meet organizational goals in the short or medium term, and at the same time, consider sustainable principles. Outsourced facilities management should be beneficial to the organization in response to their needs and impactful within and outside the organization and consider sustainability imperatives. However, it is not clear what sustainability considerations should be considered by outsourced teams to ensure sustainability in facilities management. Chapter 12 assesses the consensus on sustainability considerations and practices in facilities management outsourcing (operations and management phase). A semi-systematic review was undertaken using literature from Scopus and Web of Science, published within 10 years. Environmental issues, social responsibility, quality of service, competence, performance, relationships, and time and cost savings were identified as the considerations. The identified practices were leveraging core competencies, monitoring and performance measurement, contingency relationship model adoption, technology adoption, stakeholder collaboration, alignment with organizational objectives, provider selection based on standards and records, clear expectations and agreements and flexible strategies, data or information management and supportive policies. The study's findings are beneficial to facilities management organizations and stakeholders in devising strategies to ensure sustainability in operations and management in a building's lifecycle.

It has been a pleasure to participate in these two volumes of "Outsourcing in Management Science and Operations Research" with Springer, the authors and the editors, Prof. Benjamin and Prof. Huchang Liao, excellent colleagues but better friends. Editors from Spain, the USA, and China, three continents. Also authors from many countries, e.g., South Africa, Spain, Turkey, India, France, Italy, USA, Saudi Arabia, Brasil, ... with different religions, political ideas, cultures, ... but something in common, the interest to contribute with their hard work done for the science to the acknowledgements of the humanity, which does not understand about borders. I feel very grateful and fortunate to be part of that process. My last words, but not least, I would like to dedicate this book to my mother, who will be always in my heart (Prof. Fausto Pedro Garcia Marquez, Universidad de Castilla-La Mancha, Spain).

It is with an enormously grateful heart that I share the publication of these two volumes of "Outsourcing in Management Science and Operations Research". My academic journey on a quest to share information, improve the functions of humanity, and gain wisdom in the process has been and continues to be an abiding source of joy in my life. I continue to enjoy watching the seeds of learning grow in unexpected directions around our beautiful planet with the inspirational generations of young people I have the privilege of teaching and learning from. Finally, as always, I want to recognize the greatest roles I ever played outside of academia and the classroom given to me by those I will forever hold most dear: husband, father, and grandfather. That first role began with my beloved wife Debbie 65 years ago whose memory remains a blessing in all our lives. Debbie gave me the precious gift of fatherhood through my loving son Ron (M.D), and devoted daughter Nurit (J.D., Lieutenant Colonel Retired, USAF). They in turn brought Melitza and Jim (Colonel Retired, USAF) into our lives leading to the paramount gift, our beloved grandchildren: Hannah (Carnegie Mellon University, B.S., Neuroscience), Jimmy (Virginia Polytechnic Institute, B.S. Clinical Neuroscience), Veronica, Sebastian, and Arya. I will close with a sincere thank you for the many years of continued professional and personal support, and a wish that your journey toward knowledge and wisdom may be as rich and enduring (Prof. Benjamin Lev, Drexel University, USA)

It was a really brilliant and enjoyable journey to work with Professor Fausto and Professor Benjamin Lev for editing these two volumes of "Outsourcing in Management Science and Operations Research". The insightful thoughts shared in those chapters were just like fresh air for me. I would like to express my highest gratitude to the authors who supported these two volumes. The experience of working with Professor Fausto and Professor Benjamin Lev will be unforgettable for me forever (Prof. Huchang Liao, Sichuan University, China).

Fausto Pedro Garcia Marquez
Benjamin Lev
Huchang Liao

UNIVERSITI MALAYA
Springer
THE EIGHTEENTH INTERNATIONAL CONFERENCE
ON MANAGEMENT SCIENCE AND ENGINEERING MANAGEMENT

Contents

About the Editors

Fausto Pedro Garcia Marquez Fausto works at UCLM as a Full Professor (Accredited as Full Professor from 2013), Spain, an Honorary Senior Research Fellow at Birmingham University, UK, a Lecturer at the Postgraduate European Institute, a Research Fellow at INTI International University & Colleges, Malaysia, and has been Senior Manager in Accenture (2013–2014). He obtained his European PhD with maximum distinction. He has been distinguished with the prices: Runner Prize (2023), Nominate Prize (2022), Gran Maestre (2022), Grand Prize (2021), Runner Prize (2020) and Advancement Prize (2018), Runner (2015), Advancement (2013) and Silver (2012) by the International Society of Management Science and Engineering Management (ICMSEM), First International Business Ideas Competition 2017 Award (2017), etc. He has published more than 283 journal papers (187 JCR: 92-Q1; 52-Q2; 39-Q3; 9-Q4), some recognized as: "Progress in Photovoltaics: Research and Applications" (Q1, IF. 8.49, one of the most downloaded in first 12 months of publications, 2023), "Applied Energy" (Q1, IF 9.746, as "Best Paper 2020"), "Renewable Energy" (Q1, IF 8.001, as "Best Paper 2014"); "ICMSEM" (as "excellent"), "Int. J. of Automation and Computing" and "IMechE Part F: J. of Rail and Rapid Transit" (most downloaded), etc. He is the author and editor of over 55 books (Elsevier, Springer, Pearson, McGraw Hill, Intech, IGI, Marcombo, AlfaOmega, . . .), >115 international chapters, and 6 patents. He is the Editor of 5 Int. Journals,

Committee Member more than 70 Int. Conferences. He has been the Principal Investigator in 5 European Projects, 8 National Projects, and more than 150 projects for Universities, Companies, etc. He is being: Expert in the European Union in AI4People (EISMD), and ESF; Director of https://ingenium.uclm.es; Senior Member at IEEE, 2021–...; Honoured Honourary Member of the Research Council of Indian Institute of Finance, 2021–...; Committee Chair of The International Society for Management Science and Engineering Management (ISMSEM), 2020–...; Research Fellow at INTI International University & Colleges, Malaysia, from 2023–...; Visiting Professor at Sheyang University (China) from 2024–2027; Advisory Board of the EU Project SunBio (Id: ID 101157493) 2024–2027. His main interests are: Artificial Intelligence, Maintenance, Management, Renewable Energy, Transport, Advanced Analytics, and Data Science. More information can be found at https://blog.uclm.es/faustopedrogarcia.

Benjamin Lev Professor Benjamin Lev is the University Trustee Professor 2014–2021 at LeBow College of Business, Drexel University, Philadelphia, Pennsylvania, USA. He holds a PhD in Operations Research from Case Western Reserve University. Prior to joining Drexel University, Dr. Lev held academic and administrative positions at Temple University, University of Michigan-Dearborn, and Worcester Polytechnic Institute. He is the Editor-in-Chief of OMEGA—The International journal of Management Science www.OmegaJournal.org; Co-Editor-in-Chief of International Journal of Management Science and Engineering Management; and serves on several other journal editorial boards (INFORMS JAA (formerly Interfaces), IAOR, ORPJ, Financial Innovation, OPSEARCH, IDIM, IIE-Transactions, ERRJ, INFORMS JOR). He currently holds faculty appointments at seven Chinese universities (Beijing Jiaotong University, Chengdu University, Nanjing University of Aeronautics and Astronautics, Nanjing University of Information Science and Technology, Nanjing Audit University, Xidian University, Tianjin University). Professor Lev is the former TIMS VP-

Meetings and INFORMS VP- Meetings. INFORMS Senior Fellow since 2003. He has published eighteen books, numerous articles and organized many national and international conferences including ORSA/TIMS Philadelphia; INFORMS Israel; IFORS Scotland; ALIO-INFORMS Buenos Aires; ICMSEM Philadelphia. https://en.wikipedia.org/wiki/Benjamin_Lev.

Huchang Liao Huchang Liao is a Research Fellow at the Business School, Sichuan University, Chengdu, China. He received his PhD degree in Management Science and Engineering from the Shanghai Jiao Tong University, Shanghai, China, in 2015. He has published 4 monographs, and more than 380 peer-reviewed papers, many in high-quality international journals including *Decision Analysis*, *European Journal of Operational Research*, *Omega, IEEE Transactions on Fuzzy Systems, IEEE Transactions on Engineering Management, IEEE Transactions on Systems, Man, and Cybernetics: Systems*, *IEEE Transaction on Cybernetics,* etc. He has been a Highly Cited Researcher (2019–2023), and a Highly Cited Chinese Researcher (2020–2023). He ranked within the top 2% Ranking of Scientists in the World by Stanford University (2020–2023). His main research interests include multiple criteria decision analysis, group decision analysis, fuzzy decision analysis, machine learning based decision analysis, and medical decision analysis. Prof. Liao has been elected to be the National Young Talent in China, the Fellow of IFSA, IET, and BCS. He is the Area Editor of *International Journal of Information Technology & Decision Making*, Associate Editor or Editorial Board Member of many top-tier international journals, including *Omega—The International Journal of Management Science*, *IEEE Transactions on Fuzzy Systems,* and *Applied Soft Computing*.

Outsourcing and Domestic Cleaning Services: Insights from Clients and Domestic Workers in South Africa

David du Toit

1 Introduction

This chapter has a dual focus. Firstly, it addresses the advantages and disadvantages for clients who outsource their domestic work to external domestic cleaning service providers providing cleaning in teams of three to five domestic workers. Secondly, it explores the advantages and disadvantages for domestic workers, who are employed by outsourced domestic cleaning service providers in South Africa. Paid domestic work is a global phenomenon, where mainly middle- and upper-class households employ mostly women from marginalized and poor backgrounds as domestic workers to perform domestic work duties such as cleaning, cooking, and care labor for payment (Du Toit & Casanova, 2025). Yet, the landscape of domestic work has transformed, with outsourced domestic cleaning service providers emerging as key players in the paid domestic work sector worldwide, including in South Africa. This shift has challenged the traditional dominance of privately employed domestic workers. Outsourced domestic cleaning service providers are formal commercial suppliers that render domestic work encompassing activities such as sweeping, vacuuming, dusting, scrubbing, tidying up, and laundering by professionally trained domestic workers (Abasabanye et al., 2016; Bailly et al., 2013; Du Toit & Heinecken, 2021). Outsourced domestic cleaning service providers highlight the necessity for rigorous screening and training processes, for more effective and efficient household cleaning. By positioning themselves as specialists in domestic work, they strive to differentiate their services from others (Bailly et al., 2013; Du Toit, 2016; Souralova, 2015).

D. du Toit (✉)
University of Johannesburg, Auckland Park, Johannesburg, South Africa
e-mail: daviddt@uj.ac.za

F. P. García Márquez et al. (eds.), *Outsourcing*, International Series in Operations Research & Management Science 370, https://doi.org/10.1007/978-3-031-95393-4_1

The following excerpt from a website of an outsourced domestic cleaning service supplier in South Africa highlights their approach to domestic work:

> The ironing basket is full, the living room looks like a bomb went off, the kitchen is a mess, and the bathroom, well, it's best to avoid speaking about the bathroom. But that's where our professional domestic cleaning services come in to transform your home back to its sparkling condition. With our professional house cleaning services, your home will be spotless and you'll have more time to spend with your family instead of doing household chores. We do everything from one-time deep cleaning to regular domestic cleaning. (Website—*Skitterblink Cleaning*)

Most outsourced domestic service cleaning providers compete against cheap private domestic workers, particularly migrants, and other domestic cleaning service providers offering perhaps similar services at more competitive rates. Employing various business strategies, such as advertising their firm's niche market, these suppliers seek to differentiate their products and services from others (Devetter, 2015; Hochschild, 2012; Lair, 2012). Some of these strategies include offering cleaning services on a flexible contracting arrangement for clients who seek household cleaning on an ad hoc basis. Some providers distinguish themselves by exclusively using environmentally friendly cleaning products, targeting clients who prioritize sustainability and eco-friendliness (Bittman et al., 1999; Souralova, 2015).

Not only is cleaning standardized, efficient and convenient for clients but outsourced domestic cleaning service providers also transform the bipartite personal employment relationship between employers and domestic workers into an outsourced tripartite employment relationship between clients (households who use these domestic cleaning services), domestic workers employed through domestic cleaning service providers and the managers or owners of these providers. This means that the outsourced domestic cleaning service providers are the *sui generis* employers of the domestic workers. However, clients still hold the authority to request certain tasks and may be held responsible if any unfortunate incidents occur involving domestic workers while on their premises. In essence, outsourcing provides clients with the advantage of being liberated from the intricacies of domestic work, as the selection, training, hiring, and termination of domestic workers become the responsibility of the domestic cleaning service providers (Du Toit & Heinecken, 2021; Hondagneu-Sotelo, 2007; Raz-Yurovich & Marx, 2019; Safuta & Camargo, 2019). Clients pay a fee for the service, while the management remunerates the domestic worker and derives profit from their labor power (Camargo, 2015; Napierski-Prancl, 1998).

In addition, several other factors contribute to the growth of outsourced domestic cleaning service providers. Firstly, contracting a domestic worker can be daunting, with unfamiliar labor legislation requirements adding stress, time, and costs for employers. For people who want to sidestep these complexities, outsourcing domestic work to cleaning service firms that handle all legal employment matters, is beneficial (Du Toit & Heinecken, 2021; Safuta & Camargo, 2019). Secondly, in European countries like Belgium, and France, engaging in outsourced domestic service providers brings financial benefits through state-initiated measures such as cash-for-care schemes, vouchers, subsidies, and tax incentives to clients (Bruck et al., 2003; Camargo, 2015; Devetter, 2015; Pérez & Stallaert, 2016; Safuta & Camargo, 2019). Thirdly, the flexibility offered by outsourced domestic cleaning service providers caters to unpredictable work schedules and job demands, providing clients with adaptable care and non-care options. Clients can book, terminate, or adjust services easily, fostering a harmonious balance between professional and personal life (Chung & Van der Lippe, 2018; Guendouzi, 2006; Lair, 2007; Lott, 2018; Morel, 2012). Finally, changes in family dynamics, particularly among middle-class households opting for smaller families or choosing not to have children, impact the demand for domestic work. In such cases, employing a regular domestic worker may seem unnecessary, making the flexible hiring of an outsourced domestic cleaning supplier a more practical solution (Du Toit, 2023a, b; Du Toit & Heinecken, 2021).

Outsourced domestic cleaning service providers play a vital role in facilitating employment opportunities for domestic workers (Sibiya & Du Toit, 2022). These providers often serve as formal employers, establishing work arrangements through legally binding contracts. By formalizing these agreements, domestic workers gain protection under labor laws, ensuring job security and stability to some extent. Additionally, regular vocational training programs, focusing on both physical and emotional domestic work skills, enhance the overall employability of domestic workers and contribute to the quality of service they deliver to clients. For migrant domestic workers, accessing employment through outsourced domestic cleaning service providers offers a crucial entry point into the workforce, particularly when conventional job search avenues are challenging (Du Toit, 2012; Du Toit, 2013).

However, limited studies have been done on the supply and demand for outsourced domestic cleaning service firms specializing in household cleaning in South Africa. In a country where domestic workers are available and affordable, what makes outsourced domestic cleaning service providers a role player in the domestic work sector in South Africa and what are the underlying issues of outsourcing domestic work? One way to answer this question is to explore the insights of clients buying into the outsourced domestic work services and the domestic workers who are employed by outsourced domestic cleaning service providers. Grounded in an ongoing process of data collection, this study draws on qualitative interviews with clients and domestic workers conducted over a decade. An argument is made that, despite some disadvantages, outsourcing offers instrumental advantages for clients and domestic workers that direct employment does not offer. To unpack this, the first section looks at the practice of outsourcing, followed by the nature of paid domestic work and outsourced domestic cleaning service providers in South Africa. Hereafter the research methodology and findings of the study are discussed.

2 The Practice and Theories of Outsourcing

Outsourcing can be defined as "a strategic relationship where an external organization brings value to another by taking contractual ownership of another's internal processes for a given time" (Mederos, 2021). Since the emergence of the post-Fordist era in the 1970s, characterized by a departure from traditional manufacturing practices, various factors such as neoliberalism, technological advancements, evolving consumer demands, and intensified global competition have driven organizations to cultivate greater flexibility, adaptability, and efficiency (Lair, 2019; Majumder-Russell & Burden, 2021; McIvor, 2010). Initially applied to manufacturing jobs, outsourcing has expanded over time to encompass service-related tasks. To bolster adaptability and efficiency, organizations have differentiated their workforce into a core group, associated with core competencies, and a peripheral workforce handling non-essential functions such as human resources, information technology, security, and cleaning (Halim et al., 2017; McIvor, 2010; Mederos, 2021; Zalewski, 2018).

The literature surrounding outsourcing explores various motivations prompting organizations to engage in outsourcing. A primary driver is a desire to limit labor expenses, achieved by delegating peripheral activities to specialized external suppliers (McIvor, 2010). Thus, organizational structures transform, adopting a leaner core comprised of permanent full-time employees alongside a larger peripheral workforce consisting of part-time, temporary, and outsourced workers, that comes with lower overhead costs (Davis-Blake & Broschak, 2009; Majumder-Russell & Burden, 2021; Strangleman, 2016; Vidal, 2016; Zalewski, 2018). This rationale aligns with the transaction cost theory, which posits that firms opt for outsourcing to minimize transaction costs associated with in-house production (Williamson, 1979). According to this theory, outsourcing becomes a viable strategy when the costs of coordinating and managing external suppliers are lower than those incurred through internal production. Still, critics argue that this theory only focuses on cost reduction while overlooking the strategic and relational dimensions of outsourcing (McIvor, 2010).

A second driver of outsourcing includes the strategy for organizations striving to adapt to the ever-changing market dynamics. It provides that flexibility is needed to navigate changing conditions effectively (Kalleberg, 2001; Mederos, 2021). The core competency theory, proposed by Prahalad and Hamel (1990) suggests, among others, that firms' core should be competitively unique, cater to changing customer demands and be accessible to a range of markets. In other words, firms should prioritize their core activities and delegate non-core functions to specialized external providers to give them a competitive edge. Consequently, firms achieve functional flexibility by hiring experts on a contract basis instead of maintaining costly full-time employees. Numerical flexibility is also achieved as firms adjust their workforce size in response to fluctuations in product or service demand through mechanisms like overtime, part-time work, shifts, and short-term and temporary contracts (Kalleberg, 2001; Majumder-Russell & Burden, 2021; McIvor, 2010; Mederos, 2021).

Thirdly, outsourcing also introduces a tripartite employment relationship involving clients, service workers, and external service providers (Alvarez-Galvan, 2012). Thus, the shift transfers physical activities and the legal, social, and psychological conditions of employment to the external supplier (Du Toit & Heinecken,

2021; Rubery et al., 2002). Legal contracts between clients and employees are largely absent, shifting most contractual obligations to the external supplier. These agreements typically cover matters like grievances, health and safety protocols, pay structures, and employee disciplinary actions, thereby alleviating clients of potentially burdensome responsibilities (Belcourt, 2006; Mederos, 2021).

However, the labor market segmentation theory provides a framework for understanding the drawbacks of outsourcing for employees (Doeringer & Piore, 1971). This theory argues that the labor market is divided into two distinct segments: the primary segment, characterized by stable, well-paid jobs with good working conditions and opportunities for advancement, and the secondary segment, exemplified by low-wage, insecure jobs with poor working conditions. According to this theory, outsourcing is a strategy used by firms to shift employment from the primary segment to the secondary segment (Doeringer & Piore, 1971; Webster, 2023). By outsourcing non-core activities to external providers, firms can reduce their internal labor costs and increase flexibility, but this comes at the expense of job security and stability for the outsourced workers (Theron, 2005; Webster, 2023). Outsourcing providers, driven by the imperative to minimize costs and maximize profits, often resort to short-term, temporary, or fixed-term contracts with limited job protection and service benefits (McIvor, 2010; Sibiya & Du Toit, 2022). This segmentation can reinforce existing social and economic inequalities, as the peripheral workers are often drawn from disadvantaged groups, such as women, minorities, and immigrants (Webster, 2023). Therefore, the labor market segmentation theory provides a critical perspective on the drawbacks of outsourcing for employees, emphasizing the need for policies and practices that promote decent work and equitable outcomes for all workers.

3 Domestic Work and Outsourced Domestic Cleaning Service Providers in South Africa

Similar to organizations outsourcing non-core functions, households increasingly rely on external service providers for domestic and care work. This includes hiring professional nannies, using surrogacy services, and outsourcing tasks such as gardening, pet waste management, and event planning (Ehrenreich, 2002; Hochschild, 2012; Lair, 2007). This section, however, first provides a background to the paid domestic work sector in South Africa, followed by a discussion of the practice of outsourcing within this sector, focusing on domestic cleaning service providers.

Paid domestic work is part of the fabric of South Africa, where slaves, and later on, indigenous and marginalized Black African women mainly performed domestic work for employers. The racial segregation of the White and Black people during the apartheid years, that occurred between 1948 and 1994, exemplified the notorious exploitation of Black African domestic workers by White employers. Without any rights, Black African female domestic workers were mainly employed as full-time live-in domestic workers, where they lived on the premises of their White employers in backyard rooms (Ally, 2010). Wages were precariously low and working hours long, often exceeding 16 h a day, usually 6 days per week (Du Toit, 2020; Jansen, 2015). In the last few years of apartheid, there was an increase in both full-time and part-time live-out domestic work. In this arrangement, domestic workers did not reside on their employers' premises but returned to their own homes at the end of the workday. The nature of the work changes little, where domestic workers have to manage time pressure to complete all the domestic work tasks within a workday and then travel long distances to their dwellings often on the periphery of urban areas (Du Toit, 2013).

When apartheid ended in 1994, rights were provided to all South Africans. For the first time, domestic workers were protected by labor laws. For example, the Labor Relations Act 66 of 1995 (LRA), the Basic Conditions of Employment Act 75 of 1998 (BCEA) and the Employment Equity Act 55 of 1998 (EEA) regulates the employment relationship and working conditions of domestic workers. In addition, Sectoral Determination 7 (SD7) was launched in 2002 and applied to all domestic workers. The SD7 aims to regulate and enforce minimum employment standards for paid domestic workers (Du Preez et al., 2010; Du Toit & Huysamen, 2013). The SD7 requires an employment contract between employers and domestic workers, specifying working conditions, duties and employment obligations (Matjeke et al., 2012; Persson, 2006). A minimum wage is to be paid to domestic workers, daily, weekly or monthly (Du Toit & Huysamen, 2013). Advance notice periods are mandatory and typically entail additional payments and obligations, as stipulated by the Department of Labour (2012).

Working hours are specified and standardized. Full-time domestic workers (whether live-in or live-out) are restricted to 9 h of work per day and 45 h per week from Monday to Friday. Part-time domestic workers are limited to 35 h per week, with overtime pay, if exceeded. Work on public holidays or weekends comes with additional payments (Department of Labour, 2012; Matjeke et al., 2012). Domestic workers are entitled to paid annual leave, maternity leave, and paid leave for family responsibility duties (e.g., funerals and weddings). Employers are also required by the Unemployment Insurance Act 63 of 2001 to make monthly contributions towards domestic workers' unemployment insurance fund (UIF). Employers are only allowed to deduct medical insurance and UIF payments from the salaries of domestic workers, and may not deduct any money for breakages of or damages to household items or clothing, meals, uniforms or work equipment (Department of Labour, 2012; Du Toit & Huysamen, 2013). Recently, the Department of Labor has introduced the uFiling system, a secure online platform designed to simplify the process for employers to register, declare, and pay UIF contributions for their domestic workers. This system offers convenience and efficiency. Additionally, domestic workers can use the uFiling system to apply for various benefits, including unemployment, maternity, and illness benefits.

As labor legislation was extended to domestic workers, there was a simultaneous rise in the presence of outsourced domestic cleaning service providers in South Africa. It is generally perceived as relatively easy to start a cleaning firm. Interviews with owners of such services indicate that initiating an outsourced domestic cleaning service firm involves several steps. These include registering the business with the Companies and Intellectual Property Commission (CIPC), obtaining tax clearance certificates or company tax verification documents, acquiring membership certificates from the National Contract Cleaning Association of South Africa, and securing compensation for occupational injuries and diseases (COID) certificates (Du Toit, 2020). These prerequisites are essential before engaging in employment and marketing activities within the domestic cleaning service sector.

The owners of outsourced domestic cleaning service providers tend to be White women whose incentive to start household cleaning services often stems from their experiences of being employers of domestic workers privately. Some are sizeable nationwide franchise domestic cleaning providers that operate in different regions in the country, while others are smaller, individually owned businesses, where household cleaning is provided in a specific area only, targeting particular domestic needs. Some specialize in a single service or provide a combination of domestic and laundering duties (Du Toit & Heinecken, 2021; Mendez, 1998; Souralova & Jelinek, 2018). Some domestic cleaning service providers render household cleaning through a sole domestic worker, while others perform domestic work through teams.

In the first case of sole domestic workers, one domestic worker performs agreed-upon domestic work duties that last a few hours. The service provider employs a domestic worker, but the client provides all the cleaning supplies and often instructs domestic workers on cleaning matters. Clients pay a fee for the services rendered, whereby the service provider pays a wage for the domestic worker and keeps the rest to cover expenses and for profit making (Fudge & Hobden, 2018). In the second case, cleaning is rendered through supervised teams, usually comprising three to five uniformed domestic workers, where cleaning is performed quickly within 2 or 3 h. Duties are divided among the team members, where (for example) one domestic worker cleans the bedrooms and scrubs the bathrooms, one sweeps the floors and tidy up the lounge and dining areas, and one cleans the kitchen and wash the dishes (Du Toit, 2012, 2013; Du Toit & Heinecken, 2021).

4 Research Design and Methodology

Since 2010, I have conducted research with outsourced domestic cleaning service providers in two economically and demographically distinct provinces in South Africa: Gauteng, the economic hub that includes Johannesburg and Pretoria, and the Western Cape, a tourist destination home to Cape Town and the Winelands. Although the exact number of outsourced domestic cleaning service providers in these areas is unknown, I have engaged in qualitative and quantitative research with approximately 20 such providers across both provinces over the years.

Applying an intersectional lens to the research reveals striking patterns at the intersection of race, class, and gender. Most of the outsourced domestic cleaning service providers in my study have been operating successfully for over two decades, indicating their long-term viability in the market. Notably, these businesses are predominantly owned by White women, while the domestic workers they employ are exclusively Black African or Colored (Mixed-race) women. This division of labor along racial and gender lines reflects the persistent inequalities and power dynamics that have shaped South Africa's domestic work sector historically (Ally, 2010; Jansen, 2015).

Most of the domestic cleaning service providers in the study employ between 20 and 40 domestic workers, typically on annually renewable fixed-term contracts. The clientele of these providers is primarily middle- and upper-class households, with most providers serving 50–80 clients per month. Clients engage these services on varying schedules, from weekly or bi-weekly to twice-monthly or ad hoc basis. Prices per cleaning session range from R350 (USD 18) to R800 (USD 40), depending on the dwelling's size and the specified duties. These rates are nearly triple the cost of directly employing a domestic worker at the state-mandated minimum wage, highlighting the class-based nature of outsourced domestic cleaning services.

All interviews with domestic cleaning service providers' owners, managers, clients, and domestic workers were conducted with informed consent, recorded, transcribed, and thematically analyzed. To protect participants' identities and maintain confidentiality, pseudonyms were used throughout the qualitative research process, following ethical research practices.

By employing an intersectional framework to analyze the outsourced domestic cleaning industry, this research sheds light on the intricate interplay of race, class, and gender in shaping experiences and power dynamics within the sector. The stark racial and gender disparities between business owners and domestic workers, alongside the class-based profile of clientele, highlight how intersecting systems of oppression and privilege persistently influence the dynamics of domestic work in post-apartheid South Africa.

5 Clients' Experiences of Using Outsourced Domestic Cleaning Services

5.1 Positive Views on Outsourced Domestic Cleaning Services

This section outlines clients' positive experiences of outsourced domestic cleaning services. Most clients agreed that domestic cleaning service providers provide access to professionally trained and qualified domestic workers which is not always possible when hiring domestic workers directly. Ms. Brown, for instance, expressed this sentiment by stating:

> The companies put all the domestics through a training course and advertise that they are trained. They get certificates for each course that they've passed. They are professional and I don't have to train anyone how to iron or mop a floor. I've seen that they clean the bathroom

> from top to bottom, left to right. I believe the training of domestics sets these companies apart from ordinary domestic workers.

Domestic workers employed by outsourced domestic cleaning service providers undergo training emphasizing effective cleaning techniques, time management skills and attention to detail during the cleaning process. Clients can avoid overseeing or supervising domestic workers during home cleaning, as they trust that the trained professionals possess the necessary skills to clean their homes thoroughly and efficiently. A manager corroborated these sentiments by saying the following:

> I usually have an interview with clients before we start working there, to make sure what the client wants and expects from us in terms of cleaning. I also transfer this information to workers and then they know what clients expect. They also know the methods of cleaning. They know where they have to start and where they need to end so that the work is done fast, effective and professional.

Secondly, clients benefit from the quality control measures implemented by outsourced domestic cleaning service providers. These companies ensure adherence to high cleaning standards through sporadic inspections conducted by managers, supervisors, or team leaders. During these inspections, the quality of the cleaning work is assessed against established benchmarks. If any areas are found to be below the expected standards, the domestic workers are instructed to revisit and re-clean those specific areas. By outsourcing their cleaning needs to professional service providers, clients can have confidence in the consistent delivery of high-quality results. The service providers' commitment to maintaining strict quality control standards sets them apart from individual domestic workers, who may not be subject to the same level of oversight and accountability.

A third benefit of outsourcing domestic work is that clients have access to reliable and trustworthy domestic workers. This assurance is a direct result of management's meticulous selection and recruitment process when hiring domestic workers. This process involves thorough background checks, scrutiny of work permits, and verification of relevant documentation, all of which are standard practices before an individual is employed as part of the cleaning staff. The implementation of such a rigorous recruitment process not only ensures the competence and reliability of the domestic workers but also significantly enhances the overall level of professionalism within the domestic cleaning supplier. By choosing outsourced domestic cleaning services, clients are relieved of the complex and time-consuming tasks associated with the traditional hiring process for domestic workers. They can bypass the need to conduct interviews, assess qualifications, and navigate the intricacies of work permits and employment contracts.

Fourthly, clients also benefit from the safety and security offered by outsourced domestic cleaning services. Given the intimate nature of domestic work, which takes place within the private sphere of individuals' homes, many clients expressed unease about directly hiring domestic workers due to safety concerns. In response to these fears, domestic cleaning service providers prioritize employing reputable and trustworthy domestic workers. Through rigorous screening processes and background checks, clients mitigate risks knowing that the domestic workers entering their homes have been thoroughly vetted. Numerous clients acknowledged feeling safer engaging the services of domestic cleaning companies compared to hiring someone directly.

Fifthly, outsourcing proves advantageous for clients, offering more than just technical proficiency from domestic workers. The competency of these professionals is notably evident in their adeptness with crucial soft skills, further enhancing the overall quality of service. For example, communication with clients is managed by both domestic workers and the management of outsourced domestic cleaning service providers in a professional manner. Despite English not being the primary language for some domestic workers, the management ensures that all workers can effectively communicate in English when interacting with clients. In a country like South Africa, where domestic workers are often from poor educational backgrounds, where communication problems might occur, outsourced domestic cleaning service providers attempt to avoid this problem by employing domestic workers who understand and speak English, mitigating potential language barriers. Domestic workers employed by outsourced cleaning service providers also receive training in emotional labor skills, which encompasses learning how to interact with clients professionally and respectfully. Interviews with clients often highlighted how professional and friendly the team of domestic workers are. Professionalism extends to the communication between managers and clients too. Interviews with clients unveiled a practice where the management informs clients about any changes within the company, such as fee increases, alterations in training practices, changes in cleaning sessions or staff rotation. This proactive approach to communication contributes to a transparent and professional client-manager relationship.

Another advantage of outsourcing is the tripartite employment relationship that shifts contractual and emotional responsibilities from clients to management, minimizing involvement, dependency, and financial obligations between clients and domestic workers. Outsourced domestic cleaning service suppliers provide clients with contractual flexibility. During interviews, clients consistently highlighted the benefits of having limited involvement in the legal and administrative obligations of employing domestic workers. As one client emphasized, "One of the main benefits is that I do not get involved with the labor laws. I just pay the manager of this company a certain amount, and that's it. All the administration is given to her." Similar sentiments were shared in interviews with other clients too. Therefore, clients circumvent the legal, social, financial, and medical aspects of the employment relationship with domestic workers by contracting domestic cleaning service providers, where the management assumes these responsibilities. An owner of a domestic cleaning service supplier highlighted the benefit that clients have by outsourcing domestic work:

> People also choose household cleaning companies, because they do not want to get involved in the drama of employment contracts, unemployment insurance benefits or the hiring and firing of domestic workers. It is a lot of stress if you get involved with this and with household cleaning companies, clients avoid this stress. The client knows that everything becomes the responsibility of the company. They don't have any responsibility regarding the workers such as sick leave, pension payments and holiday leave.

Finally, outsourced domestic cleaning services provide clients with flexibility. Contractual flexibility is particularly advantageous for clients who go on extended vacations, allowing them to temporarily halt services while away and resume upon their return, often without any payment penalty. As explained by a client, "They know we leave for four months every year to go to our house in Greece, then we stop the services. When we come back, they work here again, and we don't need to look for someone new." This feature not only caters to the specific needs of clients but also adds convenience and continuity to the domestic cleaning arrangement. Domestic cleaning services also offer numerical flexibility for clients who need cleaning services on an ad hoc basis. For example, clients requiring a deep cleaning of their homes can utilize the services of an outsourced domestic cleaning provider on an ad hoc basis, without the obligation of a long-term commitment. This flexibility allows clients to address specific cleaning needs without the ongoing responsibilities associated with directly employing a domestic worker. However, despite the advantages, some clients have also reported negative experiences and consequences related to outsourcing their domestic cleaning needs to these cleaning service providers.

5.2 *Negative Views of Outsourced Domestic Cleaning Services*

This section delves into the negative consequences of outsourcing domestic work to domestic cleaning service providers, examining these repercussions from the perspective of clients. Insights gathered through interviews with clients have highlighted three prominent issues that emerge within the outsourced relationship when employing domestic cleaning service providers. Firstly, the challenge of trusting domestic workers surfaces as a concern for some clients. Multiple clients emphasized the significance of understanding a person's background, family dynamics, and previous work experience as crucial elements for establishing trust in the employer-employee relationship. Engaging domestic help through a domestic cleaning service supplier introduces a potential risk, as clients potentially find themselves in a situation where trust is placed in a third party, compromising security and safety. As one client pointed out, "If you don't know them and you haven't established a relationship with them, you don't know if they are trustworthy to be in your house."

Secondly, another concern among some clients is the perceived lack of control. In the context of an outsourced tripartite employment relationship, the management exercises authority over the roles and responsibilities of domestic workers, and clients are restricted from requesting additional favors directly from the domestic workers unless otherwise specified. While some individuals are content to surrender control, others find it challenging. The lack of control over specific tasks means that clients may find accommodating their changing needs and preferences challenging. This inflexibility can strain the outsourcing relationship, as clients may feel that the service provider is not responsive to their evolving requirements. When clients cannot customize the cleaning services to their liking, they may become frustrated and dissatisfied with the outsourced arrangement. This lack of adaptability can potentially impact the long-term viability and success of the outsourcing partnership. As a result, some clients may seek alternative solutions that better align with their cleaning needs. As expressed by one client:

> There is a lack of a clear understanding of what I as a client want and what they offer. They are also too strict in terms of what is included and excluded from what they offer. Everything I want extra, I need to pay extra for. With a maid, I can ask her to clean, and she does, without additional payment. With the company, I must pay for anything I want extra.

Clients may experience a sense of disempowerment when their concerns are not addressed or when the outsourcing company appears to prioritize its own interests over client satisfaction. This lack of control also extends to clients' limited ability to influence how domestic workers perform their duties. Despite the expectation that domestic workers receive training to carry out cleaning tasks effectively and efficiently, many clients have expressed doubts about the adequacy of this training. Some have voiced dissatisfaction, claiming that their homes were not cleaned to the desired standard, leading them to question the domestic workers' capabilities and the promises made by the outsourcing company (Du Toit, 2023a).

Furthermore, clients' lack of control is evident in the scheduling of cleaning services. When directly employing domestic workers, individual employers can set working hours that suit their preferences and schedules. However, this level of autonomy is often absent when relying on outsourced domestic cleaning services. As one client frustratedly noted, "The timeslot is not great, but I cannot change it. I had to take what I could. It is that slot or nothing." This inflexibility in scheduling can be a significant drawback for clients who value the ability to customize their cleaning services to fit their specific needs and routines. The lack of control over both the quality of the cleaning and the scheduling of services can lead to a strained relationship between clients and the outsourcing company. This could potentially undermine the overall satisfaction with the outsourced arrangement.

In an outsourced arrangement, the power dynamics shift significantly, with the management of the domestic cleaning service provider assuming control over key aspects of the service. The management determines the pricing structure and sets the standards for the quality of cleaning sessions, leaving clients with limited influence over these crucial factors (Du Toit, 2023a). The management also holds the authority to decide on the wages and employment contracts of the domestic workers, further solidifying their power within the outsourced relationship.

Given the vulnerability of the domestic work sector, some clients harbor hopes for improved treatment and upliftment of domestic workers when they are employed by an outsourced cleaning service provider. These clients believe that the formalized nature of the outsourced arrangement should lead to better working conditions and fairer employment practices for domestic workers. Yet, despite the expectation that management will adhere to legal requirements and ethical standards in their treatment of domestic workers, some clients are aware of instances where management has abused its power through inadequate compensation, lack of benefits, or unfair disciplinary practices (Du Toit, 2023a). Clients who prioritize the well-being of domestic workers may find themselves grappling with the realization that the outsourced arrangement while offering certain advantages, does not necessarily guarantee the improved treatment they had envisioned. One notable concern is the issue of inadequate payment for domestic workers, as illustrated by a client:

> I spend R350 [USD 25] per session. The lady that I've had ... she doesn't seem to get transport money, and that worries me terribly. How can they afford to, in today's circumstances, in the current economic times? I mean even the basics, bread, milk, all those ordinary things are expensive, and everything gets more expensive, including transport. I stopped using the company.

The unethical treatment of domestic workers by outsourcing company management can have profound and wide-ranging consequences. When domestic workers are subjected to mistreatment, it not only takes a toll on their physical and emotional well-being but also has the potential to impact the quality of service they provide. Domestic workers who are overworked, underpaid, or facing unfair treatment may struggle to maintain the high standards of cleaning and professionalism expected by clients. As a result, client satisfaction may suffer, as the quality of the cleaning services may decline due to the domestic workers' diminished morale and motivation. Furthermore, clients who become aware of the mistreatment of domestic workers may experience ethical concerns and a sense of moral unease. They may feel complicit in perpetuating unjust labor practices by continuing to use the services of an outsourcing company that engages in unethical treatment of its employees. In the next section, we will delve into the insights provided by domestic workers, shedding light on their experiences, aspirations, and the impact of outsourcing arrangements on their lives.

6 Domestic Workers' Experiences of Working for Outsourced Domestic Cleaning Services

6.1 Positive Views of Outsourced Domestic Cleaning Services

Scholarly literature frequently highlights the absence of written employment contracts for domestic workers, a mandatory safeguard that is often overlooked, leading to the precarious nature of their employment. However, insights gathered from interviews with domestic workers employed by outsourced domestic cleaning service providers revealed a different reality. Most of these workers have fixed-term employment contracts with the cleaning service supplier, that are renewed annually. This arrangement ensures a degree of job security and stability. One domestic worker expressed this sentiment, stating, "I know that I have a job. If one of the families moves away, I know I still have a job." This observation sheds light on the tangible advantages that formalized employment agreements within the outsourcing framework can offer to domestic workers, mitigating the uncertainties associated with traditional employment arrangements.

Entering into an employment contract with an outsourced domestic cleaning service supplier rather than an individual family not only provides a sense of job security but also serves as a possible deterrent against unjustified control and exploitation by clients. Within the traditional employer-domestic worker dynamic, the characterization of the domestic worker as "one of the family" is often a facade concealing underlying exploitation, abuse, and discrimination (Ally, 2010; Jansen, 2015). This relationship tends to be fluid, with employers fluctuating between contractual and familial perspectives based on convenience (Anderson, 2001). However, under an outsourced employment arrangement, clients are prohibited from negotiating with domestic workers to undertake tasks beyond the explicit terms outlined in their contracts with the domestic cleaning service supplier. If clients find themselves inclined toward a power struggle, they should address such concerns directly with the management of the domestic cleaning service supplier, who will try and solve it professionally. This contractual clarity establishes boundaries, mitigating the potential for exploitative practices within the employer-worker relationship.

Interviews with domestic workers employed by an outsourced domestic cleaning service provider further highlight the benefits of formalized employment, including assurances of wages, stipulated working hours, 15 days of paid leave annually, provision for sick leave, and the prospect of additional service bonuses. The contractual nature of their engagement with these service providers ensures adherence to labor laws, a safeguard that may not consistently apply in private employment arrangements. For instance, a domestic worker shared the following perspective:

> I know I will get my money at the end of the month. I know my working hours and it is fair. I usually take my leave at Christmas time to see my family. But the manager pays me for the whole month because that is what the contract says.

This quote reflects a sense of job security and fair employment terms for the domestic worker expressing it, sentiments shared by many other domestic workers too. The domestic worker seems confident about receiving their salary at the end of each month, indicating a reliable and consistent payment schedule. Working hours are transparent and fair, while there is the flexibility to take paid leave during the year. This not only speaks to the contractual agreements in place but also suggests a positive and supportive work environment where the manager honors the terms and conditions of employment and provides financial stability even during periods of leave.

In contrast to the traditional personal employer-domestic worker relationship, where domestic workers faced limited prospects for upward mobility and were reliant on the benevolence of their employers, outsourced domestic cleaning service providers present avenues for professional advancement. Notably, these domestic cleaning providers proactively offer growth opportunities, exemplified by promoting certain domestic workers to middle management or supervisory positions. This strategic move aims to cultivate loyalty and commitment to the domestic cleaning supplier but at the same time also elevate the status of these domestic workers. Domestic workers in supervisory roles are remunerated at a higher rate. Team leader positions are also available where they supervise team members and quality control in situations where direct managerial intervention may be impractical. This paradigm shift not only enhances the professional standing of domestic workers but also contributes to a more structured and supportive work environment. In addition, regular training also adds to their status of being professional workers. As one domestic worker said, "The training is good. I know what to clean when I go into a room. How to clean the rooms fast. I did not know everything before working here." An argument can be made that the skills of domestic workers undergo improvement when employed by outsourced domestic cleaning services, potentially equipping them with valuable capabilities for future employment opportunities if necessary.

Finally, being employed by a company alongside fellow domestic workers serves as an effective remedy to both isolation and monotony associated with domestic work. Certain domestic cleaning service providers go a step further by organizing cleaning teams comprising up to five members, tailored to the size of the homes they service. Insights from interviews with domestic workers highlight the significance of this team-based approach and formal employment. Working collaboratively in teams and being part of a larger organizational structure not only diminishes feelings of isolation but also mitigates the perceived monotony of exclusive employment with a single family. The friendships forged with co-workers in such team-oriented environments transform the domestic work experience, rendering it less alienating and mundane. However, not all domestic workers find employment in outsourced domestic cleaning services favorable. The next section focuses on the negative consequences that some domestic workers experience in an outsourced relationship.

6.2 *Negative Views of Outsourced Domestic Cleaning Services*

A primary challenge within the outsourced relationship is that some domestic workers lack autonomy in determining both the manner and timing of their cleaning duties. In private employment scenarios, domestic workers frequently have the liberty to decide the sequence of tasks, opting, for instance, to start with more physically demanding chores in the morning and saving activities like ironing for the afternoon. However, in the context of outsourced relationships, domestic workers find themselves directed on what tasks to undertake. For example, one domestic worker who was employed full-time by a family before said:

> Before this job here, I worked for a family from Mondays to Fridays. I only did laundry work on Tuesdays and Fridays. The other days I clean the rooms and kitchen. Now in this company, I have to do what they want [referring to the management].

The absence of the freedom to choose when and how cleaning tasks are performed could potentially lead to worker dissatisfaction and an overall decline in well-being. This issue is intertwined with another concern, namely the increased pace of work. Outsourced domestic cleaning service providers operate within a highly competitive market, competing with both rival cleaning providers and other domestic workers. The intense demand for efficiency and swift turnaround times in outsourced cleaning services can push domestic workers toward a rushed approach. Cleaning multiple homes in a tight timeframe may also compromise attention to detail, resulting in poor outcomes and the potential for client dissatisfaction. This situation could potentially affect domestic workers, leading them to feel obligated to apply extra effort to ensure client satisfaction. One domestic worker said the following: "We clean the house in two and a half hours, and then clean the next one. Every day, we clean three houses. At the end of the day, we are tired. I am very tired." The demanding pace of work can be strenuous and pose potential health risks for domestic workers.

Another issue raised by some domestic workers is the strict and unsympathetic behavior showed by certain managers toward their circumstances and needs. Many domestic workers come from economically disadvantaged backgrounds, often residing in informal settlements located far from the middle-class suburbs where they provide their services. The reliance on unreliable public transport can lead to situations where domestic workers arrive late to work or in some cases, may not be able to attend at all. Unfortunately, such occurrences are often met with hostile reactions from both management and clients. As one domestic worker said:

> I need to take the train or taxi and that is very inconvenient because some days, the trains and taxis strike a lot, then I cannot go to work and then everybody is mad at you. But it is not my fault. I want to work, but there is nothing I can do about it.

Domestic workers face additional pressure and economic strain to adhere to punctuality standards, as they may incur financial penalties for lateness, deducted from their already modest salaries. To avoid these consequences, they often need to find alternative transport arrangements when public transport is unreliable. Furthermore, living far from the middle-class suburbs where they work means that many domestic workers, particularly mothers, must leave their homes early. This can have a significant impact on their family life, as they may have to leave their children unsupervised or in the care of others, which can be emotionally taxing and financially burdensome.

Interviews with some domestic workers have emphasized that their working conditions have not improved significantly since joining a domestic cleaning service supplier. One of the primary issues faced by domestic workers is the issue of low wages, despite wage rates being regulated by the state. Several domestic workers disclosed that their earnings are insufficient to maintain a decent standard of living. However, the challenge is compounded by the fear that resisting poor wages, especially under an unsympathetic manager, might jeopardize their positions, as replacements are readily available. Thus, the outsourced relationship could expose domestic workers to exploitative management practices leading to poor working conditions, lack of job security, and limited avenues for workers to voice concerns, ultimately impacting their well-being.

7 Concluding Remarks

This chapter explored the effect of outsourced domestic cleaning service providers on the paid domestic work sector, highlighting the advantages and disadvantages for both clients and domestic workers compared to traditional employer-domestic worker relationships. In South Africa, societal shifts, such as more women engaging in full-time jobs, changes in household sizes, and flexible employment patterns, have created a demand for professional domestic cleaning services. Simultaneously, the paid domestic work sector has evolved from an informal, unprotected realm to a formalized industry regulated by labor legislation. As a result, individuals, particularly middle-class and white households, opt to delegate their domestic tasks to professional cleaning service providers, ensuring efficient, effective, and hassle-free cleaning services.

Domestic workers, who are predominantly black and from poor backgrounds, experience some advantages when employed by outsourced domestic cleaning service providers. Working in teams, specializing in tasks, building friendships and support networks, and receiving training can enhance their skills and overall work experience. However, an intersectional approach reveals that outsourcing may perpetuate and even exacerbate existing power imbalances and inequalities based on race and class.

For middle-class, white clients, outsourcing provides a convenient solution to their domestic labor needs, allowing them to maintain their privileged lifestyles without the burden of directly managing domestic workers. However, this arrangement can also reinforce a sense of entitlement and distance from the realities faced by black, poor domestic workers. Clients may prioritize their own comfort and satisfaction over the well-being and fair treatment of domestic workers.

Domestic workers, on the other hand, may find that the additional layer of authority introduced by the outsourced relationship adversely affects their agency, leading to heightened stress and poor well-being. The lack of control over the pace of work, increased workload, and fear of job loss can contribute to job dissatisfaction and compromised health. Moreover, the power dynamics inherent in the outsourced arrangement, with predominantly white managers and clients controlling the labor and working conditions of black domestic workers, echo the historical oppression and exploitation of black labor in South Africa.

The outsourced domestic cleaning services also introduce a deeper cultural shift in South African society, impacting the nature of relationships within employers' homes, which are also the workplaces of domestic workers. The traditional exchange of cultural and personal nuances in domestic work is diminishing, replaced by an impersonal, instrumental, and clinical tripartite employment relationship. This depersonalization is concerning as it erodes the societal fabric and reinforces the marginalization of black, poor domestic workers.

In conclusion, while outsourcing domestic work to cleaning service providers offers some benefits, it also perpetuates and even intensifies the intersectional inequalities faced by domestic workers in South Africa. Outsourcing does not fundamentally elevate the status or improve working conditions for domestic workers, who continue to bear the brunt of race and class-based discrimination. To truly address these issues, a more comprehensive and intersectional approach is needed, one that recognizes and challenges the structural inequalities that shape the domestic work sector and prioritizes the well-being and empowerment of black, poor domestic workers.

References

Abasabanye, P., Bailly, F., & Devetter, F. X. (2016). Does contact between employees and service recipients lead to socially more responsible behaviours? The case of cleaning. *Journal of Business Ethics, 153*(3), 813–824.

Ally, S. (2010). *From servants to workers: South African domestic workers and the democratic state*. University of KwaZulu-Natal Press.

Alvarez-Galvan, J. L. (2012). *Outsourcing and service work in the new economy: The case of call centres in Mexico City*. Cambridge Scholars Publishing.

Anderson, B. (2001). Just another job? Paying for domestic work. *Gender and Development, 9*(1), 25–33.

Bailly, F., Devetter, F. X., & Horn, F. (2013). Can working and employment conditions in the personal services sector be improved? *Cambridge Journal of Economics, 37*, 299–321.

Belcourt, M. (2006). Outsourcing—The benefits and the risks. *Human Resource Management Review, 16*, 269–279.

Bittman, M., Matheson, G., & Meagher, G. (1999). The changing boundary between home and market: Australian trends in outsourcing domestic labour. *Work, Employment & Society, 13*(2), 249–273.

Bruck, T., Haisen-DeNew, J. P., & Zimmerman, K. F. (2003). *Creating low-skilled jobs by subsidizing market-contracted household work. The future of labor*, Discussion Paper No. 958, December 2003. Available online: www.iza.org

Camargo, B. (2015). Outsourcing housework: Clients, agencies and the voucher system in Brussels. In A. Triandafyllidou & S. Marchetti (Eds.), *Employers, agencies and immigration: Care work in Europe*. Ashgate.

Chung, H., & Van der Lippe, T. (2018). Flexible working, work–life balance, and gender equality: Introduction. *Social Indicators Research*, 1–17.

Davis-Blake, A., & Broschak, J. P. (2009). Outsourcing and the changing nature of work. *Annual Review of Sociology, 35*, 321–340.

Department of Labour. (2012). *Domestic workers: What you should know, minimum wages and conditions of employment.* Available online: https://www.labourguide.co.za/workshop/161-domesticworker2012pdf-1/file

Devetter, F. X. (2015). Can public policies bring about the democratisation of the outsourcing of household tasks? *Review of Radical Political Economics, 48*(3), 363–395.

Doeringer, P. B., & Piore, M. J. (1971). *Internal labor markets and manpower analysis*. Lexington. D.C. Heath.

Du Preez, J., Beswick, C., Whittaker, L., & Dickinson, D. (2010). The employment relationship in the domestic workplace in South Africa: Beyond apartheid legacy. *Social Dynamics, 36*, 395–409.

Du Toit, D. (2012). *"For better or worse": Domestic work and outsourced housecleaning services in Stellenbosch*. Unpublished Master's thesis. Stellenbosch University.

Du Toit, D. (2013). From "Cinderella cleaners" to "maids from heaven": Clients' and domestic workers' perceptions of housecleaning services in Stellenbosch. *South African Journal of Labour Relations, 37*(1), 97–114.

Du Toit, D. (2016). "We cannot discriminate against someone without an eye or a leg... But I do look at obesity": Statistical discrimination and employers' recruitment strategies at housecleaning companies in Johannesburg. *South African Journal of Labour Relations, 40*(1), 25–41.

Du Toit, D. (2020). *Cleaning up: The use of outsourced domestic cleaning services in South Africa*. Unpublished PhD Dissertation. University of Stellenbosch.

Du Toit, D. (2023a). Paid domestic work and outsourcing in South Africa: Clients' views on trust, control and power relations. *Current Sociology, 71*(6), 1063–1081.

Du Toit, D. (2023b). Do different types of households use outsourced domestic cleaning Services for Different Reasons? An explorative study in South Africa. *Sociological Research Online, 28*(3), 681–697.

Du Toit, D., & Casanova, E. (2025). Polishing the pearl of the pacific and the city of gold: Paid domestic work in Guayaquil, Ecuador and Johannesburg, South Africa. Women's Studies: International Forum, 109, 103055.

Du Toit, D., & Heinecken, L. (2021). Is outsourcing better? Client's views of contracting in domestic cleaning services. *Employee Relations, 43*(5), 1147–1162.

Du Toit, D., & Huysamen, E. (2013). Implementing domestic workers' labour rights in a framework of transformative constitutionalism. In D. Du Toit (Ed.), *Exploited, undervalued- and essential: Domestic workers and the realization of their rights*. Pretoria University Law Press.

Ehrenreich, B. (2002). Maid to order. In B. Ehrenreich & A. R. Hochschild (Eds.), *Global woman: Nannies, maids, and sex workers in the new economy*. Owl Books.

Fudge, J., & Hobden, C. (2018). *Conceptualising the role of intermediaries in formalising domestic work*. International Labour Office.

Guendouzi, J. (2006). "The guilt thing": Balancing domestic and professional roles. *Journal of Marriage and Family, 68*, 901–909.

Halim, H. A., Ahmad, N. H., Ho, T. C. F., & Ramayah, T. (2017). The outsourcing dilemma on the decision to outsource among small and medium enterprises in Malaysia. *Global Business Review, 18*(2), 348–364.

Hochschild, A. R. (2012). *The outsourced self: What happens when we pay others to live our lives for us?* Picador.

Hondagneu-Sotelo, P. (2007). *Domestica: Immigrant workers cleaning and caring in the shadows of affluence* (2nd ed.). University of California Press.

Jansen, E. (2015). *Soos familie: Stedelike huiswerkers in Suid-Afrikaanse tekste. (Like family: Urban domestic workers in South African texts)*. Protea Boekhuis.

Kalleberg, A. L. (2001). Organizing flexibility: The flexible firm in a new century. *British Journal of Industrial Relations, 39*, 479–504.

Lair, C. D. (2007). *The outsourcing of intimate affairs*. Unpublished PhD dissertation. The University of Maryland.

Lair, C. D. (2012). Outsourcing and the contracting of responsibility. *Sociological Inquiry, 82*(4), 557–577.

Lair, C. D. (2019). Outsourcing and the risks of dependent autonomy. *SAGE Open*, 1–12.

Lott, Y. (2018). Does flexibility help employees switch off from work? Flexible working-time arrangements and cognitive work-to-home spillover for women and men in Germany. *Social Indicators Research*, 1–24.

Majumder-Russell, D., & Burden, K. (2021). *Outsourcing: A practical guide*. Globe Law and Business Limited.

Matjeke, A., Viljoen, J. M., & Blaauw, P. F. (2012). The effect of labour market regulation on domestic workers in orchards and Soshanguve, Pretoria. *South African Journal of Human Resource Management, 10*(1), 1–7.

McIvor, R. (2010). *Global service outsourcing*. Cambridge University Press.

Mederos, L. A. (2021). *The future of outsourcing: Strategic outsourcing controls and the backsourcing evolution*. Springer International Publishing.

Mendez, J. (1998). Of mops and maids: Contradictions and continuities in bureaucratized domestic work. *Social Problems, 45*(1), 114–135.
Morel, N. (2012). *The political economy of domestic work in France and Sweden from a European perspective*. Online available: https://hal-sciencespo.archives-ouvertes.fr/hal-01070392/document
Napierski-Prancl, M. (1998). *From domestic servant to service firm employee: An investigation into the occupational restructuring of the job of maid*. Unpublished Ph.D. thesis. State University of New York at Albany.
Pérez, I., & Stallaert, C. (2016). The professionalization of paid domestic work and its limits: Experiences of Latin American migrants in Brussels. *European Journal of Women's Studies, 23*(2), 155–168.
Persson, A. J. (2006). The contract of employment. *Ethical Dimensions, 66*(4), 407–415.
Prahalad, C. K., & Hamel, G. (1990). The core competence of the corporation. *Harvard Business Review, 68*(3), 79–92.
Raz-Yurovich, L., & Marx, I. (2019). Outsourcing housework and highly skilled women's labour force participation: An analysis of policy intervention. *European Sociological Review, 35*(2), 205–224.
Rubery, J., Earnshaw, J., Marchington, M., Cooke, F. L., & Vincent, S. (2002). Changing organisational forms and the employment relationship. *Journal of Management Studies, 39*(5), 645–672.
Safuta, A., & Camargo, B. (2019). The more things change, the more they stay the same? The impact of formalising policies on personalisation in paid domestic work - the case of the service voucher in Belgium. *Comparative Migration Studies, 7*(14), 1–18.
Sibiya, W., & Du Toit, D. (2022). Sweeping up decent work: Paid domestic work and digital platforms in South Africa. *Gender and Development, 30*(3), 637–654.
Skitterblink Cleaning. Available online: https://cleaningsouthafrica.co.za/
Souralova, A. (2015). An employer sui generis: How placement agencies are changing the nature of paid childcare in The Czech Republic. In A. Triandafyllidou & S. Marchetti (Eds.), *Employers, agencies and immigration: Care work in Europe*. Ashgate.
Souralova, A., & Jelinek, M. (2018). Constructing professional services: For-profit care and domestic work agencies in The Czech Republic. *Women's Studies International Forum, 70*, 53–61.
Strangleman, T. (2016). The disciplinary career of the sociology of work. In S. Edgell, H. Gottfried, & E. Granter (Eds.), *The Sage handbook of the sociology of work and employment*. Sage.
Theron, J. (2005). Employment is not what it used to be: The nature and impact of work restructuring in South Africa. In E. Webster & K. Von Holdt (Eds.), *Beyond the apartheid workplace: Studies in transition*. University of KwaZulu-Natal Press.
Vidal, M. (2016). Fordism and the golden age of Atlantic capitalism. In S. Edgell, H. Gottfried, & E. Granter (Eds.), *The Sage handbook of the sociology of work and employment*. Sage.
Webster, E. (2023). *Recasting workers' power: Work and inequality in the shadow of the digital age*. University of Bristol: Bristol University Press.
Williamson, O. (1979). Transaction cost economics: The governance of contractual relations. *Journal of Law and Economics, 22*, 233–261.
Zalewski, J. M. (2018). *Working lives and in-house outsourcing chewed-up by two masters*. Routledge.

Outsourcing and Time-Related Dimensions of Job Quality: Evidence from the Facility Management Business

Alejandro Godino and Álvaro F. Junquera

1 Introduction

The decentralization and outsourcing of economic activities are not only a defining feature of the network society, but also has experienced an important expansion in its mechanisms, the actors engaged and its results (Autor, 2003; Harrison & Kelley, 1993). Nowadays, there is an extension of new forms of outsourcing mostly based on the opportunities offered by new technologies, including the growth of (bogus) self-employment, crowd employment through platforms and the expansion of facility management companies (Drahokoupil, 2015; Aloisi & De Stefano, 2020; Beuker et al., 2019; Molina et al., 2023). It is increasingly common to find companies relying on several of these mechanisms. Moreover, it is not rare to observe provider organizations further outsourcing some of the services they provide to clients, therefore contributing to a cascading subcontracting effect. The changing and varied nature of outsourcing practices is explained by the companies' features, the sectoral background, the implementation of technologies facilitating remote and automated control, and the institutional and regulatory framework. Moreover, outsourcing drivers are equally varied, relaying on gaining flexibility and efficiency, while

A. Godino (✉)
Sociological Research Centre on Everyday Life and Work (QUIT), Autonomous University of Barcelona (UAB). Edifici B, Carrer de la Fortuna – Campus de la UAB, Almería, Barcelona, Spain
e-mail: Alejandro.Godino@uab.cat

Á. F. Junquera
Sociological Research Centre on Everyday Life and Work (QUIT), Autonomous University of Barcelona (UAB). Edifici B, Carrer de la Fortuna - Campus de la UAB (Despatx B3-075), Barcelona, Spain
e-mail: alvaro.junquera@uab.cat

F. P. García Márquez et al. (eds.), *Outsourcing*, International Series in Operations Research & Management Science 370, https://doi.org/10.1007/978-3-031-95393-4_2

reducing costs and evading fiscal or labour market regulations (Doellgast & Gospel, 2013; Godino & Molina, 2022).

In this context, the growth and expansion of facility services companies is probably one of the most interesting developments in relation to outsourcing and its implications for employment. Outsourcing is far from being a new phenomenon, but only since the early 2000s has there been a significant expansion of facility management companies in Europe, though uneven across countries. Facility management (FM) companies provide integrated services and the management of those services to other companies or facilities. Even though the integration and management components constitute the distinctive traits of this form of outsourcing, the reality is that FM firms very often compete as any other service company providing just one service to client companies. As a matter of fact, rather than competing in the integrated service providers market, FM companies often take advantage of the diversity of services provided to engage in cost competition, thus undermining the working conditions of some groups of workers through the application of lower standards in collective bargaining. While most of the literature on industrial relations has focused on these gaps between outsourced and internal workers in relation to collective agreement coverage (Godino & Molina, 2022) and wages (Dube & Kaplan, 2010), few have addressed an increasingly key aspect of job quality: the time dimensions of employment (Recio et al., 2015a, b).

This chapter examines firstly the degree of outsourced workers in selected occupations common in facility services. Secondly, it observes working conditions of facility management workers in Spain in comparison to in-house workers to explore gaps in relation to working time, stability, and work-shifts. The analysis serves to illustrate the differential conditions in these three dimensions, although showing better standards in comparison to in-house workers for certain dimensions (e.g. permanent work) while observing worse job quality in relation to the extent of part-timers, having a later impact on salaries.

The first section of the chapter discusses FM in light of the literature on the characteristics and impact of outsourcing and the specific characteristics of FM. Section 2 then discusses the methodology and the analytical strategy used, including the job quality approach adopted when studying time dimensions. Section 3 shows the results of the logistic regression models carried out. This is then followed by some concluding remarks, showing three different scenarios for outsourced workers in FM businesses in relation to time-related dimensions of job quality.

2 Outsourcing Practices and the Facility Management Business

Most production and service provision processes are sequential and require establishing the so-called value chain, i.e. a relationship between the different processes required to produce a good or service (Antràs & Chor, 2013; Huws, 2012). The design of the economic value-added formula in the 1990s advocated that companies were more efficient when they removed as many items as possible from their balance sheets (Marchington et al., 2005). Outsourcing should accordingly be interpreted first and foremost as a business strategy with a financial/economic rationale. First, outsourcing is aimed at reducing costs in the short term (suppliers base their business on economies of scale, reusing models already developed for different clients). Second, it is also aimed at transforming companies' long-term cost structures by eliminating the fixed structures that support the internal control of the outsourced processes. Third, outsourcing constitutes a mechanism to enhance organizational flexibility, as it allows for a quicker adaptation to production requirements. Finally, the greater specialization of provider companies allows for efficiency gains (Doellgast & Gospel, 2013; Godino & Molina, 2022; Kotlarsky et al., 2011).

Since the 1980s, the modularization of tasks and processes in the value chain has been required to eliminate workers engaged in ancillary activities through outsourcing practices (Flecker & Meil, 2010; Harrison & Kelley, 1993). In turn, this allowed the organization of production around networks of supplier companies, increasingly favouring the market over organizations' internal competences (Kirchner, 2015; Ricart et al., 2011). Through outsourcing, the delivery of non-core activities is extracted from the central organizations as well as the responsibility over labour and social issues of the workers completing these activities, thus dualizing workers' organizational and employment relations (Doerflinger & Pulignano, 2015; Moreno-Colom et al., 2014; Mori, 2015; Rivero et al., 2006). In this way, the reduction of labour-related risks and costs (including wages, absenteeism and conflicts, among others) mainly through vertical disintegration strategies is an important driver for outsourcing, which moves workers out of well-organized sectors and/or organizations to spaces with weaker structures of worker representation and lower capacity for collective action (Doellgast et al., 2009; Huws, 2012; Recio et al., 2015a, b; Mori, 2015; Hyman, 2015; Benassi & Dorigatti, 2020). Therefore, client companies tend to trade the control of some internal work processes for low-pay strategies (Godino & Molina, 2022).

FM businesses appear to be opportunities for companies to compensate for this organizational fragmentation of work processes by integrating most of their outsourced activities in the same supplier firm. Therefore, FM allows simplification of interorganizational coordination and reduction of transaction costs; either FM firms provide the outsourced services, or they procure services from external suppliers and manage the output from the service providers. Moreover, the management and delivery of these integrated outsourced services is increasing with the internationalization of contract procurement by multinationals, as FM companies sign contracts with large clients at the European level, facilitating standard processes with providers.

2.1 Facility Management: Definition, Characteristics, and Practices

The conceptual and empirical delimitation of FM poses several challenges, as it is a relatively new business strategy that spans traditional sectoral classifications and points to greater changes in relations between organizations, space, and work (Grimshaw, 1999). Moreover, FM companies adopt very different practices and strategies across countries, therefore making it even more difficult to define FM based on a set of common dimensions. Notwithstanding these problems, there is some consensus around the idea of an integrated management (and delivery) of non-core services and processes supporting the core business of an organization (Ferri & Pala, 2009; IOS, 2017; Redlein, 2004; Redlein & Zobl, 2014). What is accordingly distinct from other service providers is the effective integration and coordination of these ancillary activities (Avenali et al., 2010). However, a relevant trend within FM managerial literature highlights that the coordination, rather than the provision of services, is the "bread and butter" of FM activity and notes its potential in contributing to wider business outcomes (Drion et al., 2012).

In light of the above, a distinction can be made between internal and external facility management. FM activities (i.e. those tasks developed by professionals integrating and coordinating outsourced services) are not completely outsourced in the European market. A total of 49.5% of facility managers develop their activity internally (Global FM, 2018). Internal facility managers operate within client organizations while coordinating external supplier companies. In contrast, outsourced facility managers externally coordinate the integrated supply of outsourced services. These services can be delivered by the same company that coordinates externally or by other provider firms contracted by the FM company.

In terms of services provided, facility management traditionally covered infrastructure and maintenance, equipment and furniture management, efficient resource supply, waste removal and security services. However, other functions, such as supervising environmental aspects or managing IT systems, are increasingly common, especially in those countries with more developed FM. This wide range of activities supplied by FM companies explains the growth of FM in recent years and why it is becoming one of the largest business services markets in Europe (Global FM, 2016, 2018).

FM companies are generally classified according to their territorial scope (distinguishing companies that supply outsourced services to client organizations at the local, regional, and global levels) but also in relation to the extent and complexity of activities supplied. In that sense, the literature distinguishes between multi-service suppliers, facility services suppliers, and FM companies based on the number of activities covered and the level of integration and coordination between the services provided (Ferri & Pala, 2009; Hodge et al., 2014).

Moreover, there are important differences across countries in relation to the development of the FM business and the type of services provided, allowing us to differentiate several market stages (Ferri & Pala, 2009): pre-emerging markets (mostly composed of single-service supply firms and client-supplier relationships based on multiple single-service and short-term contracts), emerging markets (with an incipient set of multi-service supply companies and a fragmentary supply concerning activities, territory coverage and clients, as well as a small number of multinationals with pan-European contracts), developed markets (where single-service supply co-exists beside multi-service supply, consolidating large supply operators), and advanced markets (with a large amount of integrated-service supply and the implementation of public-private partnership projects).

The services supplied by FM firms are generally labour intensive and carried out by predominantly unskilled workers who are typically paid low wages (Price, 2015), and the rates of employment are higher for women and migrant workers. In that sense, a facility management business gathers activities and workers frequently ascribed to the secondary segments of labour markets within the same organization, thus functioning as a parallel company of the client organizations supplying the ancillary activities. The question is accordingly whether FM contributes to maintaining the segmented pattern in the labour market or facilitates an upgrade in workers' positions (Godino & Molina, 2022).

This potential pattern of segmentation is reflected in the labour practices of FM companies in Spain. The country has developed notably its FM market since the late 2000s. This was followed by attempts to bargain a specific FM business collective agreement. Sectoral coordination of collective bargaining prevailed until the 2012 labour law reform opened the door to a decentralization of collective bargaining through the extension of opting out clauses in company-level agreements. This allowed FM companies to prioritize company-level agreements to set lower standards than sectoral agreements. Trade unions responded to these challenges first by appealing to justice. Second, gradually introducing clauses aimed to solve the problem of indeterminacy of the collective agreement to be applied to FM workers while discouraging the arbitrary application of collective agreements in the FM business. Meanwhile, some of the largest FM employers had contacts to launch their own employer organization to promote sectoral negotiations for the FM businesses. According to employers, having a specific sectoral collective agreement would allow all workers in FM companies to enjoy similar conditions. However, trade unions interpreted this move as a further attempt at eroding employment conditions. This proposal was finally dismissed due to unfruitful negotiations with unions and the multiple judgements cancelling FM company agreements (Godino & Molina, 2022).

3 Time Dimensions of Job Quality

To our knowledge, the literature on the association of outsourcing with quality of employment has mainly focused on wages, whereas other labour inequalities between internal and external workers have been hardly studied: for example, identifying a common increasing workload intensification of outsourced public services in different national industrial relations regimes (Mori, 2019). Or finding how subcontracting companies in the call centres sector offer less secure jobs, higher use of invasive monitoring practices, and less worker control over schedules and breaks compared to similar "in-house" call centres (Doellgast & Pannini, 2015). This happens particularly with those aspects of job quality inherently related to the organization and quality of time. The debate on working time has always been present since the origin of factories (Hobsbawn, 1984), with an initial academic focus on the duration of working time (Boulin, 2001), which has subsequently adopted a more multidimensional approach (Muñoz De Bustillo et al., 2011).

Ancillary activities (e.g. industrial cleaning) demand flexible, customer-driven work in specific ways. As many service activities are outsourced, there is a double pressure on time schedules designed by both the firm and its clients. Employees are usually required to adapt to time-specific arrangements and have limited capacity to bargain these conditions. Each branch of activity has its own model of working time and employees consider it as the sectoral standard, though they sometimes aim to adapt their working hours to their own requirements (Recio et al., 2015a, b).

Among the several social sciences traditions to analyse job quality, the institutional and the work-life balance approaches are particularly key concerning the consideration of time dimensions. These traditions include aspects related to contractual stability, working time duration and scheduling to understand what job quality is and how it might be measured (Muñoz De Bustillo et al., 2011). This has been a path followed by the most important studies addressing the multidimensionality of job quality (Eurofound, 2002; Leschke et al., 2008; Prieto et al., 2009; Grimshaw & Lehndorff, 2010; Muñoz De Bustillo et al., 2011).

Labor market segmentation theories have traditionally considered stability, along with wages, as one of the fundamental dimensions that shape and differentiate each of the segments into which the labour market is divided (López, 1994; López et al., 1998). When the job is not temporary, it leads to the creation of communities with internal rules that are different from the rest (Doeringer & Piore, 1970). In this way, we understand stability as the different capacity to maintain employment that the various groups of workers have (López et al., 1998).

Beyond these formal aspects that shape the duration of the employment contract, various factors have substantially modified the working time for decades: the crisis in industrial employment, the rise of the service sector, and the quantitative increase of women wage-earners (Miguélez et al., 2005). Thus, working time has become one of the most discussed aspects of job quality. A dimension under which not only issues related to the number of hours worked per week, but also concerning the regulation and organization of annual working hours, scheduling, and unsocial shifts (Miguélez et al., 2005). The increasing demand of availability of facility services companies might imply challenges for the job quality of these workers.

4 Data and Methods

4.1 Data

This chapter was aimed at answering the following research questions: (1) What is the degree of outsourced workers in occupations under FM companies? And (2) what is the relation between outsourcing and time dimensions of job quality in these occupations? To answer these questions, we employed two data sources. Firstly, we used the annual version of the Spanish Labour Force Survey (EPA) microdata for 2018 and 2020 (INE, 2019, 2021). These cross-sectional datasets pool in the same file the subsample of each of the four quarters that is subjected to the annual questions. Thereby, in the microdata coming from LFS, one fourth of the individuals answers the questions during the first quarter, one fourth during the second, one fourth during the third, and one fourth during the fourth. Secondly, we also exploited the cross-tabulations of the Population and Housing Censuses of Spain for 2011 and for 2021 (INE, 2012, 2023). We could not use their microdata to run the regressions, since three-digit versions of the occupational or economic activity classifications were not available. Nevertheless, we used their published tables to assess the reliability of the survey estimates. Furthermore, the Census of 2021 has the advantage that it collected the occupational and sectoral information from administrative registers and not from personal surveys. This avoids measurement errors that might occur with workers confusing occupational classification and/or the specific sectoral classification of their employers.

Following the strategy of Dube and Kaplan (2010), we defined an outsourced worker as the one who "works for an employer that provides labour services mainly as an intermediate input to a primary firm, when that individual could in principle provide the same labour services as a direct employee of the primary firm" (p. 290). First, this analysis crosscuts the economic sector of the employer and the occupation of the employee. Then, it qualifies as outsourced any worker employed in one of these sectors who is exclusively engaged in the provision of labour-based services. In our case, the sector is measured through the CNAE-09 at three digits, the Spanish classification of economic activities, which is a further disaggregation of NACE Rev. 2. The occupation of workers is measured through the CNO-11 at three digits, the Spanish classification of occupations, which presents a close correspondence to the ISCO-08.

Specifically, we focused on three occupations within facility services because they allowed a clear identification of outsourced workers. Cleaners, with the CNO-11 equal to 921, are considered as outsourced if they worked in the economic activity 812. Security guards, those with CNO-11 equal to 594, are described as outsourced if the sector of their firm was 801, 802, or 803. Gardeners, with CNO-11 equal to 612, are categorized as outsourced if they were employed in a company with sector 813.

We considered other variables during the analysis as well. Regarding the socio-demographic variables, some of them were recoded due to sample size following common classifications like ISCED for levels of education or NUTS for regions. To analyse some time dimensions of job quality, we followed the work of Muñoz de Bustillo et al. (2011). Specifically, we studied three dimensions: contractual stability, working time duration, and working time scheduling. We retained the subsample of employed individuals and then we constructed the first two outcomes through binary variables that registered if the employee had a temporary contract (first dimension) and was part-timer (second dimension). The third outcome was operationalized through a *good schedule* index following Muñoz de Bustillo et al. (2011). This variable was created as the sum of the scores of four items: working at night, in the evening, on Sundays, and on Saturdays. The person received for each item 1 point if she/he declared that never did, 0.5 points if he/she said that did it once a month, or 0 points when she/he did at least twice a month.

4.2 Analytical Strategy

The first analysis estimated the proportion of outsourcing in three facility services occupations. We considered the sampling design of the surveys, so estimators of the Horvitz-Thompson class were used to take into account the non-equal sampling weights of each individual (Lumley, 2010). After characterizing the temporal evolution of the prevalence of outsourcing by occupation, we crossed the outsourced status with other socio-demographic variables through contingency tables. Row proportions were estimated, and inference was carried out with the Rao-Scott second-order correction to the Pearson chi-squared test (Scott, 2007).

The second analysis explored the association between being outsourced and the above-mentioned dimensions of job quality. Our goal was to estimate the predictive ability of outsourcing, so no causal model was required.[1] To quantify the practical significance of outsourcing as a predictor versus other socio-economic variables, we performed a relative importance analysis. This analysis considers not only the predictive ability a covariate may have in companion of other predictors (in a multivariable model), but also on its own, as a good proxy of other predictors of the outcome (Johnson & LeBreton, 2004). Due to the survey character of our main dataset, we have opted for combining the results coming from multivariable and bivariable analyses instead of using other more novel interpretability statistic.

Firstly, for the partial associations, logistic regression models were estimated for the binary outcomes and a linear regression model for the good schedule dimension. The simplicity of the model structure was dictated by the nominal scale of most of the candidate predictors and by the reduced sample size we have. The specification followed the guidelines of Harrell (2015) and Riley et al. (2019a, b) for multivariate

[1] Strictly speaking, we implicitly assumed a specific causal model for the missing data: missing completely at random (Mohan & Pearl, 2021). Still, the objective of the chapter was not effect estimation.

prediction models by determining in advance the number of degrees of freedom we may spend. To facilitate the interpretation of coefficients, all estimates have been expressed in average marginal changes.[2] The standard error estimation considered the sampling weights thanks to the {survey} package implemented by Lumley (2010).

Secondly, for the total associations, we have estimated Cramér's V for each predictor and each time dimension of job quality. This statistic has been adapted to the complex sampling setting following the recommendations of Lumley (2022). The advantages of this quantity are that it is easily understandable and that it is simple to adapt to predictors with interval scale.

5 Results

In this section, we start by providing estimates regarding the extent of outsourcing for each job. Following that, we share findings from a multivariable model that measures the predictive power of certain covariates on time-related aspects of job quality. We specially focus on the importance of the outsourcing status versus other predictors easier to measure.

5.1 The Prevalence of Outsourcing

The first objective of this research was to estimate the proportion of outsourcing in the three occupations of interest. Table 1 shows the percentage of outsourced workers for each job estimated with the Labour Force Survey (2018 and 2020) and with the Census (2011 and 2021). At least from 2018, for cleaners and security guards, it is more common to be employed by a provider company than to be an internal worker. One out of two cleaners served as outsourced worker in Spain during 2018. Comparing the survey and the census proportions, the estimates are quite robust to the source and the year of measurement from 2018 onwards. These findings are consistent with the literature, identifying a trend to outsource ancillary services to businesses (Ahmed et al., 2011; Kirchner, 2015; López, 1994) particularly being the case of cleaners and security guards (Tregenna, 2008).

Looking at security guards, three out of four workers were outsourced according to the last estimate before the covid crisis. This proportion of outsourcing is the one experiencing the largest change from 2011 to the last estimate in 2020. It is also the occupation with the highest prevalence of outsourcing between the three facility services occupations analysed. On the contrary, outsourcing is not majoritarian in

[2] These quantities are more known as average marginal effects or average partial effects. We have preferred to substitute the last term by *change* to highlight the non-causal goal of our research.

Table 1 Proportion of outsourced workers by occupation (three digits)

	Census 2011	*LFS 2018*	*LFS 2020*	*Census 2021*
Cleaners	21.24	52.32 (1.75)	57.88 (1.81)	52.91
Security guards	28.53	74.39 (3.5)	84.92 (3.01)	
Gardeners	27.66	37.21 (4.25)	37.80 (4.31)	38.92

Note: Own elaboration based on INE (2012, 2019, 2021, 2023). The cells of the columns that employed survey data show the estimated proportion with its standard error in parenthesis

Table 2 Contingency tables for outsourcing and different covariates with LFS-2018

		No	Yes
Sex	Man	42.81	57.19
$\chi^2_{RS2} = 3.685,\ p = 0.055$	Woman	49.05	50.95
Nationality	EU, except Spanish	47.49	52.51
$\chi^2_{RS2} = 0.110,\ p = 0.895$	Foreign	48.8	51.2
	Spanish	46.54	53.46
Level-orientation of education	Primary or less	58.64	41.36
$\chi^2_{RS2} = 2.938,\ p = 0.013$	Lower secondary	48.55	51.45
	General upper secondary	40.45	59.55
	Vocational upper secondary	39.18	60.82
	General tertiary	45.66	54.34
	Vocational tertiary	38.82	61.18
NUTS-1 region	Community of Madrid	35.32	64.68
$\chi^2_{RS2} = 6.997,\ p < 0.001$	Canarias	59.46	40.54
	Centre	49.03	50.97
	East	43.04	56.96
	Northeast	36.79	63.21
	Northwest	39.62	60.38
	South	59.7	40.3

Note: Own elaboration based on INE (2019). Each cell shows the row proportion in percentage

the case of gardeners. The last estimate indicates that around 39% of the persons that had this occupation were outsourced. If we focus on the temporal evolution of this proportion, there is a smaller change between 2011 and 2021 compared with the other occupations. It is also interesting to observe how this proportion was not modified once the pandemic impacted in 2020.

Table 2 explores the association between being an outsourced worker and certain socio-demographic variables for the pooled sample of the LFS-2018. Looking at different prevalences by sex, we see that men are more affected by outsourcing, whereas women approximately present equal shares of in-house and outsourced workers. According to the chi-square test, this dependence is statistically significant at the 90% level. On the contrary, the test cannot reject the independence between being outsourced and the nationality of the individual. The row proportions show that the three categories present more outsourcing than in-house workers, but in the three cases the differences between proportions are quite small.

The next two panels investigate the relationship between outsourcing and two other variables: the level-orientation of education and the big region in which the individual lives. Concerning education, attending to the point estimates of these bivariate associations, the pattern that emerges is quite interesting. Once we disaggregate the levels of education by orientation (vocational or general), there is no linear relationship between the level and the proportion of outsourcing. Those with primary education or less have the lowest prevalence of outsourcing. This proportion keeps increasing in function of the level until it decreases again with those with general tertiary education. Still, the departure of both variables from the independence situation is enough to reject it at the 95% level through the chi-square test. This would raise the hypothesis that those workers with higher educational attainment may consider certain outsourced and low-skilled workplaces only as in-transition jobs. Therefore, without the possibility of developing careers within these sectors that would allow them to in-house work. Further longitudinal analysis would be required to contract this possibility.

In the last panel, the region of residence is crossed with the outsourcing status. We see how the outsourcing proportion reaches its minimum in the South region (comprising Andalusia, Region of Murcia, Ceuta, and Melilla), while has its maximum in the Region of Madrid. The prevalence is also comparatively high in the Northeast, the region that includes the Basque Country, Navarre, La Rioja, and Aragon. These results are consistent with the stages of FM markets, existing an association between more advanced markets for FM businesses and the amount of wealth created by an economic system (influencing the ability of its firms to efficiently produce high value goods and services) (Ferri & Pala, 2009).

5.2 *Outsourcing and Time-Related Dimensions of Job Quality*

The second objective of the research was to explore the association between outsourcing and time-related dimensions of job quality. To assess the predictive ability of outsourcing, we have inserted in a multivariable model other features that are usually collected through labour force surveys. We have estimated one model for each outcome variable following the modelling strategy detailed in the methodology section. To increase the available degrees of freedom, we have pooled the subsample of security guards and gardeners, since the number of events of interest they present were scarce. Note that the different sample sizes available for cleaners and for guards plus gardeners mean that the statistical tests have different power in each case. Statistical significance is more difficult to attain with small sample sizes, so predictors that were significant with the second subsample represent heavier evidence.

Firstly, we focus on the subsample of cleaners. Table 3 shows the results from three models, one for each studied dimension of job quality. These coefficients show the partial association of its covariate with the outcome, that is, having discounted the dependence between predictors. The model in the first column tries to predict the event of temporary employment. The coefficient of outsourcing is statistically significant and presents a negative association. Thereby, in average, being outsourced is linked to 7.2 percentual points less of probability of being temporary worker. Nonetheless, to value the size of the relation, its predictive ability must be compared to other covariates. Holding constant the rest of covariates, the parameter of vocational tertiary education has the largest size. Compared with the primary education, in average, when the individual has such level has 16 p.p. extra of probability of being temporary. There are also two coefficients that are statistically significant showing a negative relationship with the probability of having a temporary employment, the factors of *age* and *Spanish* nationality. As an example, for an interquartile contrast (from 45 to 54 years), the linear parameter of *age* predicts, in average, 9 p.p. less of probability of being temporary. These findings are coherent with the existence of European legislation on employees' rights in situations of changing employers since 1977 under the well-known "Acquired Rights Directive". Since then, mechanisms of social dialogue have further developed in this area, with particular emphasis on the "Transfers of Undertakings Directive". Subsequently, these directives were implemented in the different member countries and later updated in the Transfer of Undertakings (Protection of Employment) Regulations (Acas, 2024). These directives primarily aimed to ensure not only the continuity of existing contracts before a succession of companies but also the conditions of those contracts. Each Member State was responsible for operationalizing these provisions within their respective legal frameworks. That is the case of Spain with the labour subrogation clauses included in collective agreements, particularly in those sectoral agreements covering outsourced activities (e.g. Industrial cleaning).

The next column presents the estimates for the model that considers *part-time* as the outcome variable. The coefficient of outsourcing is statistically significant at the 99% level, which indicates that this variable incorporates new information to the model. In average, being outsourced is related to an extra increase of 13.7 p.p. of probability of having a part-time job. This positive association between outsourcing and part-time employment is consistent with several authors remarking how subcontractors employ a larger proportion of part-timers across diverse national and regulatory settings (Doellgast & Pannini, 2015; Shire et al., 2009), commonly a cost-cutting strategy by provider businesses (Godino & Molina, 2022). Nevertheless, the variable that incorporates more original information is the *sex*. Table 3 shows that being a woman is related in average to 24.4 p.p. more of probability of being part-time. This result is logical with the largely explored higher impact of part-time work to female-related activities and occupations (Booth & van Ours, 2013; Recio et al., 2015a, b; Fagan et al., 2020), as is the case of industrial cleaning. Again, the coefficient of age is significant at the 99% level with a negative association, but this time its point estimate is lower. The rest of coefficients are not statistically significant.

Table 3 Model estimates for cleaners using LFS-2018

	Temporary	Part-time	Good schedule
Outsourced (Yes vs. No)	−0.072** (0.029)	0.137*** (0.034)	0.525*** (0.068)
Sex (Woman vs. Man)	0.017 (0.040)	0.244*** (0.046)	0.036 (0.115)
Nationality (ref.: EU, except Spanish)			
Foreign	−0.046 (0.102)	−0.037 (0.103)	0.360* (0.217)
Spanish	−0.192** (0.096)	−0.037 (0.094)	0.338 (0.211)
Age	−0.010*** (0.001)	−0.006*** (0.002)	0.005 (0.004)
Level of education (ref.: Primary or less)			
Lower secondary	0.044 (0.047)	−0.082 (0.055)	−0.099 (0.103)
General upper secondary	0.030 (0.060)	−0.050 (0.077)	−0.045 (0.146)
Vocational upper secondary	0.039 (0.064)	−0.120 (0.074)	−0.061 (0.135)
General tertiary	0.084 (0.093)	−0.034 (0.118)	0.189 (0.195)
Vocational tertiary	0.159** (0.072)	−0.100 (0.081)	0.021 (0.146)
Num. Obs.	1243	1272	1227
Design-based R^2	0.182	0.094	0.097

Note: Own elaboration based on INE (2019). NUTS-1 region included as control variable. Each cell reports the average marginal change with its standard error in parenthesis. For logistic regression models, the design-based version of the pseudo R^2 of Nagelkerke is shown. * $p < 0.1$, ** $p < 0.05$, *** $p < 0.01$

The last column explores the associations for the model that considers the index of *good schedule* as response variable. Note that the outcome variable has interval scale, so coefficients may be interpreted as unitary changes and not changes in probabilities. The main result of this model is that being outsourced is related in average to approximately 0.5 points more in the index of good schedule. Considering that the index is originally delimited from 0 to 4, the change associated to outsourcing is of remarkable size. This estimate is statistically significant at the 99% level. Considering that the good schedule index is composed of four dimensions, we can rerun the same analysis but now considering each dimension as outcome variable. The results from these estimations indicate that, considering sampling uncertainty, the relation between outsourcing and working at evenings or nights is virtually zero. The dependence we are observing in the third column of Table 3 comes from a positive and statistically significant association between being

Table 4 Estimates of Cramér's V for cleaners using LFS-2018

Covariate	*Temporary*	*Part-time*	*Good schedule*
Outsourced	0.011	0.015	0.104
Sex	< 0.001	0.021	0.003
Nationality	0.044	0.002	0.004
Age	0.108	0.026	0.006
Level of education	0.022	0.004	0.007
NUTS-1 region	0.01	0.004	0.015

Note: Own elaboration based on INE (2019). Variable *age* is categorized in six levels

an outsourced worker and working during Saturdays or Sundays.[3] This is coherent considering that provider companies tend to adapt to the calendar and schedule of their client companies, being those mostly businesses developing their activities Monday to Friday and during social working hours. In contrast, in-house workers in ancillary occupations as cleaners may work during evenings and weekends as a large part of Spanish firms are part of the commerce and tourism sectors. As we can see, except the coefficient of the foreign level of *nationality*, the rest of coefficients are not statistically significant. For this variable, we find that compared with those with a European citizenship (other than the Spanish) foreign cleaners have in average better time-shifts.

Whereas the estimates of a multivariable model present coefficients of partial association, it is also interesting to consider the total association linked to each predictor. Table 4 presents the estimates of the Cramér's V for cleaners during year 2018. Regarding temporary employment, we see that the variable that collects more information to predict it is *age* ($\hat{V}_{Y_1 \sim A} = 0.108$). Our variable of interest, *outsourced*, is far from that estimate. Considering the previous results on partial associations, this points that the outsourcing status might be associated to bad predictors of temporary employment that we would need to held constant. Concerning part-time work, the predictive ability of the different variables is more similar. Consistent with the multivariable model, *age* and *sex* appear to be the best predictors. Still, their sizes are small and not so distant from the coefficient of outsourcing ($\hat{V}_{Y_2 \sim O} = 0.015$). Lastly, the estimates of the third column go in line with Table 3 and confirms that the best prediction of an outsourced situation is, in average, an improved schedule. The Cramér's V for outsourcing is the highest among the candidates, although of modest magnitude. Therefore, this indicates that outsourcing might be a good predictor of a better time-shifts after holding constant other covariates (partial association), but also on its own when considered alone (total association).

Secondly, we concentrate on the subsample of security guards and gardeners. Notice that the sample size did not allow us to control for the level of education or the NUTS-1 region. Table 5 shows the results of our estimations. Concerning

[3] The results from these additional estimations are available upon request.

Table 5 Model estimates for security guards and gardeners using LFS-2018

	Temporary	Part-time	Good schedule
Outsourced (Yes vs. No)	−0.115**	0.046	0.331**
	(0.051)	(0.031)	(0.129)
Sex (Woman vs. Man)	−0.026	0.169**	0.169
	(0.070)	(0.075)	(0.194)
Nationality (Spanish vs. not Spanish)	−0.166*	−0.037	−0.081
	(0.096)	(0.059)	(0.175)
Age	−0.008***	−0.003**	−0.002
	(0.002)	(0.001)	(0.006)
Num. Obs.	368	440	432
Design-based R^2	0.167	0.120	0.316

Note: Own elaboration based on INE (2019). Each cell reports the average marginal change with its standard error in parenthesis. The third model includes a coefficient for the occupation. For logistic regression models, the design-based version of the pseudo R^2 of Nagelkerke is shown. * $p < 0.1$, ** $p < 0.05$, *** $p < 0.01$

temporary employment, as for cleaners, being outsourced is associated in average with a decrease in the probability of being temporary. This difference of probability between outsourced and in-house workers is of 11.5 p.p., being statistically significant at the 95% level. We also found a statistically significant difference among the probabilities of being a temporary worker in function of being Spanish. The average marginal change is of 16.6 p.p. less, but we should be cautious as it is only significant at the 90% level. Variable *age* seems to add non-redundant information if we want to predict fixed-term contracts. To interpret its coefficient, consider that a contrast in its interquartile range (52 vs. 42 years old) is related in average to an 8 p.p. decrease in the probability of being temporary.

Regarding the association of outsourcing and part-time work, the group of guards and gardeners seem to have a different behaviour in comparison to what we found with cleaners. As we can see in the second column of Table 5, the coefficient of outsourcing is not statistically significant. This indicates that we cannot reject that in-house and outsourced workers had the same average probability of participating in a part-time job. As is well known in the literature, holding constant the rest of covariates, women have in average higher probability of part-time work. We also detect through a linear term a negative association between age and part-time employment, although this time the size of the coefficient is lower.

The third model in Table 5 tried to estimate partial associations in order to predict the index of good schedule. The main finding of this model is that, for guards and gardeners, outsourcing is again associated with better schedules, but this time the coefficient is lower. Remind that this specification also controls for the occupation, given the different prevalences of night work intrinsic to security jobs. Specifically, being outsourced is in average related to a 0.33 increase in the score of good schedules, a difference that is statistically significant at the 95% level. This result is in the same direction of what we found for cleaners. Still, it

Table 6 Estimates of Cramér's V for security guards and gardeners using LFS-2018

Covariate	*Temporary*	*Part-time*	*Good schedule*
Outsourced	0.019	0.007	0.071
Sex	0.001	0.04	0.016
Nationality	0.049	0.001	0.027
Age	0.11	0.015	0.023
Level of education	0.015	0.03	0.042
NUTS-1 region	0.053	0.009	0.031

Note: Own elaboration based on INE (2019). Variable *age* is categorized in six levels and *nationality* in three levels

is true that the set of controls employed for both specifications are not the same, so comparisons are delicate. The rest of coefficients presented in the table are not statistically significant.

Lastly, Table 6 presents the results for the estimation of total associations of each predictor with each outcome of interest for the subsample of guards and gardeners. The findings are quite similar to what we detected for cleaners. Concerning temporary work, outsourcing again plays a marginal role as good predictor on its own. Other variables like age seem to collect more information without the requirement of being inserted in a multivariable model. Something similar occurs with the part-time outcome, although now all the candidate predictors have modest total associations with the response variable. Sex is highlighted again as the best predictor for part-time. Outsourcing really shines as the best predictor for the dimension of good schedule. The total association is not large ($\hat{V}_{Y_3 \sim O} = 0.071$), but also for these occupations serve as the variable with the highest relationship with the index of good schedule.

6 Conclusions

The observed data regarding time-related dimensions of job quality shows ambivalent results. Nevertheless, we can synthesize the analysis into three scenarios to identify different paradigmatic situations for outsourced workers compared to in-house employees. First of all, we found a scenario of better working conditions for outsourced workers due to institutional frameworks statutory mandatory. Coordination mechanisms can intervene in buffering market challenges and minimizing inequalities between workers of internal and outsourced services, such as the application of Transfer of Undertakings-Protection of Employment legislation, further impacting in lower levels of temporary work within outsourced workers covered by labour subrogation clauses in collective agreements.

Secondly, we found a scenario of better working conditions for outsourced workers in comparison to in-house employees due to the alignment of provider companies to certain practices of client organizations. This is the case of outsourced employees adjusting their working hours to the scheduling of these client companies. In this way, blue-collar outsourced workers engaged in auxiliary activities end up benefiting from this adaptation, in a flexible way, to standardized working hours for white-collar workers engaged in core activities of client companies.

And lastly, a common scenario of worse working conditions for outsourced workers in comparison to in-house employees is due to the implementation of labour cost-cutting strategies, particularly through the increasing of part-timers in these outsourced activities and the use of overtime work as adjustment mechanisms to the client's demand. Supplier companies operate based on economies of scale, optimizing work processes through high specialization and a concentration of clients with similar demands, thereby reducing costs for these non-core functions for organizations. However, these supplier companies also optimize resources through a reduction in labour costs and the arbitrary application of collective agreements that allow for a discretionary implementation of minimum working hours. Precisely, the limited leeway for facility services provider companies to dismiss employees due to the mandatory application of labour subrogation clauses leads these companies to concentrate their strategies for adjusting labour costs on other employment dimensions. Primarily, this involves reducing working hours, thereby reducing salary costs, while commonly intensifying the work pace to maintain the contracted service by client companies.

The chapter also contains important policy insights. More specifically, ensuring the predominance of sectoral collective bargaining would help to set limits on wage-undercutting strategies. Another element contributing to reaching this goal is the implementation of national and EU regulations on tendering, public procurement, and codes of conduct. This is the case for the Barcelona City Council, which implements a social assessment of its providers and gives a weighted importance of 30% to social criteria and 70% to the offered price (Ajuntament de Barcelona, 2016). Thus, if the City Council detects that the offered price is abnormally low (and therefore implies working conditions below those agreed by collective negotiations), the offer will be excluded.

In that sense, it would be appropriate to consider these types of mechanisms across all government administrations. One way would be through the State's Advisory Board on Administrative Contracting. This body makes both recommendations and instructions to public administrations regarding the public contracting of third parties. One of the mechanisms of this board is precisely the establishment of a series of requirements for companies that are contracted (from a certain amount in construction and service contracts). These requirements are primarily financial, but we understand that, following the example of the Barcelona City Council, the introduction of new requirements for companies is necessary, mainly concerning the application of collective agreements, thereby conducting a prior social assessment.

These policy pointers can not only imply improvements in terms of job quality, but also in the quality of the service provided, particularly in the case of essential workers (as is the case of many facility services workers). Particularly in the health sector, Bacigalupea et al. (2015) found that the implementation of austerity and privatization policies during the great recession followed parallel patterns in Spain. This was later evidenced during the first wave of the pandemic in 2020, when there was a correlation between the incidence of COVID-19 mortality in residential care service and the trend to privatizing and increasing the number of users in nursing homes (Barrera-Algarín et al., 2021).

Beyond the results achieved, this study has several limitations that should be highlighted to address them in future research. In substantive terms, we envision two possible streams of future research. Firstly, the study is limited to the Spanish case, which restricts the generalization of the results considering that FM practices vary significantly across countries. Therefore, further research should address comparisons with other countries with diverse stages of FM market development. Secondly, there are other time-related dimensions relevant to the improvement of job quality such as overtime, work intensity, schedule predictability, and control over working time. Although the consideration of the three variables analysed in the chapter responds to a focus in the literature precisely on stability, working time and unsocial schedule (particularly in the case of those theoretical approaches that have paid more attention to time-related dimensions), future steps expanding the current research should widen the dimensions considered.

In methodological terms, we think that there are two possible paths to continue the research. On the one hand, the objective of the analysis might move from description to effect estimation. To estimate the impact of outsourcing at firm level, Bilal and Lhuillier (2021) used an instrumental variable strategy to bypass the selection bias that presumably confounds conventional regressions. At the worker level, it is possible that jobseekers with low productivity self-select in a contractor firm because they tend to pay less and also accept worse job quality conditions for the same reason. On the other hand, this causal inference strategy might also be assisted by the analysis of qualitative data gathered through interviews or focus groups. The potential of these extensive datasets is that they can support or raise suspicions on the causal assumptions of an instrumental variable identification. Beyond evaluating the exogeneity assumption of instruments, qualitative data might also suggest hypotheses on the mechanisms (causal paths) that might explain the effects estimated with instrumental variable regressions.

References

Acas. (2024). *TUPE transfers*. https://www.acas.org.uk/tupe

Ahmed, S. A., Hertel, T. W., & Walmsley, T. L. (2011). Outsourcing and the US labour market. *The World Economy, 34*(2), 192–222.

Ajuntament de Barcelona. (2016). *Guía de contratación pública social*. https://ajuntament.barcelona.cat/contractaciopublica/es/contratacion-publica-social

Aloisi, A., & De Stefano, V. (2020). Regulation and the future of work: The employment relationship as an innovation facilitator. *International Labour Review, 159*(1), 47–69.

Antràs, P., & Chor, D. (2013). Organizing global value chain. *Econometrica, 81*(6), 2127–2204.

Autor, D. (2003). Outsourcing at will: The contribution of unjust dismissal doctrine to the growth of employment outsourcing. *Journal of Labor Economics, 21*(1), 1–42.

Avenali, A., Matteucci, G., & Nonino, F. (2010). *Outsourcing of Facility Management Activities and Procurement Design*. Technical Report, 13. Dipartimento di Informatica e Sistemistica Antonio Ruberti. Sapienza. Università di Roma.

Bacigalupea, A., Martín, U., Font, R., González-Rábagoa, Y., & Bergantinos, N. (2015). Austeridad y privatización sanitaria en época de crisis: ¿existen diferencias entre las comunidades autónomas? *Gaceta sanitaria: Órgano oficial de la Sociedad Española de Salud Pública y Administración Sanitaria, 30*(1), 47–51. https://doi.org/10.1016/j.ga-ceta.2015.10.003

Barrera-Algarín, E., Estepa-Maestre, F., Sarasola-Sánchez-Serrano, J. L., & Malagón-Siria, J. C. (2021). COVID-19 y personas mayores en residencias: Impacto según el tipo de residencia. *Revista Española de Geriatría y Gerontología, 56*(4), 208–217.

Benassi, C., & Dorigatti, L. (2020). Out of sight, out of mind: The challenge of external work arrangements for industrial manufacturing unions in Germany and Italy. *Work, Employment and Society, 34*(6), 1027–1044.

Beuker, L., Borghi, P., Bureau, M. C., Corsani, A., Gazier, B., Godino, A., Koene, B., Martín-Artiles, A., Molina, O., Mori, A., Naedenoen, F., Norbäck, M., Širok, K., Stanic, M., & Walter, L. (2019). The place of self-employment in the European context. Evidence from nine country case studies: Belgium, France, Germany, Italy, The Netherlands, Slovenia, Spain, Sweden and the United Kingdom. In R. Semenza & F. Pichault (Eds.), *The challenges of self-employment in Europe* (pp. 77–139). Edward Elgar Publishing.

Bilal, A., & Lhuillier, H. (2021). *Outsourcing, inequality and aggregate output (No. w29348)*. National Bureau of Economic Research.

Booth, A. L., & van Ours, J. C. (2013). Part-time jobs: What women want? *Journal of Population Economics, 26*, 263–283. https://doi.org/10.1007/s00148-012-0417-9

Boulin, J. Y. (2001). Working time in the new social and economic context. *Transfer, 2*(1), 197–209.

Doellgast, V., & Gospel, H. (2013). *Outsourcing and human resource management*. Cornell University, ILR School.

Doellgast, V., & Pannini, E. (2015). The impact of outsourcing on job quality for call Centre workers in the telecommunications and call Centre subcontractor industries. In J. Drahokoupil (Ed.), *The outsourcing challenge* (pp. 117–136). ETUI Publications.

Doellgast, V., Holtgrewe, U., & Deery, S. J. (2009). The effects of National Institutions and collective bargaining arrangements on job quality in frontline service workplaces. *Industrial and Labor Relations Review, 62*(4), 489–509.

Doerflinger, N., & Pulignano, V. (2015). Outsourcing and collective bargaining in the recent crisis: Implications for employment in multinationals. In J. Drahokoupil (Ed.), *The outsourcing challenge organizing workers across fragmented production networks*. ETUI.

Doeringer, P. B., & Piore, M. J. (1970). *Internal labor markets and manpower analysis*. Harvard University, Massachusetts Institute of Technology.

Drahokoupil, J. (2015). *The outsourcing challenge organizing workers across fragmented production networks*. ETUI.

Drion, B., Melissen, F., & Wood, R. (2012). Facilities management: Lost, or regained? *Facilities, 30*(5/6), 254–261.

Dube, A., & Kaplan, E. (2010). Does outsourcing reduce wages in the low-wage service occupations? Evidence from janitors and guards. *ILR Review, 63*(2), 287–306.

Eurofound. (2002). *Quality of work and employment in Europe: Issues and challenges. Foundation paper, 1*. Office for Official Publications of the European Communities.

Fagan, C., O'Reilly, J., & Rubery, J. (2020). Part-time work: Challenging the "breadwinner" gender contract. In *The gendering of inequalities* (pp. 174–186). Routledge.

Ferri, A., & Pala, F. (2009). The facility management market in Europe and Italy. In A. De Toni, A. Ferri, & M. Montagner (Eds.), *Open facility management. A successful implementation in a public administration* (pp. 3–28).

Flecker, J., & Meil, P. (2010). Organisational restructuring and emerging service value chains: Implications for work and employment. *Work, Employment and Society, 24*(4), 680–698.

Global FM. (2016). *Global FM market report 2016*. International Facility Management Association.

Global FM. (2018). *Global FM market report 2018*. International Facility Management Association.

Godino, A., & Molina, O. (2022). The industrial relations chameleon: Collective bargaining in the facility management business. *Employee Relations, 44*(7), 1–18.

Grimshaw, B. (1999). Facilities management: The wider implications of managing change. *Facilities, 17*(1/2), 24–30.

Grimshaw, D., & Lehndorff, S. (2010). Anchors for job quality: Sectoral systems of employment in the European context. *Work Organisation, Labour & Globalisation, 4*, 24–40.

Harrell, F. E. (2015). *Regression modeling strategies. With applications to linear models, logistic and ordinal regression, and survival analysis*. Springer.

Harrison, B., & Kelley, M. R. (1993). Outsourcing and the search for 'flexibility. *Work Employment & Society, 7*(2), 213–235.

Hobsbawn, E. (1984). *Workers: Worlds of labour*. Pantheon Books.

Hodge, G., Poglitsch, R., & Ankerstjerne, P. (2014). *Perspectives on the FM market development*. White Paper, ISS.

Huws, U. (2012). *Outsourcing and the fragmentation of employment relations: the challenges ahead*. Acas Future of Workplace Relations discussion paper series.

Hyman, R. (2015). Three scenarios for industrial relations in Europe. *International Labour Review, 154*, 5–14.

INE. (2012). *Censo de Población y Viviendas 2011—Consulta de tablas a medida*. https://www.ine.es/censos2011/tablas/Inicio.do

INE. (2019). *Encuesta de Población Activa 2018 - Fichero anonimizado anual para usuarios de ficheros especiales con Ocupación y Actividad a tres dígitos*. Instituto Nacional de Estadística.

INE. (2021). *Encuesta de Población Activa 2020 - Fichero anonimizado anual para usuarios de ficheros especiales con Ocupación y Actividad a tres dígitos*. Instituto Nacional de Estadística.

INE. (2023). *Censo de Población y Viviendas 2021—Consulta de tablas a medida*. https://www.ine.es/Censo2021/Inicio.do?L=0

IOS. (2017). *Facility management*. Definition 41011:2017.

Johnson, J. W., & LeBreton, J. M. (2004). History and use of relative importance indices in organizational research. *Organizational Research Methods, 7*(3), 238–257.

Kirchner, S. (2015). Who performs outsourcing? A cross-national comparison of companies in the EU-28. In J. Drahokoupil (Ed.), *The outsourcing challenge. Organizing workers across fragmented production networks*. ETUI.

Kotlarsky, J., Oshri, I., & Willcocks, L. P. (2011). *The handbook of global outsourcing and offshoring*. Palgrave Macmillan.

Leschke, J., Watt, A., & Finn, M. (2008). *Putting a number on job quality? Constructing a European job quality index. Working paper 2008.03*. European Trade Union Institute.

López, P. (1994). *La construcción de tipologías en sociología: propuesta metodológica de construcción, análisis y validación. Aplicación a la segmentación del mercado de trabajo de la "Regió Metropolitana de Barcelona"*. Servei de Publicacions de la UAB.

López, P., Miguélez, F., Lope, A., & Coller, X. (1998). La segmentación laboral: hacia una tipología del ámbito productivo. *Papers, 55*, 45–77.

Lumley, T. (2010). *Complex surveys: A guide to analysis using R*. John Wiley & Sons.

Lumley, T. (2022, December 6). A short note on effect sizes. *Biased & Inefficient*.https://notstatschat.rbind.io/2022/12/06/a-short-note-on-effect-sizes/

Marchington, M., Grimshaw, D., Rubery, J., & Willmott, H. (2005). *Fragmenting work. Blurring organizational boundaries and disordering hierarchies*. Oxford University Press.

Miguélez, F., Torns, T., Borrás, V., Moreno, S., & Recio, C. (2005). El tiempo de trabajo ¿la última frontera? *Revista universitaria de ciencias del trabajo, 6*, 83–104.

Mohan, K., & Pearl, J. (2021). Graphical models for processing missing data. *Journal of the American Statistical Association, 116*(534), 1023–1037.

Molina, O., Butollo, F., Makó, C., Godino, A., Holtgrewe, U., Illsoe, A., Junte, S., Larsen, T. P., Illésy, M., Pap, J., & Wotschack, P. (2023). It takes two to code: A comparative analysis of collective bargaining and artificial intelligence. *Transfer: European Review of Labour and Research, 29*(1), 87–104.

Moreno-Colom, S., Godino, A., & Recio, A. (2014). Servicios externalizados y condiciones laborales: de la competencia de precios a la presion de los tiempos de trabajo. *Sociología del Trabajo, 81*, 50–67.

Mori, A. (2015). Outsourcing public services: Local government in Italy, England and Denmark. In J. Drahokoupil (Ed.), *The outsourcing challenge* (pp. 137–156). ETUI.

Mori, A. (2019). *Employment relations in outsourced public services: Working between market and state*. Springer.

Muñoz De Bustillo, R. M., Fernández-Macías, E., Antón, J. I., & Esteve, F. (2011). E pluribus Unum? A critical survey of job quality indicators. *Socio-Economic Review, 9*(3), 447–475.

Price, I. (2015). *People Make, and Patterns Break, FM*. EuroFM, Research Papers.

Prieto, C., Arnal, M., Caprile, M., & Potroni, J. (2009). *La calidad del empleo en España: una aproximación teórica y empírica*. Ministerio de Trabajo e Inmigración.

Recio, A., Moreno-Colom, S., & Godino, A. (2015a). Out of sight: Dimensions of working time in gendered occupations. In *Hard work in new jobs: The quality of work and life in European growth sectors* (pp. 189–207). Palgrave Macmillan UK.

Recio, A., Moreno-Colom, S., & Godino, A. (2015b). Out of sight: Dimensions of working time in gendered occupations. In M. Ramioul, V. Kirov, & U. Holtgrewe (Eds.), *Hard work in new jobs. The quality of work and life in European growth sectors*. Palgrave Macmillan.

Redlein, A. (2004). *Facility management: Business process integration*. Diplomica Verlag.

Redlein, A., & Zobl, M. (2014). Outsourcing: a cost-saving approach in FM? In *Proceedings CIB Facilities Management Conference* (pp. 21–23).

Ricart, J. E., Agnese, P., Pisani, N., & Adegbesan, T. (2011). *Offshoring in the global economy: Management practices and welfare implications*. Fundación BBVA.

Riley, R. D., Snell, K. I., Ensor, J., Burke, D. L., Harrell, F. E., Jr., Moons, K. G., & Collins, G. S. (2019a). Minimum sample size for developing a multivariable prediction model: Part I–continuous outcomes. *Statistics in Medicine, 38*(7), 1262–1275.

Riley, R. D., Snell, K. I., Ensor, J., Burke, D. L., Harrell, F. E., Jr., Moons, K. G., & Collins, G. S. (2019b). Minimum sample size for developing a multivariable prediction model: PART II-binary and time-to-event outcomes. *Statistics in Medicine, 38*(7), 1276–1296.

Rivero, J., de Val, A. L., & de Val, J. J. (2006). *La negociación colectiva en el sector de empresas multiservicios*. Ministerio de Trabajo y Asuntos Sociales Subdirección General de Información Administrativa y Publicaciones, Colección Informes y Estudios. Serie Relaciones Laborales, 73.

Scott, A. (2007). Rao-Scott corrections and their impact. In *Proceedings of the 2007 joint statistical meetings, Salt Lake City, Utah*.

Shire, K. A., Mottweiler, H., Schönauer, A., & Valverde, M. (2009). Temporary work in coordinated market economies: Evidence from front-line service workplaces. *ILR Review, 62*(4), 602–617. https://doi.org/10.1177/001979390906200407

Tregenna, F. (2008). Quantifying the outsourcing of jobs from manufacturing to services. *South African Journal of Economics, 72*(2), 222–238.

Ensuring Circularity through Outsourcing Decisions in Solar Photovoltaic Supply Chains

Ismail Erol, Iskender Peker, Tolga Benli, and Ilker Murat Ar

1 Introduction

Unlike finite fossil fuels like coal, crude oil, and natural gas, renewable energy supplies are ones that may be replenished over a time period. Among renewable alternatives for the generation of electricity, solar energy is the most abundant energy resource on earth (Bodkhe et al., 2020). The global demand for solar electricity from households and businesses has been rising at an exponential rate. There are two main elements driving this spike in demand: (a) Cost saving: By switching to clean energy, businesses that use a significant amount of power, such as data centers, cement, textile, paper, chemicals, etc., may save a lot of money. (b) A strong commitment to net zero and an increasing emphasis on sustainability (IEA, 2024).

According to Chowdhury et al. (2020), SPv energy is one of the most appealing forms of renewable energy. More specifically, more than half of the growth in renewable energy worldwide may be attributed to SPv (IEA, 2024). China is now leading the Pv equipment manufacturing business, having displaced the USA, Japan,

I. Erol (✉)
Baskent University, Faculty of Economics and Administrative Sciences, Ankara, Turkey
e-mail: ierol@baskent.edu.tr

I. Peker
Gumushane University, Faculty of Economics and Administrative Sciences, Gumushane, Turkey
e-mail: iskenderpeker@gumushane.edu.tr

T. Benli
Atilim University, Faculty of Business Administration, Ankara, Turkey
e-mail: tolga.benli@atilim.edu.tr

I. M. Ar
Ministry of Industry and Technology, Ankara, Turkey
e-mail: ilkermurat.ar@sanayi.gov.tr

F. P. García Márquez et al. (eds.), *Outsourcing*, International Series in Operations Research & Management Science 370, https://doi.org/10.1007/978-3-031-95393-4_3

and Europe in terms of size and geographic distribution during the past 10 years (IEA, 2024). In order to assist achieve global energy and climate goals, the IEA (2024) contends that SPv technology is a crucial component of the clean energy transition. Some of the elements of an SPv supply chain include energy generators, panel suppliers, assemblers, and material processors. System resilience may be negatively impacted by inefficiencies in any area of an SPv supply chain and/or disruptions in its surrounding environment (Foster et al., 2010). Note that the yearly SPv capacity additions by 2030 need to more than triple to 630 gigawatts in order to stay up with the IEA's Roadmap to Net Zero Emissions by 2050. Furthermore, by 2030, the production capacity for polysilicon wafers, ingots, cells, and modules has to more than quadruple from what it is now (IEA, 2022). The world's ability to generate enough SPv panels in the near future is called into question because of the necessity to greatly increase production capacity in order to satisfy future demand.

SPv supply chains should be simplified wherever feasible to increase resilience, paying special attention to the obsolete and unsustainable linear business models that are frequently utilized in the industry (Erol et al., 2021). Opstal et al. (2022) suggested that supply chain and sourcing obstacles, legal challenges, a lack of trust and acceptability in the market, restricted access to funding, and liability concerns as a result of few certification options are significant obstacles to the introduction of circular solar business models in general. In another study, Opstal and Smeets (2023) argued that the main challenges to the introduction of a sustainable photovoltaics industry are as follows: "a lack of strong policies," "a lack of public and market acceptance and trust," "weak regulations," "limited financing," "a lack of necessary data and technology," "inefficient waste management," "liability risks due to limited certification opportunities," and "monitoring, maintenance, and operational costs."

Note that even with their exponential expansion, solar panels won't last forever. Industry guidelines state that a solar panel's productive lifespan is normally between 25 and 30 years (Tao & Yu, 2015). Simply put, more will be taken out of service every year, meaning that we will soon need to deal with "tens of millions of metric tons of end-of-life materials." The International Renewable Energy Agency (IRENA) projects that by 2050, solar panels would produce between 60 and 78 million tons of material, necessitating one of three end-of-life possibilities: "recycling, reuse, or disposal." To address this, companies in SPv supply chains should implement circular outsourcing strategies (IRENA and IEA-PVPS, 2016).

Circular outsourcing is, in general, the practice of contracting out a supply, service, or job while accounting for the principals of circularity aiming to recover as many resources as possible. To achieve the effective circular outsourcing deployment, note that examining the critical success factors (CSFs) is crucial. Utilizing CSFs helps an organization or supply chain achieve its objectives and mission. Put differently, poor execution of these factors will result in a mediocre bottom-line for an organization or a supply chain. In addition, to utilize CSFs effectively, decision-makers must address the interdependencies between them, which will help to address a probable cause and effect structure of the CSFs.

The goal of this study, therefore, is to systematically explore CSFs for ensuring effective circular outsourcing in SPv supply chains. This study focuses on the following research questions:

RQ_1: What are the CSFs for enabling circular outsourcing in SPv supply chains?
RQ_2: What are the associations among the CSFs?
RQ_3: What implications are provided to improve circular outsourcing in SPv supply chains?

To respond to the research questions, in this study a methodology is developed through integrating qualitative methods with quantitative ones. First, a list of CSFs for ensuring effective circular outsourcing in SPv supply chains are identified with the help of a systematic literature review and the opinions of an expert group. Then, the causality among CSFs are scrutinized using Decision-Making Trial and Evaluation Laboratory (*DEMATEL*), a type of structural modeling approach that is useful in analyzing the cause-and-effect relationships among the constituents of a system. To tackle the ambiguity of expert views, traditional *DEMATEL* is improved by neutrosophic sets in this study. Finally, several implications resulting from the findings of this study are provided to achieve circularity in outsourcing decisions of SPv supply chains.

2 CSFs for Circular Outsourcing in SPv Supply Chains

In this section, a literature analysis was first conducted to identify CSFs for enabling CE and circular outsourcing in SPv and various supply chains. To this end, the criteria for searching the extant studies were set up. We consider the following two criteria for the inclusion of the research: (1) The research should discuss CSFs for enabling CE and circular outsourcing in SPv and other supply chains. (2) The research should be published in refereed journals included in database, such as Science Direct, Springer, Taylor and Francis, Emerald, and Wiley.

The following search terms serve as the foundation for the literature review: "CSFs for circularity," "CSFs for circular outsourcing in SPv supply chains," "CSFs for circular supply chains," "CSFs for circular economy," and "CSFs for sustainable supply chains." More specifically, the following keywords combination was employed: (("critical success factors") AND ("key success factors") AND ("enablers") AND ("supply chain") AND ("circular economy" OR "circular supply chain" OR "circular outsourcing") AND ("review") AND ("quantitative")).

The review shows that researchers have performed several studies on CSFs, enablers, and barriers for various types of supply chains in the context of CE. However, surprisingly, researchers have not focused on the CSFs of improved circularity in outsourcing in any industry. More explicitly, no study has been conducted to explore CSFs of ensuring circular outsourcing in SPv supply chains.

However, a few existing studies have been performed on CSFs, enablers, and barriers for CE and sustainability adoption for several industries. For example,

Zhao et al. (2021) proposed a framework to prioritize the CSFs for implementing sustainability and CE in energy industries. They concluded that atmosphere for innovation is the most important CSF. According to the review of Feldman et al. (2024), there are 21 distinct barriers to the circular economy in Australia. The authors suggested that the most common ones are the ones that are already in place, such as the high cost of transportation, the absence of government incentives, the lack of government standards and regulations, incomplete or erroneous data, and the failure of businesses to prioritize the changes that are necessary for the circular economy. The authors finally further categorized the obstacles according to a stage in the material's lifespan (or supply chain) until its depletion or disposal, since this facilitates the identification of areas for further study, feasible solutions, and barriers that are more manageable. Nyffenegger et al. (2024) addressed the current objectives, obstacles, and enablers for the shift towards CE using the findings of 20 interviews with representatives of European Pv supply chains. They concluded that "reducing virgin material consumption," "reinserting internal by-products," "exploiting rising market interest for sustainable products," "increasing traceability and monitoring PV module performance while in usage," "engaging in PV module design for circularity," and "using sustainable positioning as unique selling proposition" are some of the main enablers. In another study, DeSousa et al. (2023) discussed photovoltaic waste in Brazil. To this end, they analyzed the challenges to implementing circularity principles in photovoltaic industry. They concluded that lack of regulatory requirements turn out to be the most significant challenge.

Based on the studies we have reviewed, Table 1 that includes a list of CSFs for enabling circular outsourcing is built.

3 Methodology

This study aims to systematically investigate CSFs for ensuring circular outsourcing in SpVSCs. In this study, qualitative and quantitative methods are combined to achieve this goal. To this end, first, a literature analysis and the opinions of a group of experts are used. Using relevant keywords such as "circular outsourcing in SPv supply chains," "circularity in outsourcing," and "circular economy in outsourcing" we searched Science Direct, Springer, Taylor and Francis, Emerald, and Wiley between 2000 and 2024. Table 1 provides the specific details of the CSFs identified in this study.

Next, the causality between CSFs is examined by means of the Decision-Making Trial and Evaluation Laboratory (*DEMATEL*). *DEMATEL* is a type of structural modeling approach used to analyze the cause-and-effect relationships between the constituents of a system. In this study, neutrosophic sets improve traditional DEMATEL (*N-DEMATEL*) to address the vagueness of expert opinions. The proposed methodology is presented in Fig. 1.

Table 1 A list of CSFs for enabling circular outsourcing

CSFs (C)	Description	References
Enabling increased supply chain visibility and traceability for better circular outsourcing (C_1)	Increasing visibility and traceability will support the supply chain to be more agile, reduce risks and ensure circularity by managing resources more efficiently	Shen and Chen (2020), Mageto (2022) and Nyffenegger et al. (2024)
Ensuring improved circularity index of outsourced products and materials (C_2)	Ensuring circularity in outsourced products and materials can eliminate environmental concerns, increase economic efficiency and hopefully build consumer confidence	Stål and Corvellec (2018), Oliveira Silva and Morais (2022) and Nyffenegger et al. (2024)
Developing effective strategies to improve circular outsourcing (C_3)	Achieving organizational goals with effective strategies will bring resilience and competitive advantage to the business, making it easier to increase circularity in outsourcing	Feng et al. (2021) Zarbakhshnia et al. (2023) and Feldman et al. (2024)
Building collaborative partnerships with outsourcing companies towards circularity (C_4)	Establishing collaborative relationships with outsourcing companies encourages a closed-loop structure in an environment of mutual trust.	Chen et al. (2019) and Shen and Chen (2020)
Ensuring enhanced top management commitment towards effective circular outsourcing (C_5)	Corporate priorities are shaped by top management commitment, which influences corporate culture, reduces resistance to change, increases stakeholder trust and supports circular supply chain practices	Shen and Chen (2020) and Ensslin et al. (2020)
Developing circular business models to boost circular outsourcing (C_6)	Circular business models can align outsourcing practices with circular economy principles, promote efficient resource use, extract value from waste, and incentivize reusability	Tamás (2018), Oliveira Silva and Morais (2022) and Zhao et al. (2021)
Implementing proper information technologies to support circular outsourcing (C_7)	Implementation of appropriate information technologies can provide visibility, traceability and secure transactions. Integration of technologies such as IoT, Blockchain, RFID with ERP systems can benefit from optimizing circular outsourcing processes	Mageto (2022) and Chen et al. (2021)

(continued)

Table 1 (continued)

CSFs (C)	Description	References
Building an effective measurement system to evaluate circular outsourcing performance (C_8)	To evaluate circular outsourcing performance, it is crucial to implement an effective measurement system which enables continuous monitoring, goal alignment, data-driven decision-making, and benchmarking	Agrawal and Singh (2020) and Chen et al. (2021)
Training outsourcing personnel effectively for ensuring better circular outsourcing (C_9)	Providing training to outsourcing personnel can enhance their understanding of circular principles, facilitate implementation of circular practices, and enable them to adapt to changing circumstances effectively	Shen and Chen (2020) and Stek (2022)
Maintaining a strategic alignment between outsourcing and business strategies (C_{10})	In order to successfully implement outsourcing strategies, it is important to align them with business strategies. This promotes integration of decision-making and ensures a consistency in organizational goals	Stål and Corvellec (2018) and Zarbakhshnia et al. (2023)
Ensuring regulatory compliance in circular outsourcing (C_{11})	Regulatory compliance in circular outsourcing ensures legal obligations are fulfilled, ethical behavior structures are preserved, and processes are adapted to the environment	Russo et al. (2021), Mageto (2022), Feldman et al. (2024) and DeSousa et al. (2023)
Understanding the actual implications of not converting to circular outsourcing (C_{12})	Possible consequences of not switching to circular outsourcing include regulatory compliance risks, resource scarcity, waste management costs, damage to reputation, failure to meet stakeholder expectations, and risk of adaptation to market conditions. Avoiding these requires companies to build a circular structure in outsourcing	Russo et al. (2021) and Nguyen et al. (2022)

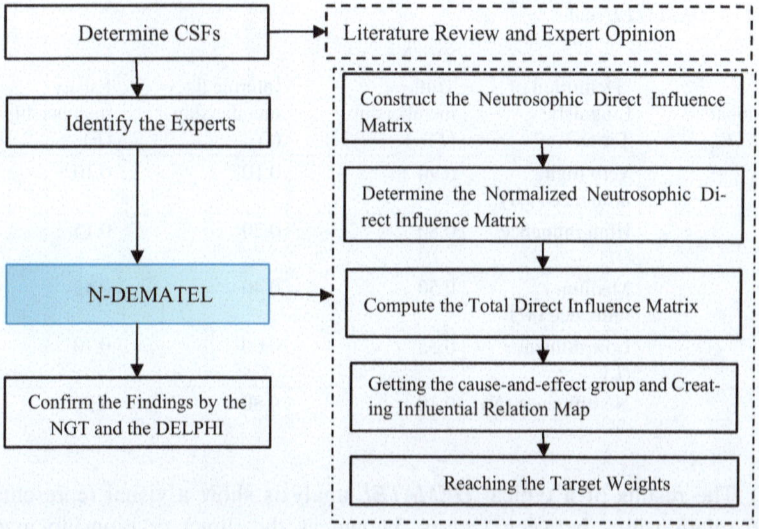

Fig. 1 The proposed methodology

3.1 Neutrosophic-DEMATEL

Golcuk and Baykasoglu (2016) claimed that criteria reliance and interaction are two different ideologies. Three subcategories of criteria reliance exist; preferred dependency, causal dependency, and structural dependency. Hierarchical TOPSIS, ANP, and AHP all exhibit structural dependency. The dominance and dependent relationships in the criteria's structure are implied by structural dependency. For example, determining the criteria structure a priori (i.e., which criterion or cluster effects the other criteria and/or clusters, including feedback) is necessary for pairwise comparison and criteria weights calculations. The fundamental differences between both approaches in the causal dependency are cause and effect linkages. Decision analysis models causal dependency using a variety of methodologies, including causal maps, DEMATEL, Fuzzy Cognitive Map (FCM), Bayesian networks, System Dynamics, Interpretive Structural Modeling (ISM), and Structural Equation Modeling (SEM) (Golcuk & Baykasoglu, 2016). DEMATEL is one of these criteria interaction modeling techniques that has gained enormous popularity in the last several years. A thorough method for creating a structural model that incorporates causal connections between intricate drivers is called *DEMATEL* (Ghag et al., 2023). This method can divide the drivers into "cause and effect" and turn the interactions between them into a comprehensible structural model of the system. In order to make long-term strategic decisions and identify areas for improvement, examining the interrelated interactions among factors in a complex system and categorize them it is a practical and helpful approach (Fakhry et al., 2023). DEMATEL method is able to solve individual perception of experts (Tseng,

Table 2 *N-DEMATEL* scale

Traditional *DEMATEL*	"Definition of Linguistic Terms"	SVNN Truth-membership (*T*)	Intermediacy-membership (*I*)	Falsity-membership (*F*)
4	Very high influence (*VH*)	0.90	0.10	0.10
3	High influence (*H*)	0.80	0.20	0.15
2	Medium influence (*M*)	0.50	0.40	0.45
1	Low influence (*L*)	0.35	0.60	0.70
0	No influence (*N*)	0.10	0.80	0.90

2009). The results of a typical *DEMATEL* analysis show a visual representation of the relationships between factors, known as the direct relationship map. In addition, according to Saleh et al. (2023), neutrosophic sets are remarkably capable of handling ambiguity and indeterminacy in the decision-making process. In this study, the neutrosophic *DEMATEL* (*N-DEMATEL*) approach is employed to obtain the factors' (CSFs) importance.

The followings are the steps of the *N-DEMATEL* approach (Abdel-Basset et al., 2018; Abdullah et al., 2021; Kilic et al. 2021) used in this research:

(i) Establish the factors and objective of the study.
(ii) Using the evaluation scale described in Table 2, construct "the Neutrosophic Direct Influence Matrix," represented by A^H. The experts provide the appropriate values for each criterion's truth, intermediacy, and falsity membership rating in terms of single-valued neutrosophic numbers (SVNN) (Table 2).

Table 2 compiles the opinions of all experts regarding the relative weight of each component.

$$A^G = \begin{bmatrix} a_{11} & \cdots & a_{1n} \\ \vdots & \ddots & \vdots \\ a_{m1} & \cdots & a_{mn} \end{bmatrix} \tag{1}$$

In the matrix, a_{ij} which is an SVNN in the form of < Tij, Iij, Fij > denotes the degree of influence that the factor *i* has on the factor *j*.

(iii) Using Eqs. (2–3), determine the Normalized Neutrosophic Direct Influence Matrix (*B*).

$$\boldsymbol{B} = \boldsymbol{k}.\boldsymbol{A}^{\boldsymbol{G}} \tag{2}$$

$$k = \text{Min}\left(\frac{1}{\mathbf{max}\sum_{j=1}^{n}\left|\check{X}_{zij}\right|}, \frac{1}{\mathbf{max}\sum_{i=1}^{n}\left|z_{\check{X}_{z}j}\right|} \right) i \ and \ j = 1, 2, 3, \ldots, \text{n} \tag{3}$$

Therefore, note that that the truth-membership values of the aggregated direct influence matrix are used to determine the "k" value during the normalization process. The multiplication is then carried out to obtain the normalized matrix.

(iv) Utilizing Eq. (4), compute "the Total Neutrosophic Direct Influence Matrix (S)." I denotes the matrix of identities.

$$S = B + \text{B}^2 + \text{B}^3 + \text{B}^4 + \cdots + B^{\text{m}} = B.(\text{I} - B)^{-1} \ (\text{m} \to \infty) \tag{4}$$

On the other hand, in a neutrosophic set, comparable operations such as the truth-membership (T), indeterminacy-membership (I), and falsity-membership (F) functions are carried out independently for every element by using Eqs. (5) through (7).

$$\left[T_{\text{ij}}\right] = B_T.(\text{I} - B_T)^{-1} \tag{5}$$

$$\left[I_{\text{ij}}\right] = B_I.(\text{I} - B_I)^{-1} \tag{6}$$

$$\left[F_{\text{ij}}\right] = B_F.(\text{I} - B_F)^{-1} \tag{7}$$

(v) Using the Eqs. (8–9), get the vectors D and R.

$$D = [d_{\text{i}}]_{\text{nx1}} = \left[\sum\nolimits_{\text{j}=1}^{\text{n}} S_{\text{ij}}\right]_{\text{nx1}} \tag{8}$$

$$\text{R} = \left[r_{\text{j}}\right]_{\text{nx1}} = \left[\sum\nolimits_{\text{i}=1}^{\text{n}} S_{\text{ij}}\right]_{\text{1xn}} \tag{9}$$

The symbol d_{i} represents the sum of the i_{th} row, which demonstrates the overall impact of the i_{th} factor on other factors. The entire influence of the factor by other factors is represented by "the sum of the j_{th} column," which is denoted by r_{j}. The highest $(D + R)$ value indicates that the factor has a strong association and plays a significant role. The factors are called the cause group if its "(D-R) value" is positive and has a major influence on other factors. The factors with negative (D-R) are impacted by the rest, which are referred to as the effect group.

Equation (10), which provides the transformation formula, is used to obtain the defuzzy *T*, *I*, and *F* values.

$$X = T_{ij} - I_{ij} + (2\alpha - 1)\, F_{ij} \tag{10}$$

(vi) Apply Eqs. (11–12) to standardize the data and get the final importance weights of the factor's relevance.

$$w_i = \left[(D_i + R_i)^2 + (D_i - R_i)^2\right]^{0,5} \tag{11}$$

$$W_i = \frac{w_i}{\sum w_i} \tag{12}$$

High relevance scores D + R for *prominent factors* indicate a stronger association with the other factors. With the highest D + R value, *influencing factors* appear to have stronger links with the other components. The most impacted factors are referred to as *resulting factors*. Stated differently, businesses might prioritize these aspects after taking into account the others. This is not to say they should be disregarded; rather, the contributing elements ought to be thoroughly looked into.

(vii) In order to create an Influential Relation Map (*IRM*), set a threshold value: The experts or decision-makers must determine a threshold value (α) to shorten the *S* and prevent the intricacy of little effects. Setting a suitable threshold (α) is very important. The impact on the *IRM* won't show up if the threshold (α) is found too high. However, if it turns out to be too low, the IRM's criterion count rises, and the map gets overly complicated. Equation (13) is used to compute the threshold (α). The total of the components in the *S*-matrix is represented by *N*.

$$\alpha = \frac{\sum_{i=1}^{n} \sum_{j=1}^{n} t_{ij}}{N} \tag{13}$$

4 Validate the Results

In this step, the findings of this study are validated. To achieve that, first a list of prioritized actions and/or recommendations is ultimately produced via the Nominal Group Technique (NGT). The NGT is a qualitative method for gathering feedback from stakeholders based on both individual and group reflection (Rankin et al., 2016). Huge and Mukherjee et al. (2018) state that virtual meetings can be used to validate the findings. This study used NGT based on the virtual meetings, as utilized by Hugé and Mukherjee (2018) and Rankin et al. (2016). Then, the DELPHI method is also used to test or reinforce the validation results obtained from the NGT. The Delphi procedure involves several rounds. Throughout this

Table 3 "The expert group"

Group	Size	Features
"Academicians"	6	They work as professors in Turkey in a variety of departments, who published research on circular economy, circular supply chain management, and outsourcing in renewable energy supply chains
"Company managers"	5	They have hands-on experience in outsourcing, procurement, and circular supply chain management in solar photovoltaic supply chains

procedure, a 7-point Likert scale—where 1 denotes strong disagreement and 7 denotes complete agreement—is used to gauge the experts' level of agreement with the findings. Using the responses from the first round, the statistics for "the median, first quartile, third quartile, and range" were computed. In the other phases, additional questionnaires are created. Experts are informed about the general trend of judgments based on statistical data from the previous rounds and are given the opportunity to reevaluate their remarks.

4.1 Application and the Results

This study aims to methodically examine CSFs to ensure successful circular outsourcing in SPv supply chains. The proposed approach shown in Fig. 1 is used in this study. The followings are the details of the application.

4.1.1 Identify the Expert Group

A single individual may not be able to effectively appraise the dynamics impacting a strategy due to personal biases and inadequate knowledge. Understanding how the CSFs would affect a suggested plan is also improved through group discussion (Thomas, 1985). Table 3 exhibits the expert group based on their experience in the field. Furthermore, it is contended that no set guideline for obtaining the ideal sample size of experts to consult. Stated differently, the size of an expert group in similar investigations is frequently unknown (Bulut & Duru, 2018). It is crucial to choose experts who are knowledgeable and experienced enough with the SPv supply chains to respond to the questionnaire. Experts should also be knowledgeable about CE both theoretically and practically. In light of these two factors, the present study defines experts as a group of respondents including researchers, decision-makers, and/or practitioners who possess adequate knowledge, research, and practical experience with both SPv supply chains and CE. We employed a purposive sample enhanced by snowball recruiting to identify experts who fulfilled the aforementioned requirements. Our initial step was to search the Internet for professionals with the necessary expertise in both SPv supply chains and CE. We discovered throughout this search procedure that while many scholars and practitioners have an experience on SPv supply chains, some of them lack sufficient knowledge of CE and circular outsourcing and vice versa. Following 2 months of phone conversations, in-person meetings, and Internet searches, 16 individuals were identified to satisfy our requirements and create a varied composition. At last, we managed to administer the survey to eleven respondents.

Once the expert group was built, the rest of the steps of the methodology were achieved as follows.

4.1.2 N- DEMATEL

In this study, the CSFs shown in Table 1 are used for *N-DEMATEL* analysis. To achieve that, *N-DEMATEL* questionnaire was built and provided to the expert group. The expert group used the scale in Table 2 to respond to the questions. Following the compilation of the responses, the steps of *N-DEMATEL* detailed in Sect. 3.1 were conducted.

4.1.3 Construct the Neutrosophic Direct Influence Matrix

In this step, the assessments from the experts were combined to create the neutrosophic direct influence matrix (A^G) as demonstrated in Appendix A.

4.1.4 Determine the Normalized Neutrosophic Direct Influence Matrix

Appendix B displays "the normalized neutrosophic direct influence matrix (B)," which was constructed employing Eqs. (2–3).

Calculate "the Total Direct Influence Matrix (S)".

Equations (4–7) were used to create the total direct influence matrix (S) as displayed in Appendix C.

4.1.5 Get the Cause-and-Effect Group and Creating the Influential Relation Map

"Equations (8) and (9)" were utilized to compute ($D + R$) and (D-R) values of the CSFs. The results are shown in Table 4. Table 4 also displays the cause-and-effect groups. In addition, Fig. 2 illustrates the associations among CSFs.

Table 4 $D + R$ and D-R values of the CSFs

CSFs (C)	D + R	D-R	Cause (C)/Effect (E)
Enabling increased supply chain visibility and traceability for better circular outsourcing (C_1)	11.985	4.922	C
Ensuring improved circularity index of outsourced products and materials (C_2)	13.725	−0.458	E
Developing effective strategies to improve circular outsourcing (C_3)	13.369	0.067	C
Building collaborative partnerships with outsourcing companies towards circularity (C_4)	11.028	3.682	C
Ensuring enhanced top management commitment towards effective circular outsourcing (C_5)	13.330	0.004	C
Developing circular business models to boost circular outsourcing (C_6)	14.589	−1.997	E
Implementing proper information technologies to support circular outsourcing (C_7)	12.230	−1.342	E
Building an effective measurement system to evaluate circular outsourcing performance (C_8)	10.839	−0.891	E
Training outsourcing personnel effectively for ensuring better circular outsourcing (C_9)	13.565	−1.877	E
Maintaining a strategic alignment between outsourcing and business strategies (C_{10})	11.949	0.190	C
Ensuring regulatory compliance in circular outsourcing (C_{11})	11.530	4.003	C
Understanding the actual implications of not converting to circular outsourcing (C_{12})	19.440	0.693	C

4.1.6 Reaching the Target Weights

The weights of the CSFs were obtained using Eqs. (10–12) as shown in Table 5.

As shown in Table 5 and Fig. 2, the results of this analysis concluded that the associations amongst the CSFs for ensuring efficient circular outsourcing in SpVSCs. The CSFs are divided into three classes—"prominent," "influencing," and "resulting" ones—based on Table 5. Table 6 provides the rankings.

Table 6 indicates that the most prominent factor was C_{12} (understanding the actual implications of not converting to circular outsourcing). The most prominent CSFs may also have the longest-term effects on other CSFs with "the greatest net causal-effect (D-R) values," indicating that the success of circular outsourcing in SpVSCs mostly depends on casual CSFs. Table 6 reveals that C_{12} (understanding the actual implications of not converting to circular outsourcing) was the most important causal CSF. Finally, take notice of the effect group's CSFs with negative D-R values, which indicate that they are impacted by the other CSFs. This is not to suggest that they are trivial or should be disregarded; instead, they ought to be thoroughly examined in the latter phases of a plan aimed at enhancing the efficiency of circular outsourcing in SpVSCs. Figure 2 and Table 6 indicate that CSF_2 (ensuring improved circularity index of outsourced products and materials) was the most crucial resulting (effect) CSF.

Table 5 Weights of the CSFs

CSFs (C)	Weight
Enabling increased supply chain visibility and traceability for better circular outsourcing (C_1)	0.081
Ensuring improved circularity index of outsourced products and materials (C_2)	0.086
Developing effective strategies to improve circular outsourcing (C_3)	0.083
Building collaborative partnerships with outsourcing companies towards circularity (C_4)	0.073
Ensuring enhanced top management commitment towards effective circular outsourcing (C_5)	0.083
Developing circular business models to boost circular outsourcing (C_6)	0.092
Implementing proper information technologies to support circular outsourcing (C_7)	0.077
Building an effective measurement system to evaluate circular outsourcing performance (C_8)	0.068
Training outsourcing personnel effectively for ensuring better circular outsourcing (C_9)	0.085
Maintaining a strategic alignment between outsourcing and business strategies (C_{10})	0.075
Ensuring regulatory compliance in circular outsourcing (C_{11})	0.076
Understanding the actual implications of not converting to circular outsourcing (C_{12})	0.121

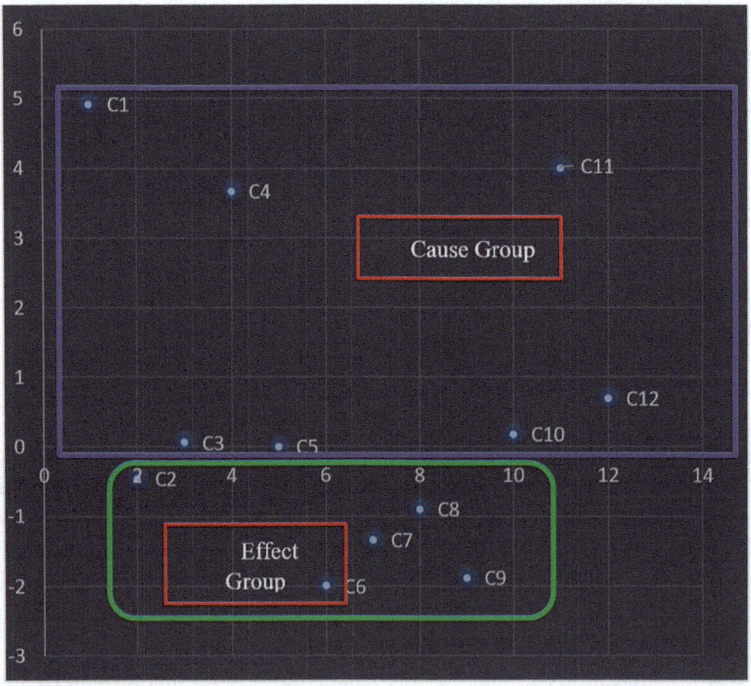

Fig. 2 Influential relation map

Table 6 "Ranking of the CSFs"

"Aspects"	"Rankings"
"Prominent"	$C_{12} > C_6 > C_2 > C_9 > C_3 > C_5 > C_7 > C_1 > C_{10} > C_{11} > C_4 > C_8$
"Influencing" (Cause)	$C_{12} > C_3 > C_5 > C_1 > C_{10} > C_{11} > C_4$
"Resulting" (Effect)	$C_2 > C_9 > C_5 > C_7 > C_8$

4.1.7 Validate the Findings

In this section, the findings of this study were validated using the NGT and the DELPHI. To this end, the expert group was initially given the results shown in Table 4. The expert group then participated in a virtual meeting for around 30 min. The expert committee discussed the findings throughout the discussion and came to an agreement that no change is necessary. To further increase the reliability of the findings, the DELPHI method was also used to test or reinforce the validation results obtained from the NGT. This method was applied to another expert group with three experts. This new group includes one senior manager working for a solar manufacturing company and two faculty members who published research on circular economy and circular supply chain management. A two-round Delphi process was used in this research. In order to prevent group members from negatively influencing one another, the first questionnaire was created and sent to the expert group via an online platform. The experts were asked to rate their agreement with the *N-DEMATEL* results on a 7-point Likert scale, where 1 represented extreme disagreement and 7 represented perfect agreement. Using the responses from the first round, the statistics for the median, first quartile, third quartile, and range were computed. In the second phase, an additional questionnaire that is unique to each expert was created. Experts were given the chance to reassess their responses and were notified of the overall trend of opinion based on the statistical data from the second survey round. It turned out that not a single expert altered their assessment in the second round. Table 5 displays the findings from the analysis. The primary measure of consensus in the Delphi analysis is range value, which is the difference between the first and third quartiles and should be less than 1.5 (Ab Latif et al., 2017). Therefore, considering the range values in Table 7 it can be claimed the results of *N-DEMATEL* were validated.

5 Discussion and Implications

As the need to cut carbon emissions and fight climate change is becoming more and more apparent, SPv supply chains are gaining attention in this regard. SPv supply chains still have a lot of obstacles to overcome in spite of this growth in renewable energy. Their attempts to transform the way the world produces and uses power may be undermined by various factors, which might vary from fierce rivalry in the markets to circularity. Outsourcing in SPv supply chains is focused on meeting the demands of solar energy enterprises. To be more precise, it entails

Table 7 Validation by DELPHI

"CSFs" (C)	"Cause (C)/Effect (E)"	DELPHI results				
		First quartile	Third quartile	Range	Median
Enabling increased supply chain visibility and traceability for better circular outsourcing (C_1)	C	6	7	1	6.67
Ensuring improved circularity index of outsourced products and materials (C_2)	E	6	7	1	6.67
Developing effective strategies to improve circular outsourcing (C_3)	C	7	7	0	7.00
Building collaborative partnerships with outsourcing companies towards circularity (C_4)	C	7	7	0	7.00
Ensuring enhanced top management commitment towards effective circular outsourcing (C_5)	C	7	7	0	7.00
Developing circular business models to boost circular outsourcing (C_6)	E	5.8	7	1.2	6.20
Implementing proper information technologies to support circular outsourcing (C_7)	E	6	7	1	6.67
Building an effective measurement system to evaluate circular outsourcing performance (C_8)	E	7	7	0	7.00
Training outsourcing personnel effectively for ensuring better circular outsourcing (C_9)	E	5.7	7	1.3	6.33
Maintaining a strategic alignment between outsourcing and business strategies (C_{10})	C	5.8	7	1.2	6.33
Ensuring regulatory compliance in circular outsourcing (C_{11})	C	7	7	0	7.00
Understanding the actual implications of not converting to circular outsourcing (C_{12})	C	5.9	7	1.1	6.33

assigning specific operations, jobs, and tasks to a third-party supplier who has the knowledge and means to complete them successfully. Through circular outsourcing, increasing productivity and streamlining processes without adding undue stress to the workloads of your own employees is possible.

Several findings from this study could help SPv supply chains develop effective circular outsourcing. This section offers further in-depth analysis of the findings with references to the earlier studies. To be more precise, the findings of this study are first compared with those of previous research. But keep in mind that there aren't any studies focusing exactly on the CSFs that analyze the foundations of effective circular outsourcing in various industries. It should be noted that the results of the previous research are not entirely consistent with our findings because they were conducted in different industries with distinct sets of CSFs.

Given that, for instance, according to the experts, this study suggests that understanding the actual implications of not converting to circular outsourcing (C_{12}), developing circular business models to boost circular outsourcing (C_6), training outsourcing personnel effectively for ensuring better circular outsourcing (C_9), ensuring improved circularity index of outsourced products and materials (C_2), developing effective strategies to improve circular outsourcing (C_3), and enabling increased supply chain visibility and traceability for better circular outsourcing (C_1) are the most crucial CSFs based solely on the conventional rankings. According to Nguyen et al. (2022) cooperative behavior along supply chains is the most important factor for outsourcing performance. On the other hand, Zarbakhshnia et al. (2023) stated that along with economic criteria, compliance with local rules and policies also important for circular outsourcing operations. Similarly, Wang et al. (2021) emphasize the importance of economic criteria for better circular outsourcing performance. Omair et al. (2022) is another study that focuses on the significance of the economic dimension of circular outsourcing. Finally, Agrawal and Singh (2020) concluded that circular outsourcing practice positively affects the sustainability dimensions of businesses.

In this study, the CSFs were also categorized into cause and effect in addition to the standard rankings of the CSFs. Cause and effect are influenced in the same way when one factor impacts the another. This process is referred to as causality. A cause is an action that comes before an event or incidence. Given the definition, the present study provided the associations among the variables to answer the RQ_2. According to the results of the *N-DEMATEL* analysis, Understanding the actual implications of not converting to circular outsourcing (C_{12}), ensuring regulatory compliance in circular outsourcing (C_{11}), enabling increased supply chain visibility and traceability for better circular outsourcing (C_1), building collaborative partnerships with outsourcing companies towards circularity (C_4), developing effective strategies to improve circular outsourcing (C_3), ensuring enhanced top management commitment towards effective circular outsourcing (C_5), and maintaining a strategic alignment between outsourcing and business strategies (C_{10}), are the cause CSFs. That means building effective circular outsourcing entails addressing these CSFs first. While some studies (Agrawal & Singh, 2020; Nguyen et al., 2022) in the literature focus on different drivers of circular outsourcing (such as increasing sustainability and collaboration), the majority (Mageto, 2022; Moreira & Rodrigues, 2023; Omair et al., 2022; Wang et al., 2021; Zarbakhshnia et al., 2023) emphasize the economic criteria. However, the results of this study expand the scope by drawing attention to different drivers in circular outsourcing, such as regulatory compliance, top management commitment, and understanding the actual implications of not converting to circular outsourcing.

Furthermore, an effect is the result or consequence of a cause. This implies that cause CSFs must be addressed before effect CSFs may be ensured. According to the findings of this study, developing circular business models to boost circular outsourcing (C_6), training outsourcing personnel effectively for ensuring better circular outsourcing (C_9), implementing proper information technologies to support circular outsourcing (C_7), and building an effective measurement system to evaluate circular outsourcing performance (C_8) are the effect CSFs. More specifically, for example, C_9 and C_7 can only be addressed if the cause CSFs regarding, for example, "legal and regulatory structure, top management commitment, supply chain visibility, collaborative partnerships" are achieved. On the other hand, Oliveira Silva and Morais (2022) focuses on circular business models on outsourcing decisions. The authors propose a multi-criteria decision-making model for business managers to classify circular strategies as either utilizing outsourcing or not.

Several managerial implications are also provided by the study's findings to address RQ_3. First note that enabling increased supply chain visibility and traceability for better circular outsourcing (C_1), building collaborative partnerships with outsourcing companies towards circularity (C_4), developing effective strategies to improve circular outsourcing (C_3), ensuring enhanced top management commitment towards effective circular outsourcing (C_5), and maintaining a strategic alignment between outsourcing and business strategies (C_{10}) are significant to an effective transition to circular outsourcing. To elaborate, note also that recovery related activities alone won't be enough to create a circular economy. It necessitates a fundamental shift in the sourcing of materials and the design, production, sale, usage, and disposal of things. Closing, delaying, and shrinking resource loops successfully frequently requires extensive planning and collaboration across organizational boundaries.

More specifically, a company's dedication to moving away from linear patterns is essential, but a transformation cannot be completed on its own. Systems and loops must be taken into consideration for a circular supply chain to function in SPv industries. To achieve this understanding the actual implications of not converting to circular outsourcing (C_{12}) is crucial. Therefore, we suggest that businesses involved in SPV supply chains need to research the effects of both implementing and not using circular business models. Then, maintaining a strategic alignment between outsourcing and business strategies (C_{10}) is also required to accomplish a successful transition to CE and circular outsourcing.

Ensuring regulatory compliance in circular outsourcing (C_{11}) is another crucial factor. More specifically, the effectiveness of outsourcing towards CE for SPv supply chains is largely dependent on a nation's incentive structure and laws. Given that, it may be claimed that policies that actively encourage circular outsourcing in SPv supply chains can bolster their business justifications, depending on the degree of support. Therefore, keep in mind that governments should implement legislative frameworks that include incentive programs to raise the degree of circular outsourcing. First, direct incentives make circular outsourcing more financially viable right now by lowering the requirement for an upfront investment. Subsidies are guaranteed by government loans, although low-cost financing is usually provided during the first investment stage. Over a number of years, further incentives could also be offered. Nonetheless, indirect incentives can be used to make an environment that is suitable for investment by promoting development-friendly conditions or eliminating barriers to circular outsourcing in SPv supply chains. Financial incentives for R&D, innovation, and human capital make up the first group. R&D funding can be utilized to develop new outsourcing technologies or boost the effectiveness of ones that already exist. Innovation and skill building do contribute to improved supply chain infrastructure, even though they may not necessarily result in sustained economic activity at the outset.

Moreover, increased supply chain visibility and traceability for better circular outsourcing (C_1), more effective strategies to improve circular outsourcing (C_3), and improved circularity index of outsourced products and materials (C_2) should be ensured along with an improved legal framework and incentives. Note that a number of solar panel recycling schemes have lately been launched globally to enhance the circularity of SPv supply chains. While these programs benefit companies and the industry indirectly by preserving their positive image, current recycling methods may not be profitable, which hinders their wider use. Hence, we contend that in order to increase the capacity for recycling solar panels, legal frameworks that outline stakeholder responsibilities, outsourcing approaches, financial models for end-of-life management, and minimal requirements for collecting and recycling must be constructed. Lastly, since solar panel recycling is still a technological challenge, further studies on circular outsourcing in SPv supply chains is needed to improve material value conservation and raise recovery rates that pave the way for effective circular business models to boost circular outsourcing (C_6).

6 Conclusions

Researchers contend that achieving net zero emissions requires the use of solar energy. As a result, the number of solar panel installations is increasing rapidly on a global scale, raising questions regarding the efficacy and long-term viability of the supply chains for solar photovoltaic energy. For instance, resource inefficiency brought about by the typical linear supply chain method makes supply chain performances unstable in terms of sustainability. Scholars and policymakers alike maintain that in order to tackle the present issues, a new paradigm must be developed. The CE is a solid plan of action that might offer innovative methods to address resource inefficiencies. But keep in mind that, while having a strong basis, CE still need a variety of supports from other departments in order to work effectively. For example, it is possible that circular outsourcing will be of great help in enabling the efficacy of SPv supply chains. To achieve this, it is maintained that studying critical CSFs for ensuring circular outsourcing in SPv supply chains is crucial. The literature review suggests that not much research have been done recently on this topic, which is surprising given its significance. Thus, more research on the CSFs of improving outsourcing in the context of CE is required.

The purpose of this research is to examine the CSFs of circular outsourcing in SPv supply chains. To this end, using the state of the art at the time, a set of CSFs was initially listed. Next, the relationships between the CSFs were discovered using *N-DEMATEL*. The findings of this study revealed the perceived cause-and-effect CSFs to improve the circularity of outsourcing. Specifically, while ensuring regulatory compliance in circular outsourcing (C_{11}), enabling increased supply chain visibility and traceability for better circular outsourcing (C_1), building collaborative partnerships with outsourcing companies towards circularity (C_4) are the most important cause CSFs, developing circular business models to boost circular outsourcing (C_6), training outsourcing personnel effectively for ensuring better circular outsourcing (C_9), and implementing proper information technologies to support circular outsourcing (C_7) are the most significant effect CSFs. It should be noted that because resolving effect CSFs is only feasible once cause CSFs have been met, this collection of results is extremely important for decision-makers.

Future research potentials exist as well, some of which stem from this study's shortcomings. The first shortcoming relates to the research's geographic emphasis, which is the SPv supply chain in Türkiye. As a result, the findings of our research do not immediately apply to other SPv supply chains worldwide. Future study would thus benefit from obtaining perspectives from various geographical areas to pinpoint potential commonalities and divergences with the European photovoltaic sector. Since circular activities, in particular, are still in their early stages in the downstream processes of supply chain, they lack expertise and efficiency when it comes to best practices. In addition, quantitative findings from various geographic scopes would be required to evaluate the applicability of our approach.

In addition, this study does not mainly focus on how to implement CSFs. Therefore, more research is needed to demonstrate how to implement circular outsourcing considering the CSFs for enhanced circularity. Further conceptual research is also required to clarify terms such as "drivers," "barriers," and "enablers" in relation to circular SPv supply chains. New research should be conducted to scrutinize these factors that will pave the way for building better circular strategies, business models, and legal and incentive framework. It is also recommended that more research on effective circular outsourcing, business models, product design, and improved recovery methods be carried out in SPv supply chains as well as across a range of industries in developing and emerging nations. This will allow for a more thorough analysis of the relationships between the various sets of CSFs in the context of circular economy and circular outsourcing. Finally, new quantitative techniques grounded on statistics, operations research, and multi-criteria methods with improved extensions may be applied to further investigate CSFs and enablers of circular SPv supply chains.

Appendix A Neutrosophic Direct Influence Matrix (A^G)

CSFs (C)	C_1			C_2			C_3			C_4			C_5			C_6		
	T	I	F	T	I	F	T	I	F	T	I	F	T	I	F	T	I	F
C_1	0.10	0.80	0.90	0.83	0.17	0.13	0.10	0.80	0.90	0.57	0.40	0.40	0.10	0.80	0.90	0.57	0.40	0.40
C_2	0.10	0.80	0.90	0.10	0.80	0.90	0.53	0.43	0.50	0.53	0.43	0.50	0.53	0.43	0.50	0.53	0.43	0.50
C_3	0.83	0.17	0.13	0.47	0.47	0.50	0.10	0.80	0.90	0.63	0.33	0.37	0.10	0.80	0.90	0.63	0.33	0.37
C_4	0.37	0.57	0.63	0.47	0.47	0.50	0.45	0.50	0.57	0.10	0.80	0.90	0.10	0.80	0.90	0.10	0.80	0.90
C_5	0.90	0.10	0.10	0.47	0.47	0.50	0.90	0.10	0.10	0.90	0.10	0.10	0.10	0.80	0.90	0.37	0.57	0.63
C_6	0.37	0.57	0.63	0.47	0.47	0.50	0.45	0.50	0.57	0.37	0.57	0.63	0.63	0.33	0.37	0.10	0.80	0.90
C_7	0.90	0.10	0.10	0.42	0.53	0.58	0.45	0.50	0.57	0.33	0.60	0.65	0.63	0.33	0.37	0.47	0.47	0.50
C_8	0.70	0.27	0.25	0.42	0.53	0.58	0.45	0.50	0.57	0.60	0.33	0.35	0.63	0.33	0.37	0.47	0.47	0.50
C_9	0.73	0.23	0.23	0.68	0.30	0.32	0.45	0.50	0.57	0.73	0.23	0.23	0.63	0.33	0.37	0.83	0.17	0.13
C_{10}	0.63	0.33	0.37	0.47	0.47	0.50	0.45	0.50	0.57	0.47	0.47	0.50	0.63	0.33	0.37	0.60	0.37	0.38
C_{11}	0.57	0.40	0.40	0.23	0.67	0.75	0.45	0.50	0.57	0.10	0.80	0.90	0.63	0.33	0.37	0.10	0.80	0.90
C_{12}	0.83	0.17	0.13	0.47	0.47	0.50	0.87	0.13	0.12	0.83	0.17	0.13	0.90	0.10	0.10	0.60	0.37	0.38

CSFs (C)	C_7			C_8			C_9			C_{10}			C_{11}			C_{12}		
	T	I	F	T	I	F	T	I	F	T	I	F	T	I	F	T	I	F
C_1	0.10	0.80	0.90	0.10	0.80	0.90	0.10	0.80	0.90	0.23	0.67	0.75	0.33	0.60	0.65	0.10	0.80	0.90
C_2	0.53	0.43	0.50	0.53	0.43	0.50	0.53	0.43	0.50	0.53	0.43	0.50	0.72	0.27	0.30	0.53	0.43	0.50
C_3	0.63	0.33	0.37	0.63	0.33	0.37	0.63	0.33	0.37	0.23	0.67	0.75	0.60	0.37	0.38	0.10	0.80	0.90
C_4	0.57	0.40	0.40	0.10	0.80	0.90	0.10	0.80	0.90	0.23	0.67	0.75	0.83	0.17	0.13	0.10	0.80	0.90
C_5	0.37	0.57	0.63	0.37	0.57	0.63	0.37	0.57	0.63	0.50	0.43	0.48	0.37	0.57	0.63	0.10	0.80	0.90
C_6	0.63	0.33	0.37	0.63	0.33	0.37	0.63	0.33	0.37	0.63	0.33	0.37	0.90	0.10	0.10	0.63	0.33	0.37
C_7	0.10	0.80	0.90	0.37	0.57	0.63	0.37	0.57	0.63	0.60	0.37	0.38	0.73	0.23	0.23	0.37	0.57	0.63
C_8	0.23	0.67	0.75	0.10	0.80	0.90	0.57	0.40	0.40	0.23	0.67	0.75	0.80	0.20	0.15	0.10	0.80	0.90
C_9	0.50	0.43	0.48	0.37	0.57	0.63	0.10	0.80	0.90	0.37	0.57	0.63	0.50	0.43	0.48	0.37	0.57	0.63
C_{10}	0.23	0.67	0.75	0.33	0.60	0.65	0.63	0.33	0.37	0.10	0.80	0.90	0.10	0.80	0.90	0.10	0.80	0.90
C_{11}	0.10	0.80	0.90	0.10	0.80	0.90	0.33	0.60	0.65	0.50	0.43	0.48	0.10	0.80	0.90	0.10	0.80	0.90
C_{12}	0.57	0.40	0.40	0.63	0.33	0.37	0.60	0.37	0.38	0.90	0.10	0.10	0.37	0.57	0.63	0.10	0.80	0.90

Appendix B Normalized Neutrosophic Direct Influence Matrix (B)

CSFs (C)	C_1			C_2			C_3			C_4			C_5			C_6		
	T	I	F	T	I	F	T	I	F	T	I	F	T	I	F	T	I	F
C_1	0.00	0.02	0.02	0.02	0.00	0.00	0.00	0.02	0.02	0.02	0.01	0.01	0.00	0.02	0.02	0.02	0.01	0.01
C_2	0.00	0.02	0.02	0.00	0.02	0.02	0.01	0.01	0.01	0.01	0.01	0.01	0.01	0.01	0.01	0.01	0.01	0.01
C_3	0.02	0.00	0.00	0.01	0.01	0.01	0.00	0.02	0.02	0.02	0.01	0.01	0.00	0.02	0.02	0.02	0.01	0.01
C_4	0.01	0.01	0.01	0.01	0.01	0.01	0.01	0.01	0.01	0.00	0.02	0.02	0.00	0.02	0.02	0.00	0.02	0.02
C_5	0.02	0.00	0.00	0.01	0.01	0.01	0.02	0.00	0.00	0.02	0.00	0.00	0.00	0.02	0.02	0.01	0.01	0.01
C_6	0.01	0.01	0.01	0.01	0.01	0.01	0.01	0.01	0.01	0.01	0.01	0.01	0.02	0.01	0.01	0.00	0.02	0.02
C_7	0.02	0.00	0.00	0.01	0.01	0.01	0.01	0.01	0.01	0.01	0.01	0.01	0.02	0.01	0.01	0.01	0.01	0.01
C_8	0.02	0.01	0.01	0.01	0.01	0.01	0.01	0.01	0.01	0.02	0.01	0.01	0.02	0.01	0.01	0.01	0.01	0.01
C_9	0.02	0.01	0.01	0.02	0.01	0.01	0.01	0.01	0.01	0.02	0.01	0.01	0.02	0.01	0.01	0.02	0.00	0.00
C_{10}	0.02	0.01	0.01	0.01	0.01	0.01	0.01	0.01	0.01	0.01	0.01	0.01	0.02	0.01	0.01	0.02	0.01	0.01
C_{11}	0.02	0.01	0.01	0.01	0.02	0.02	0.01	0.01	0.01	0.00	0.02	0.02	0.02	0.01	0.01	0.00	0.02	0.02
C_{12}	0.02	0.00	0.00	0.01	0.01	0.01	0.02	0.00	0.00	0.02	0.00	0.00	0.02	0.00	0.00	0.02	0.01	0.01

CSFs (C)	C_7			C_8			C_9			C_{10}			C_{11}			C_{12}		
	T	I	F	T	I	F	T	I	F	T	I	F	T	I	F	T	I	F
C_1	0.00	0.02	0.02	0.00	0.02	0.02	0.00	0.02	0.02	0.01	0.02	0.02	0.01	0.01	0.01	0.00	0.02	0.02
C_2	0.01	0.01	0.01	0.01	0.01	0.01	0.01	0.01	0.01	0.01	0.01	0.01	0.02	0.01	0.01	0.01	0.01	0.01
C_3	0.02	0.01	0.01	0.02	0.01	0.01	0.02	0.01	0.01	0.01	0.02	0.02	0.02	0.01	0.01	0.00	0.02	0.02
C_4	0.02	0.01	0.01	0.00	0.02	0.02	0.00	0.02	0.02	0.01	0.02	0.02	0.02	0.00	0.00	0.00	0.02	0.02
C_5	0.01	0.01	0.01	0.01	0.01	0.01	0.01	0.01	0.01	0.01	0.01	0.01	0.01	0.01	0.01	0.00	0.02	0.02
C_6	0.02	0.01	0.01	0.02	0.01	0.01	0.02	0.01	0.01	0.02	0.01	0.01	0.02	0.00	0.00	0.02	0.01	0.01
C_7	0.00	0.02	0.02	0.01	0.01	0.01	0.01	0.01	0.01	0.02	0.01	0.01	0.02	0.01	0.01	0.01	0.01	0.01
C_8	0.01	0.02	0.02	0.00	0.02	0.02	0.02	0.01	0.01	0.01	0.02	0.02	0.02	0.00	0.00	0.00	0.02	0.02
C_9	0.01	0.01	0.01	0.01	0.01	0.01	0.00	0.02	0.02	0.01	0.01	0.01	0.01	0.01	0.01	0.01	0.01	0.01
C_{10}	0.01	0.02	0.02	0.01	0.01	0.01	0.02	0.01	0.01	0.00	0.02	0.02	0.00	0.02	0.02	0.00	0.02	0.02
C_{11}	0.00	0.02	0.02	0.00	0.02	0.02	0.01	0.01	0.01	0.01	0.01	0.01	0.00	0.02	0.02	0.00	0.02	0.02
C_{12}	0.02	0.01	0.01	0.02	0.01	0.01	0.02	0.01	0.01	0.02	0.00	0.00	0.01	0.01	0.01	0.00	0.02	0.02

Appendix C Total Neutrosophic Direct Influence Matrix (S)

CSFs (C)	C_1	C_2	C_3	C_4	C_5	C_6	C_7	C_8	C_9	C_{10}	C_{11}	C_{12}
C_1	1.20	0.37	0.18	0.31	0.18	0.28	0.15	0.13	0.16	0.21	0.29	0.08
C_2	0.58	1.42	0.56	0.60	0.56	0.52	0.46	0.42	0.49	0.51	0.69	0.28
3	0.70	0.50	1.38	0.58	0.40	0.52	0.46	0.43	0.49	0.39	0.63	0.16
C_4	0.32	0.28	0.28	1.19	0.19	0.17	0.26	0.12	0.16	0.21	0.42	0.07
C_5	0.75	0.51	0.61	0.67	1.36	0.45	0.40	0.35	0.41	0.45	0.57	0.14
C_6	0.77	0.61	0.63	0.66	0.69	1.48	0.55	0.52	0.60	0.62	0.82	0.34
C_7	0.77	0.50	0.51	0.52	0.56	0.48	1.31	0.36	0.42	0.50	0.65	0.22
C_8	0.60	0.43	0.44	0.52	0.48	0.41	0.31	1.23	0.40	0.34	0.59	0.12
C_9	0.79	0.63	0.58	0.70	0.62	0.63	0.50	0.41	1.40	0.51	0.70	0.26
C_{10}	0.60	0.45	0.44	0.50	0.49	0.47	0.32	0.30	0.45	1.30	0.42	0.14
C_{11}	0.38	0.25	0.30	0.23	0.34	0.19	0.15	0.14	0.23	0.28	1.21	0.06
C_{12}	0.98	0.70	0.81	0.87	0.80	0.69	0.58	0.57	0.64	0.75	0.78	1.20

References

Ab Latif, R., Dahlan, A., Ab Mulud, Z., & Mat Nor, M. Z. (2017). The Delphi technique as a method to obtain consensus in health care education research. *Education in Medicine Journal, 9*(3), 89–102. https://doi.org/10.21315/eimj2017.9.3.10

Abdel-Basset, M., Manogaran, G., Gamal, A., & Smarandache, F. (2018). A hybrid approach of neutrosophic sets and DEMATEL method for developing supplier selection criteria. *Design Automation for Embedded Systems, 22*(3), 257–278. https://doi.org/10.1007/s10617-018-9203-6

Abdullah, L., Ong, Z., & Mohd Mahali, S. (2021). Single-valued Neutrosophic DEMATEL for segregating types of criteria: A case of subcontractors' selection. *Journal of Mathematics, 2021*, 12. https://doi.org/10.1155/2021/6636029

Agrawal, S., & Singh, R. K. (2020). Outsourcing and reverse supply chain performance: A triple bottom line approach. *Benchmarking, 28*(4), 1146–1163. https://doi.org/10.1108/BIJ-09-2020-0498

Bodkhe, U., Tanwar, S., Parekh, K., Khanpara, P., Tyagi, S., Kumar, N., & Alazab, M. (2020). Blockchain for Industry 4.0: A comprehensive review. *IEEE Access, 8*, 79764–79800. https://doi.org/10.1109/ACCESS.2020.2988579

Bulut, E., & Duru, O. (2018). Analytic hierarchy process (AHP) in maritime logistics: Theory, application and fuzzy set integration. In P. T.-W. Lee & Z. Yang (Eds.), *Multi-criteria decision making in maritime studies and logistics: Applications and cases* (pp. 31–78). Springer International Publishing. https://doi.org/10.1007/978-3-319-62338-2_3

Chen, K. S., Chang, T. C., & Lin, Y. T. (2019). Developing an outsourcing partner selection model for process with two-sided specification using capability index and manufacturing time performance index. *International Journal of Reliability, Quality and Safety Engineering, 26*(3), 1–16. https://doi.org/10.1142/S0218539319500153

Chen, Z. S., Zhang, X., Govindan, K., Wang, X. J., & Chin, K. S. (2021). Third-party reverse logistics provider selection: A computational semantic analysis-based multi-perspective multi-attribute decision-making approach. *Expert Systems with Applications, 166*(August 2020), 114051. https://doi.org/10.1016/j.eswa.2020.114051

Chowdhury, M. S., Rahman, K. S., Chowdhury, T., Nuthammachot, N., Techato, K., Akhtaruzzaman, M., Tiong, S. K., Sopian, K., & Amin, N. (2020). An overview of solar photovoltaic panels' end-of-life material recycling. *Energy Strategy Reviews, 27*, 100431.

DeSousa, K., van Etten, J., Neby, M., & Solberg, S. Ø. (2023). Climate variability indices for ecological and crop models in R: The climatrends package. *Journal of Open Source Software, 8*(85), 4405. https://doi.org/10.21105/joss.04405

Ensslin, L., Mussi, C. C., Dutra, A., Ensslin, S. R., & Demetrio, S. N. (2020). Management support model for information technology outsourcing. *Journal of Global Information Management, 28*(3), 123–147. https://doi.org/10.4018/JGIM.2020070107

Erol, I., Peker, I., Ar, I. M., Turan, İ., & Searcy, C. (2021). Towards a circular economy: Investigating the critical success factors for a blockchain-based solar photovoltaic energy ecosystem in Turkey. *Energy for Sustainable Development, 65*, 130–143.

Fakhry, A. E., Ali, A. M., Abdelhafeez, A., & Tantawy, A. A. (2023). Evaluation the key success factors in emergency management using Neutrosophic DEMATEL method. *International Journal of Neutrosophic Science, 21*(4), 195–195.

Feldman, J., Seligmann, H., King, S., Flynn, M., Shelley, T., Helwig, A., & Burey, P. (2024). Circular economy barriers in Australia: How to translate theory into practice? *Sustainable Production and Consumption*. https://doi.org/10.1016/j.spc.2024.02.001

Feng, Z., Xiao, T., & Robb, D. J. (2021). Environmentally responsible closed-loop supply chain models with outsourcing and authorization options. *Journal of Cleaner Production, 278*, 123791. https://doi.org/10.1016/j.jclepro.2020.123791

Foster, R., Ghassemi, M., & Cota, A. (2010). *Solar energy: Renewable energy and the environment*. CRC Press.

Ghag, N., Acharya, P., & Khanapuri, V. (2023). Analyzing the sustainable international competitiveness factors of SMEs by fuzzy Delphi and Neutrosophic DEMATEL. *Business Strategy & Development, 6*, 447–463.

Golcuk, I., & Baykasoglu, A. (2016). An analysis of DEMATEL approaches for criteria interaction handling within ANP. *Expert Systems with Applications, 46*, 346–366.

Hugé, J., & Mukherjee, N. (2018). The nominal group technique in ecology & conservation: Application and challenges. *Methods in Ecology and Evolution, 9*(1). https://doi.org/10.1111/2041-210X.12831

IEA. (2022). *Special Report on Solar PV Global Supply Chains*. https://www.iea.org/reports/solar-pv-global-supply-chains/executive-summary. Accessed on 04 April 2024.

IEA. (2024). *Renewables 2023*. IEA. https://www.iea.org/reports/renewables-2023, License: CC BY 4.0.

IRENA and IEA-PVPS. (2016). *End-of-Life Management: Solar Photovoltaic Panels*. International Renewable Energy Agency and International Energy Agency Photovoltaic Power Systems.

Kilic, H. S., Yurdaer, P., & Aglan, C. (2021). A leanness assessment methodology based on neutrosophic DEMATEL. *Journal of Manufacturing Systems, 59*, 320–344.

Mageto, J. (2022). Current and future trends of information technology and sustainability in logistics outsourcing. *Sustainability (Switzerland), 14*(13), 141376. https://doi.org/10.3390/su14137641

Moreira, O. J., & Rodrigues, M. C. M. (2023). Sourcing third party logistics service providers based on environmental, social and corporate governance: A case study. *Discover Sustainability, 4*(1), 36. https://doi.org/10.1007/s43621-023-00149-3

Mukherjee, N., Zabala, A., Huge, J., Nyumba, T. O., Esmail, B. A., & Sutherland, W. J. (2018). Comparison of techniques for eliciting views and judgements in decision-making. *Methods in Ecology and Evolution, 9*(1), 54–63. https://doi.org/10.1111/2041-210x.12940

Nguyen, D. T., Rameezdeen, R., Chileshe, N., & Coggins, J. (2022). Effect of customer cooperative behavior on reverse logistics outsourcing performance in the construction industry—A partial least squares structural equation modeling approach. *Engineering, Construction and Architectural Management, 29*(9), 3345–3362. https://doi.org/10.1108/ECAM-11-2020-0967

Nyffenegger, R., Boukhatmi, Ä., Radavičius, T., & Tvaronavičienė, M. (2024). How circular is the European photovoltaic industry? Practical insights on current circular economy barriers, enablers, and goals. *Journal of Cleaner Production*, 141376. https://doi.org/10.1016/j.jclepro.2024.141376

Oliveira Silva, W. D., & Morais, D. C. (2022). Impacts and insights of circular business models' outsourcing decisions on textile and fashion waste management: A multi-criteria decision model for sorting circular strategies. *Journal of Cleaner Production, 370*(May), 133551. https://doi.org/10.1016/j.jclepro.2022.133551

Omair, M., Alkahtani, M., Ayaz, K., Hussain, G., & Buhl, J. (2022). Supply chain modelling of the automobile multi-stage production considering circular economy by waste management using recycling and reworking operations. *Sustainability (Switzerland), 14*(22), 15428. https://doi.org/10.3390/su142215428

Opstal, W., & Smeets, A. (2023). Circular economy strategies as enablers for solar PV adoption in organizational market segments. *Sustainable Production and Consumption, 35*, 40–54. https://doi.org/10.1016/j.spc.2022.10.019

Opstal, V., Smeets, A., Duhoux, T., Blévennec, L., & Gillabel, J. (2022). Final report on co-created circular solar business models. *Zenodo (CERN European Organization for Nuclear Research).* https://doi.org/10.5281/zenodo.7362233

Rankin, N. M., Mcgregor, D., Butow, P. N., White, K., Phillips, J. L., Young, J. M., Pearson, S. A., York, S., & Shaw, T. (2016). Adapting the nominal group technique for priority setting of evidence-practice gaps in implementation science. *BMC Medical Research Methodology, 16*(1), 110. https://doi.org/10.1186/s12874-016-0210-7

Russo, I., Pellathy, D., & Omar, A. (2021). Managing outsourced reverse supply chain operations: Middle-range theory development. *Journal of Supply Chain Management, 57*(4), 63–85. https://doi.org/10.1111/jscm.12244

Saleh, W. A., Abdelkaderb, S. M., Rashada, H., & Abdelgawad, A. (2023). Analyzing critical success factors of IoT-enabled green supply chain management using bipolar Neutrosophic-DEMATEL. *Neutrosophic Sets and Systems, 55*(1), 8.

Shen, B., & Chen, C. (2020). Quality management in outsourced global fashion supply chains: An exploratory case study. *Production Planning and Control, 31*(9), 757–769. https://doi.org/10.1080/09537287.2019.1683774

Stål, H. I., & Corvellec, H. (2018). A decoupling perspective on circular business model implementation: Illustrations from Swedish apparel. *Journal of Cleaner Production, 171*, 630–643. https://doi.org/10.1016/j.jclepro.2017.09.249

Stek, K. (2022). A soft skills experiment in an industrial engineering and management academic course. In A. Alves Carvalho & N. van Hattum-Janssen (Eds.), *Training engineering students for modern technological advancement* (pp. 20–49). IGI Global. https://doi.org/10.4018/978-1-7998-8816-1.ch002

Tamás, P. (2018). Innovative business model for realization of sustainable supply chain at the outsourcing examination of logistics services. *Sustainability (Switzerland), 10*(1), 210. https://doi.org/10.3390/su10010210

Tao, J., & Yu, S. (2015). Review on feasible recycling pathways and technologies of solar photovoltaic modules. *Solar Energy Materials and Solar Cells, 141*, 108–124. https://doi.org/10.1016/j.solmat.2015.05.005

Thomas, J. (1985). Force field analysis : A new way to evaluate your strategy. *Long Range Planning, 18*(6), 54–59. https://doi.org/10.1016/0024-6301(85)90064-0

Tseng, M. L. (2009). Using the extension of DEMATEL to integrate hotel service quality perceptions into a cause–effect model in uncertainty. *Expert Systems with Applications, 36*, 9015–9023.

Wang, C. N., Dang, T. T., & Nguyen, N. A. T. (2021). Outsourcing reverse logistics for e-commerce retailers: A two-stage fuzzy optimization approach. *Axioms, 10*(1), 34. https://doi.org/10.3390/axioms10010034

Zarbakhshnia, N., Govindan, K., Kannan, D., & Goh, M. (2023). Outsourcing logistics operations in circular economy towards to sustainable development goals. *Business Strategy and the Environment, 32*(1), 134–162. https://doi.org/10.1002/bse.3122

Zhao, G., Ahmed, R. I., Ahmad, N., Yan, C., & Usmani, M. S. (2021). Prioritizing critical success factors for sustainable energy sector in China: A DEMATEL approach. *Energy Strategy Reviews, 35*, 100635–100635. https://doi.org/10.1016/j.esr.2021.100635

Embracing Blockchain Technologies in Outsourcing Practices: Cases and Studies in Operations Research and Management Science

Mallikarjun Reddy Dorsala, Manoj Kumar Somesula, and Mahesh Kumar Morampudi

1 Introduction

Operations research and management science (OR&MS) has many applications in industry management, IT management, business management, military, supply chain management, and organizational behavior (Henderson & Nelson, 2006). The use of OR&MS methodologies and applications is ever increasing for decision-making and optimization processes in Industry 4.0 (Ivanov et al., 2021). Although the use of OR&MS methodologies in Industry 4.0 is increasing, issues like resource constraints (personnel and technology), skill gaps, and high costs hinder its wide adoption. By employing outsourcing techniques, all or some of the OR&MS tasks are outsourced to service providers that provide low-cost outsourcing solutions. The outsourcing service providers cater services ranging from supplying expert personnel to offering extensive computation and storage capacities. By outsourcing OR&MS methods, an organization can benefit from operational and cost efficiency, resulting in enhanced performance and decision-making. An organization generally outsources its OR&MS tasks to a centralized service provider (CSP). The CSPs can be any business process outsourcing (BPO) company, technology consulting company, cloud provider, human resource consulting firm, or management consulting

M. R. Dorsala (✉)
Department of Computer Science and Engineering, Indian Institute of Information Technology, Sri City, India

M. K. Somesula
Department of Computer Science and Engineering, National Institute of Technology, Jalandhar, Punjab, India
e-mail: kumarsm@nitj.ac.in

M. K. Morampudi
Department of Computer Science and Engineering, School of Engineering and Applied Sciences, SRM University-AP, Mangalagiri, India

F. P. García Márquez et al. (eds.), *Outsourcing*, International Series in Operations Research & Management Science 370, https://doi.org/10.1007/978-3-031-95393-4_4

firm. Outsourcing to a centralized service provider presents a series of challenges, including data security and privacy concerns, lack of transparency, trust and accountability issues, inefficient payment processes, and time-consuming and costly dispute resolution processes. However, the emergence of Blockchain technology has ushered in a new era of trust and transparency, offering potential solutions to these issues. Blockchain's unique properties of decentralization, trust, and transparency can be harnessed to address the problems associated with centralized service providers in outsourcing. By integrating Blockchain, we can significantly mitigate the challenges of traditional outsourcing, paving the way for a more secure and efficient future.

This chapter delves into integrating Blockchain technology within the outsourcing of supply chain processes, a widely used operations management methodology. We first discuss the effects of outsourcing to Blockchain in various supply chain processes like sourcing and manufacturing, inventory management, distribution and delivery, retail, customer experience, reverse logistics, and second-hand market. Later, we explore real-world case studies of integrating Blockchain into Walmart's food industry, payments, and delivery. However, integrating Blockchain requires trained human resources in both Blockchain and the supply chain. Platforms like Everledger[1] offer Blockchain-based supply chain solutions to ease the integration. This chapter discusses the Everledger platform's solutions for supply chains of electric batteries, diamonds, and wines and spirits.

We also explore the integration of Blockchain in some management science methods. We first discuss the benefits of integrating Blockchain in human resource management (HRM) functions like recruitment and onboarding, performance tracking, payroll and benefits, and training and development. Later, we discuss the impact of integrating Blockchain in project management and organizational behavior. Although integrating Blockchain into outsourcing offers several benefits, it presents some challenges. Therefore, at the end of the chapter, we present a detailed discussion of the challenges and potential solutions.

2 Blockchain Technology: Fundamentals, Components, Types, and Features

Blockchain is a decentralized transaction and data management technology developed first for Bitcoin cryptocurrency (Yli-Huumo et al., 2016). It is an open, distributed ledger that records transactions between parties in verifiable and immutable ways. The transactions can be financial or nonfinancial. Although the first Blockchain, Bitcoin, is used primarily to record changes in ownership of digital currency (Bitcoin), many other Blockchains can store arbitrary data along

[1] https://everledger.io/

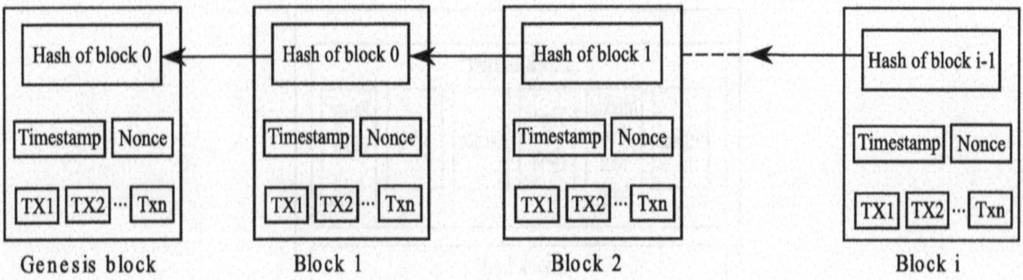

Fig. 1 Distributed ledger (Dorsala et al., 2021)

with changes in ownership of digital assets (financial/nonfinancial) in a verifiable and immutable way.

2.1 Components of a Blockchain Network

- **Distributed ledger** (Blockchain): It is a chain (sequence) of blocks. In the chain, each block is cryptographically linked to its previous block. The hash of a parent block is stored in a child block. The typical structure of a distributed ledger is presented in Fig. 1:
  - **Block:** A block consists of two parts. A block header containing meta-data and consensus information and a block body containing transactions. A typical block structure is presented in Fig. 2.
  - **Transaction:** A transaction is a record of a change of ownership of a digital asset or initiates the execution of a smart contract.
  - **Smart contract:** A smart contract is a software program (a set of functions) deployed and stored on a Blockchain. Its execution is initiated by sending a transaction to the Blockchain network on which it is deployed. The execution of a smart contract function can change the ownership of a digital asset, execute some arbitrary instructions, store some arbitrary data, or change the already stored data.
- **Nodes**: A node maintains the security and health of a Blockchain network. One of the major types of nodes is a full node, which maintains the entire history of the distributed ledger and participates in the consensus process.
- **Consensus**: A consensus algorithm governs adding new blocks to a distributed ledger. It also specifies transaction validation and execution rules, block generation and verification rules, and new digital currency generation rules. The security of a Blockchain network is governed by a consensus algorithm. Public Blockchains mainly use proof-of-work or proof-of-stake algorithms, whereas private/consortium Blockchains use PBFT (RAFT/Tendermint) or quorum consensus algorithms.

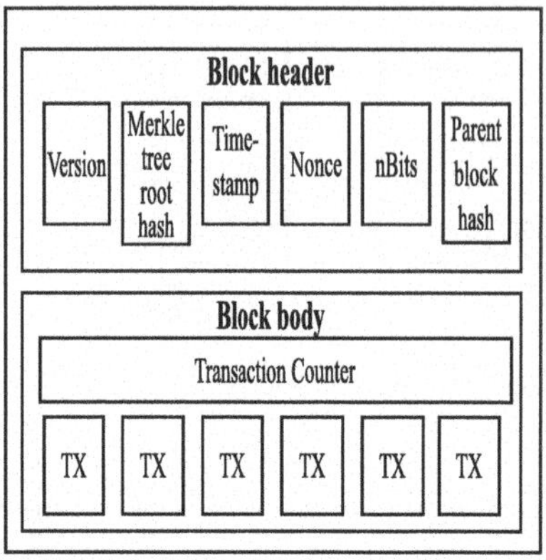

Fig. 2 Block structure (Dorsala et al., 2021)

2.2 Types of Blockchains

Blockchain technology is broadly classified into three types based on its degree of decentralization, and the level of access control (openness). The three major types of Blockchains are: (1) Public Blockchain: Allows anyone to join the network, create transactions, and add and verify blocks without restrictions. The level of decentralization is very high, with no single entity controlling the network. The network is secured through consensus algorithms like proof of work or proof of stake. Major public Blockchains are Bitcoin (Nakamoto, 2008) and Ethereum (Wood et al., 2014). (2) Private Blockchain: Participation in the network is often limited to certain participants or organizations. The level of decentralization is low, but the scalability and privacy level are high compared to a public Blockchain. Many enterprises and business-oriented organizations have developed their own private Blockchains. (3) Consortium Blockchain: Multiple organizations form as a consortium and share a common Blockchain network. Trust and security are maintained through the collaborative efforts of the consortium members. Participation is limited only to the consortium members. For example, some major financial institutions worldwide participate in the R3 Corda (Brown et al., 2016) consortium Blockchain network.

The advantages of integrating Blockchain have the following advantages:

1. **Data security and privacy:** Blockchain's decentralization nature ensures data security, and the pseudo-anonymity feature decouples the data from its source. Advanced cryptographic features like zero-knowledge proofs also provide data privacy.
2. **Data manipulation:** The cryptographic features and the inherent chaining of Blockchain data mitigate the risk of data manipulation in the outsourced tasks.
3. **Transparency:** Every data entry or transaction in the Blockchain is publicly visible and verified publicly by every participant, providing complete transparency.

4. **Trust and accountability:** Unlike centralized entities, Blockchain is decentralized by design, provides complete transparency, and ensures trust and accountability.
5. **Payment processes:** Most public Blockchains provide instant peer-to-peer payments through which multiple parties settle payments instantly without intermediaries.
6. **Dispute resolution processes:** Most Blockchain platforms offer smart contracts that can execute contractual clauses of outsourcing agreements and resolve disputes succinctly and financially prudently, eliminating legal hassles.

3 Integrating Blockchain Technology in the Outsourcing of Supply Chain Processes

Blockchain brings trust and transparency to the supply chain process (Laaper et al., 2017). For example, a simple supply chain system depicted in Fig. 3 has multiple intermediaries like suppliers, manufacturers, distributors, retailers, 3PLs, insurance providers, and end customers who do not necessarily trust or know each other. The flow of information is only between immediate entities in the chain, and the communication is fragmented throughout the life cycle of a product. The fragmented information flow due to data silos causes communication delays decreasing the speed and increasing the cost of a supply chain process. Also, the traditional supply chain process consists of many centralized entities susceptible to single point of

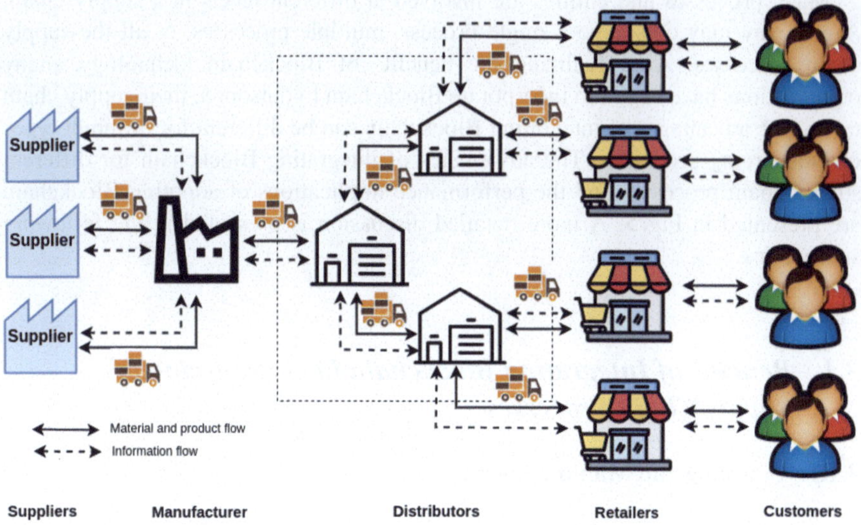

Fig. 3 A typical supply chain flow (Chen et al., 2007)

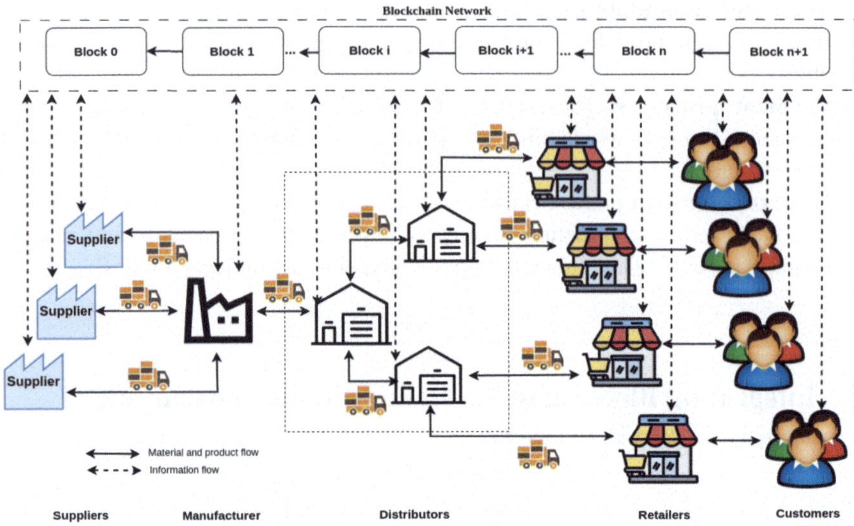

Fig. 4 Blockchain-based supply chain flow

failure. A Blockchain-based solution presented in Fig. 4 will connect all the parties through a common ledger, where the parties share data securely, reliably, immutable, and trusted. Every entity has a common view of data, and no single entity controls all the data. Also, with Blockchain-based solutions, the data is no longer maintained by a centralized authority, which brings transparency and trust to a supply chain process.

Many processes and entities are involved at different levels in a supply chain. A company may outsource a single process, multiple processes, or all the supply chain processes. After realizing the benefits of Blockchain technology, many organizations have begun to incorporate Blockchain to outsource their supply chain tasks. The advantages of integrating Blockchain can be different for different types of outsourcing processes. The advantages of integrating Blockchain for different supply chain processes and the performance implications of adopting Blockchain are presented in Fig. 5. A more detailed discussion is presented in the following subsections.

3.1 Benefits of Integrating Blockchain in Outsourcing of Supply Chain Processes

3.1.1 Sourcing and Manufacturing

One of the most critical aspects of a supply chain process is finding the source of all the product parts. This knowledge is vital in maintaining a product's quality

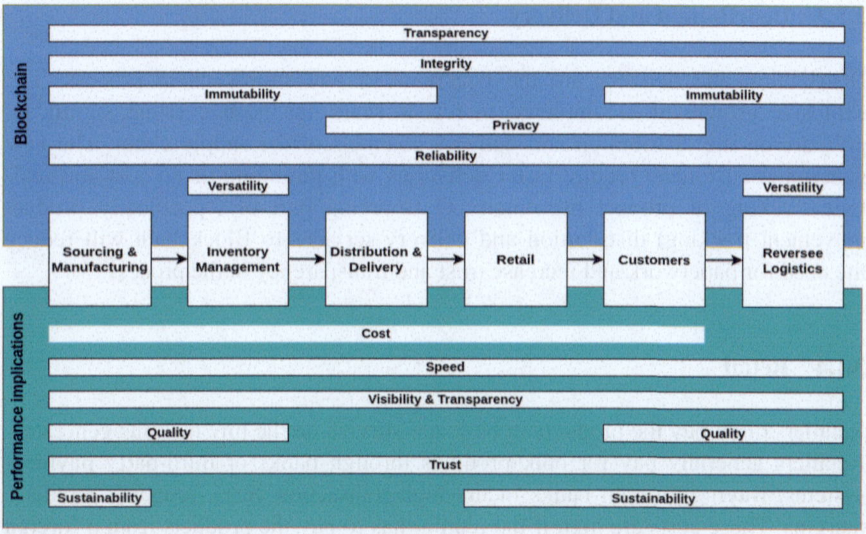

Fig. 5 Blockchain-based supply chain theoretical framework (Difrancesco et al., 2023)

and quantities and tracking the supplier if a product is defective (Zhou et al., 2022). However, tracking the origins of parts (specifically when many suppliers are sourcing the parts) is often complicated, time-consuming, and costly. Also, the origin and supplier data are stored on centralized data servers, raising concerns about the truthfulness of the data. However, if the same data is outsourced to be stored on a Blockchain network, Blockchain, with its inherent trust, transparency, and immutability properties, guarantees its truthfulness and ensures that nobody can tamper with the data. Also, every entity in the supply chain can track and access all the data regarding parts, products, and suppliers.

3.1.2 Inventory Management

Inventory management is a complex task because of a growing number of multiple stock-keeping units, several sourcing suppliers, ever-changing consumer demands, erroneous paperwork, and missing/inaccurate/outdated information. Due to mismanaged inventory, an organization may suffer from severe economic and reputation loss. Blockchain offers an innovative way of inventory management because multiple parties own no inventory item simultaneously (Difrancesco et al., 2023). When ownership of an inventory item changes (for example, supplier to manufacturer or retail to consumer), the change of ownership is recorded in Blockchain in real time. The record gives all the supply chain participants a precise and transparent end-to-end view of product information, including ownership, amount, quality, and location. As a result, companies can operate efficiently with minimum inventory errors and lower warehousing costs.

3.1.3 Distribution and Delivery

Distribution and delivery are the backbone of any supply chain process. The explosive growth of e-commerce in recent years has been exerting significant pressure on the distribution and delivery channels of the supply chain. The new generation customers require faster deliveries with minimum or no cost and real-time tracking of product movement. Outsourcing part of (specifically product movement tracking) distribution and delivery services to Blockchain will reduce the need for paperwork and increase trust and transparency in the process.

3.1.4 Retail

Retailers often buy the products in bulk and survive on the tiny margins generated. Retailers generally pay for bulk products through banks or third-party payment systems. Buying through banks incurs high transaction costs, reducing retailers' margins. These costs are high if the retailer has to buy the products from a foreign country (cross-border payments). Also, the time taken for cross-border transaction settlement is high. Outsourcing retail payments to Blockchain will reduce retailers' transaction costs and increase margins.

The cross-border products purchased by retailers will go through a customs procedure at the port of entry. This process is tedious and slow due to the manual paperwork and lack of trust in the products' origins. However, with the adoption of Blockchain, as the entire life cycle of the product is publicly available, the authenticity and provenance of the products can be established, and the entire customs process can be automated for a hassle-free and faster delivery of products to retailers.

3.1.5 Customer Experience

Blockchain-based supply chain traceability increases customer confidence in the product's authenticity and the manufacturer's brand value. For example, counterfeiting is more prevalent in the pharmaceutical domain than in other domains. To combat counterfeiting, if a company adopts a Blockchain-based solution and outsources most of the supply chain processes to Blockchain, then when a customer purchases the product, the entire data belonging to the product's life cycle is publicly visible. The customer can check the publicly visible data and have confidence in the product's authenticity without being susceptible to counterfeiting.

3.1.6 Reverse Logistics and Second-Hand Market

Blockchain provides many advantages to different supply chain processes; the same technology can be adapted for reverse logistics as reverse logistics focuses on the flow of products from end customers to manufacturers for purposes such as returns, recycling, repairs, or disposal. Blockchain mitigates fraud in product returns. For example, a fraudulent person purchases a product and returns it with some parts missing or changed (Petlee, 2017) and simultaneously claims a refund. Blockchain-based solutions would prevent such an attempt as data about every part of the product is stored immutably and available for all the stakeholders. Another advantage is tracking the disposed or recycled materials used in manufacturing new products. The tracking will instill trust when a company claims that it uses recycled material to manufacture its products, as the customers can see all the data of the recycled product.

In traditional resales, buyers need to trust the sellers on the authenticity of the products. However, with a Blockchain-based solution, buyers can check the authenticity of the product without relying on the reseller, as all the data about the product, including its historical ownership, is publicly available on the Blockchain.

3.2 *Case Study 1: Walmart*

In recent years, Walmart has built several platforms to outsource supply chain processes to Blockchain:

1. **Food industry:** In 2018, Walmart announced it was taking the initiative to build a new Blockchain-based food traceability platform to increase transparency and create shared value for all stakeholders (Ruso, 2018). Suppliers must acquire the data through the IBM Food Trust network using GS1 standard communication protocols. The acquired data, such as product ID, purchase orders, batch/lot codes, and date/time codes (harvesting, processing, shipping, and receiving), is stored in Blockchain. This new platform reduces the time to trace a product to seconds instead of days. In 2019, Walmart China tested tracing 21 of its products using VeChain's Blockchain technology.[2] That year, Walmart also launched the first-ever Blockchain platform to trace Shrimp exports from India to overseas retailers. Walmart also partnered with IBM to build a Hyperledger Fabric-based Blockchain platform[3] to trace mangoes stored in US stores. The platform reduced the time from 6 days to 2 seconds to trace mangoes, which is a humungous amount of reduction in time (Ruso, 2018).
2. **Payments:** Walmart is embracing Blockchain technology to outsource its payment data. In this regard, Walmart has filed two patent applications for digital shopping and vendor payments (De, 2018). The first application describes outsourcing encrypted payment information to Blockchain, and the second application is about a Blockchain-based payment processing system that automates

[2] https://www.vechain.org/

[3] https://www.hyperledger.org/projects/fabric

dividing the payment between parties that provide services related to obtaining and delivering the products.

3. **Delivery:** Walmart also filed a patent that describes outsourcing a part of the drone-based delivery process to Blockchain (Baydakova, 2018). Drones operate autonomously but often need to exchange information/packages with other drones/customers. The parties (drones/customers) must be mutually authenticated during the exchange. Drones rely on a database of delivery information stored on Blockchain for authentication. In summary, Walmart is leveraging Blockchain technology to infuse trust in drone-based deliveries.

3.3 Case Study 2: Everledger

Everledger is an industry-leading platform that helps companies outsource their supply chain processes to Blockchain. It offers supply chain solutions across domains ranging from luxury goods, insurance, diamonds and gemstones, fashion, batteries, and art:

1. **Electric batteries:** An immutable digital identity will be established on Everledger Blockchain for every electric battery that is manufactured. The digital identity is then used to track the battery over time. For example, by using Everledger, a repurposer can quickly and easily separate arrays from one battery for use in another without losing its origination data. Another example is that OEMs can track the battery's journey to final recovery by approved battery recyclers.
2. **Diamonds:** The traditional diamond industry suffers from counterfeiting diamonds, lack of transparency in the origins of the diamonds, and nonavailability of historical ownership data. In recent years, the diamond industry has reached a broad consensus that the solution to traditional problems is outsourcing some diamond supply chain processes to Blockchain. On Everledger, a digital twin for a diamond is maintained along with physical and virtual inventory. The digital twin is created by collecting a comprehensive set of data points related to each diamond, including its 4Cs (carat, cut, color, clarity) and other unique identifying features, and documenting the data on Blockchain. The digital twin will help the manufacturer and the retailer prove a diamond's provenance, allowing customers to make more informed and ethical purchasing decisions.
3. **Wines and spirits:** The brand value and reputation of winegrowers and distillers are often at stake due to a lack of control and visibility into their supply chain once the products leave manufacturing units. Everledger solves the counterfeiting of wine products by using Identify, a Blockchain-backed intelligent tagging for anti-counterfeit and provenance assurance platform. Using Identify, the winegrowers and distillers can create a digital identity for every product manufactured at the source. Once the digital identity is created, the manufacturer physically secures the product with various options, including traditional options (marks,

imprint, coat) and new options like IoT (chip, NFC tags). The end customers can use the security markings to authenticate, transfer, or track the product with the help of the provenance data stored in the Blockchain. A customer can verify the product's authenticity just by using his/her smartphone and the chip/tag on the product within a short time.

3.4 *Case Study 3: Two-Wheeler Bearing Supply Chain*

A simple bearing supply chain primarily has three parties: the manufacturer of the bearing, the manufacturer of the 2-wheelers, the dealers of the 2-wheelers, and the end customers. Although the supply chain is simple, it is plagued by many challenges at different levels. Some challenges of the traditional bearing supply chain are as follows:

1. Stakeholders, specifically the end customers, cannot trace the origins of the bearing.
2. Every stakeholder has a platform to record supply chain transactions of the bearings. With every stakeholder having a platform to record the bearing's data, the data can be tampered with or destroyed.
3. Payment settlements between the stakeholders are time-consuming as the payment processing has to be done manually between the stakeholders.
4. No protection mechanisms are in place to detect the counterfeiting bearings.

A real-time industry study (Ghode et al., 2023) shows that integrating Blockchain enhances transparency, increases data security, improves traceability, speeds up information retrieval, decreases nonvalue-added activities (NVA), and decreases payment settlement time. The study built a shared ledger as a common platform for all the stakeholders, and the bearings and transaction data were recorded on the Blockchain. The study shows that the impact of integrating Blockchain in decreasing the NVA has been measured as 4.5 on the Likert scale. Integrating Blockchain helped to reduce the NVA activities as follows:

1. Once the bearings data is stored and verified in Blockchain, it is available to all the stakeholders. Therefore, it reduces manual and repeated data entry and errors.
2. A smart contract verifies and confirms the bearing consignment data and then triggers an automated payment process, saving time and transaction fees.
3. The orders are also placed through a Blockchain smart contract, which automatically updates the demand and informs the manufacturer about new orders, thereby reducing the delay.
4. The rules about bearings transactions are encoded into a smart contract. The encoding improves trust among stakeholders and reduces manual intervention in decision-making about supply chain transactions.

4 Integrating Blockchain Technology in the Outsourcing of Management Science Methods

Management science explores different practices, principles, and strategies that enable organizations or individuals to guide a business toward success. Management science includes financial management, human resource management (HRM), marketing, strategic, and operational management. Traditional management science methods are becoming increasingly complex due to technological advancements and the ever-growing mutual dependence on different industries. Due to this complexity, many organizations recognize the need for strategic outsourcing of management science methods as a viable solution. More precisely, management methods like human resource management and IT project management are being outsourced by organizations to focus on their core competencies, enhance efficiency, and develop innovation. Rather than outsourcing to traditional centralized entities, by outsourcing to Blockchain, an organization can benefit from tamper-proof record management, trust, and transparency in the outsourcing process. The following subsections explore outsourcing of some management science methods to Blockchain.

4.1 Case Study 4: Human Resource Management

One of the most critical roles in any organization is human resource management (HRM) (Chanda & Singh, 2023; Zirar, 2023; Damle et al., 2023), which oversees selecting, hiring, developing, and managing human resources. Having an in-house HRM for all the HRM activities is costly due to the requirement of sizeable in-house staff, training programs, and technology infrastructure. By outsourcing some HRM functions, organizations can dedicate more resources to focus on strategic initiatives, innovation, and growth. At the same time, organizations can also outsource some HRM functions to Blockchain to enhance efficiency, transparency, and security in the HRM processes. The following subsections explore the benefits of outsourcing different HRM functions to Blockchain.

4.1.1 Recruitment and Onboarding

One major challenge in recruitment is verifying job candidates' qualifications and experience. Companies are wasting tremendous amounts of money and time due to manual verification, which is also erroneous. To reduce cost time and improve the accuracy of the process, some organizations are exploring Blockchain-based automatic verification of qualifications and experience by building the following systems:

1. **Decentralized identity management:** Every job candidate establishes a non-repudiable decentralized identity on the Blockchain, linked to his social identity

and authorized by respective authorities. A job candidate can share his/her decentralized identity with potential employers, who can verify the authenticity of the identity and reduce the risk of identity-related fraud.
2. **Skill verification:** Job candidates store their educational qualifications and work experience certificates as non-fungible tokens (NFTs) in the Blockchain, authorized by respective issuing authorities (Khati et al., 2023). Then, the job candidates can share the immutable records with potential employers, implanting trust and eliminating the need for manual verification.
3. **Decentralized talent marketplaces:** A decentralized marketplace using smart contracts and Blockchain helps employees and employers to connect and negotiate employment contracts without intermediaries, increasing the flexibility for both parties.

4.1.2 Performance Tracking

In the traditional HRM, the employee performance data is stored in a centralized and nontransparent model. Also, the process of performance evaluation is not trustworthy and lacks transparency. Outsourcing performance tracking to Blockchain enables employees to track and record their achievements, feedback, and goals transparently. The performance evaluation rules can be encoded as smart contracts, which can use the recorded data for evaluation. Smart contracts automate the evaluation process and enhance the transparency and fairness of the performance evaluations.

4.1.3 Payroll and Benefits

Similar to performance tracking, the payroll can also be outsourced to Blockchain. Smart contracts can be used to automate salary payments, incentives, loyalty programs, performance-related bonuses, and other compensation-related benefits, reducing manual errors and increasing the transparency and accountability of the payment process.

4.1.4 Training and Development

Organizations invest significant resources in employee training programs. However, maintaining the employees' historical training data can be challenging. By integrating Blockchain into employee training programs, employees can earn and store digital certificates (NFTs) of training courses. They can also share the NFTs with employers, other employees, or social media to gain visibility and recognition for their skills and expertise.

4.2 *Case Study 5: Project Management*

Project management is essential for any organization to ensure the successful initiation, planning, execution, monitoring, and closing of the project. The effectiveness of project management mainly relies on the strategic use of project management tools, which enables project managers to effectively plan and track project progress, manage resources, and ensure successful project completion. However, the existing project management tools could be more efficient in managing cross-organizational projects. In existing cross-organizational projects, the tools are stored centralized at one of the organizations, creating trust and transparency issues for the other organizations involved. Outsourcing cross-organizational project management processes to Blockchain can impart trust and transparency in all the organizations involved in the project.

4.2.1 Cross-organizational Gantt Chart

Gantt chart (Li et al., 2022) is a project management tool that is used to plan, execute, and track a project. It is widely used in IT development, production plant scheduling, educational activities, and several others to save the time and cost of a project. Nevertheless, the traditional Gantt chart systems are primarily centralized and often need to improve when multiple organizations are involved in a project. Outsourcing the storage and maintenance of the Gantt chart to Blockchain enables parties from several organizations to work on a Gantt chart collaboratively, trustlessly, and transparently. Figure 6 shows managers from different organizations collaboratively defining the project's goals, scheduling the execution, and designing the Gantt chart. The Gantt chart is then submitted to a Blockchain, which project members from different organizations can access. The project members can then complete the assigned goals according to the chart and submit the feedback to the project manager through the Blockchain. In this way, outsourcing to Blockchain helps dynamic project management across organizations.

4.3 *Case Study 6: Organizational Behavior*

Organizational behavior is the study of individuals or groups of individuals in the context of an organization. It seeks to increase organizational effectiveness, productivity, and employee satisfaction. Four significant factors influence organizational behavior (Oktriono et al., 2021): people, structure, environment, and technology. Achieving organizational success requires assessing and optimizing these four factors. However, organizations often suffer from data inconsistencies, lack of transparency, and dependency on intermediaries during evaluation. Addressing these challenges is crucial, so outsourcing organizational behavior processes

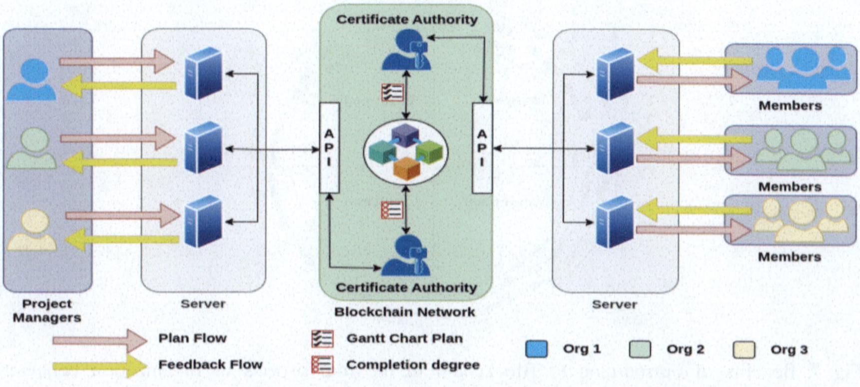

Fig. 6 Blockchain-based inter-organizational Gantt chart (from Li et al., 2022 licensed under CC-BY 4.0)

Table 1 Differences between traditional evaluation and Blockchain-based evaluation of four factors of organization behavior

Factor	Traditional evaluation	Blockchain integration
People	Analyze performance reviews, employee feedback, and human resource metrics	Outsourcing employee performance data to Blockchain ensures immutable and transparent recording
Structure	Analyze communication channels, organizational charts, and relationships	Smart contract-based communication channels can enforce and automate rules minimizing hierarchical bottlenecks and increasing consistency in decision-making
Environment	Analyze market trends, competitive landscapes, and regulatory changes	Blockchain-based Oracle networks feed real-time data of external factors like regulatory compliance, market transactions, and supply chain data to smart contracts. The smart contracts can execute encoded actions based on external real-time data, ensuring timely responses to environmental changes
Technology	Analyze compatibility, efficiency, and security of existing systems	The decentralized nature of Blockchain can foster a collaborative environment between different organizations to share the technologies for mutual development and innovation, which results in improving the overall technological landscape within the organization

to Blockchain can solve the issues. Table 1 discusses the differences between traditional evaluation and Blockchain integration concerning the four factors.

A recent study (Oktriono et al., 2021) explored the impact of outsourcing to Blockchain on the four behavioral organization aspects. The study identified 16 advantages across the four factors, as shown in Fig. 7.

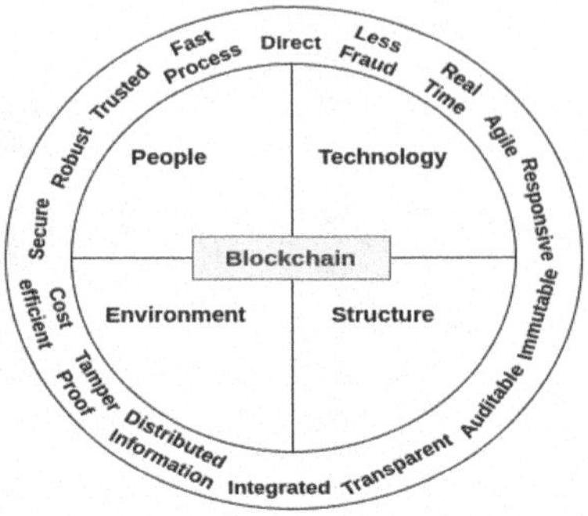

Fig. 7 Benefits of outsourcing to Blockchain to the four aspects of organization behavior (Oktriono et al., 2021)

5 Challenges of Outsourcing to Blockchain and Potential Solutions

Although outsourcing supply chain operations and management science methods to Blockchain offers several benefits compared to traditional outsourcing, there are some challenges:

- **Blockchain platform:** Several Blockchain platforms are available that differ on throughput, scalability, latency, and capacity factors. Unfortunately, none of the existing Blockchain platforms are suitable for matching the throughput and scalability of traditional outsourcing while providing trust, immutability, and transparency. However, according to an organization's outsourcing requirements, multi-criteria decision-making can be employed to select a suitable Blockchain platform.
- **Technical skills:** Since Blockchain technology is relatively new, there must be more technical skills to understand Blockchain among the organizations' upper hierarchical structures and bureaucracy. Technical skills are needed to integrate Blockchain in outsourcing processes. Comprehensive training programs, specialized skill development programs, and awareness initiatives must be conducted across the organization to improve technical skills.
- **Regulatory Compliance:** Blockchain is a unique technology that is perceived differently in different geographical locations. The regulatory landscape of Blockchain is ever-changing and becoming a barrier to its adoption. Organizations must stay updated and collaborate with legal experts to navigate frequent regulatory changes.
- **Security and privacy considerations:** Although transparency is one of the main features of Blockchain, it poses the risk of exposure to sensitive data. Therefore, the organizations must choose the data to be outsourced to Blockchain more vigilantly. Also, adhering to data protection rules is a big challenge when integrating Blockchain. Adopting robust encryption techniques, cryptographic

protocols like zero-knowledge proofs, access controls, and complying with data protection rules can enhance the security and privacy of data on Blockchain.

- **Interoperability:** Blockchain platforms often lack interoperability due to their adoption of diverse technologies and performance factors. Different organizations may adopt different Blockchains according to their needs. Organizations may face the challenge of interoperability during cross-organization collaboration. Organizations must adopt widely accepted Blockchain standards to mitigate interoperability challenges, incorporating interfaces that facilitate interoperability and develop communication channels between different systems without compromising security.
- **Smart contract:** Smart contracts are potent tools for enforcing and automating predefined rules. However, they can become complex when there is a need to translate complex business logic and diverse use cases. Complex smart contracts are often erroneous and require experienced programmers to design and develop smart contracts. Also, most of the smart contract development languages are erroneous. Therefore, a robust security audit is required, which is a costly and time-consuming process. To minimize complexity, a strong collaborative environment is required between supply chain operations or management science experts and Blockchain developers. Also, intensive testing, expert-level auditing, iterative refinement, and continuous improvements are required to overcome the challenge of smart contract security.
- **Legacy system integration:** Legacy systems often lack support for Blockchain integration, causing complexities in outsourcing processes. Therefore, integrating legacy systems with a decentralized Blockchain requires meticulous planning for smoother compatibility. During the integration, issues could relate to communication standards, security protocols, data representation formats, access controls, software/hardware incompatibility, and many others. To address these challenges, organizations can consider developing middleware solutions and interfaces with phased migration instead of a complete migration.

6 Future Directions and Emerging Trends

- **Integrating with Industry 4.0 technologies:** One primary research direction is integrating Industry 4.0 technologies like IoT, artificial intelligence, edge computing, and digital twins with Blockchain (Vilas-Boas et al., 2023) to create innovative solutions for outsourcing supply chain and management science methods.
- **Decentralized governance models:** Identifying factors that drive decentralization in traditional organizations and constructing robust Blockchain-based decentralized governance models are emerging trends.
- **User experience and adoption:** As Blockchain inherently fails to provide a sophisticated user experience, most traditional users hesitate to adopt Blockchain in their day-to-day activities. Therefore, investigating design principles and

strategies to improve the user experience in Blockchain-based outsourcing is a potential area for further exploration.
- **Security and privacy-preserving techniques:** Another key emerging trend is integrating robust privacy-preserving techniques like zero-knowledge proofs and homomorphic encryption to protect the security and privacy of data outsourced to Blockchain. Also, developing robust smart contract languages and execution environments suited explicitly for supply chain and management science methods is a topic of interest for future research.
- **Interoperability standards:** As discussed earlier, integrating legacy systems with Blockchain is complex and challenging. Therefore, developing communication protocols and interoperability standards that facilitate seamless integration is significant for future exploration.
- **Cross-domain applications:** Supply chain and management science methods have applications in most engineering, management, and science fields. Exploring cross-domain applications of Blockchain-based outsourcing is one of the emerging paradigms. For example, a novel solution can be developed by outsourcing supply chain management processes in the healthcare, finance, or government services domain to Blockchain.

7 Conclusion

Supply chain and management science fields are becoming increasingly complex, forcing organizations to outsource most supply chain and management science processes to centralized third parties. However, outsourcing to third parties fosters challenges like data privacy and security, lack of transparency, trust and accountability issues, and many others. The recent advances in Blockchain technology allow Blockchains to emulate the centralized third parties and solve the challenges associated with the centralized parties. Integrating Blockchain with the outsourcing landscape of supply chain and management science methods increases data privacy and security, provides transparency in the outsourcing process, and inculcates trust and accountability. Blockchain integration with supply chain outsourcing benefits almost all processes, from sourcing to reverse logistics. Several companies, including Walmart, are exploring the integration of Blockchain across all service domains. There are also companies like Everledger that are helping companies move their supply chain processes to Blockchain. Human resource management could benefit from Blockchain during recruitment, performance tracking, training, and development of employees. Blockchain-based outsourcing also helps organizations manage cross-organizational projects efficiently. Nevertheless, integrating Blockchain with supply chain and management science methods has several challenges, including a lack of necessary technical skills, regulatory compliance, and data security and privacy considerations. In the future, these challenges can be mitigated by investing in research and development, technology maturation, and training a large workforce. As the number of organizations adopting Blockchain in supply chain and management science is increasing, in the future, many new solutions will be developed and deployed, attracting many numbers of people working in the integrated domain of Blockchain and supply chain or Blockchain and management science.

References

Baydakova, A. (2018). Walmart explores blockchain for connecting automated delivery drones. Retrieved January 20, 2023 from https://www.coindesk.com/markets/2018/09/03/walmart-explores-blockchain-for-connecting-automated-delivery-drones/.

Brown, R. G., Carlyle, J., Grigg, I., & Hearn, M. (2016). Corda: An introduction. *R3 CEV, August, 1*(15)14.

Chanda, P., & Singh, P. (2023). Mapping the landscape of blockchain research in human resource management: A bibliometric analysis. In *Proceedings of the 2023 Fifteenth International Conference on Contemporary Computing* (pp. 115–126).

Chen, M. C., Yang, T., & Yen, C. T. (2007). Investigating the value of information sharing in multi-echelon supply chains. *Quality & Quantity, 41*, 497–511.

Damle, M., Kulkarni, P., & Damle, M. (2023). Blockchain technology in talent retention and capability development in HRM. In *2023 5th International Conference on Inventive Research in Computing Applications (ICIRCA)* (pp. 1181–1188). IEEE.

De, N. (2018). Walmart wants to store payment data on a blockchain. Retrieved January 20, 2023 from https://www.coindesk.com/markets/2018/04/19/walmart-wants-to-store-payment-data-on-a-blockchain/

Difrancesco, R. M., Meena, P., & Kumar, G. (2023). How blockchain technology improves sustainable supply chain processes: A practical guide. *Operations Management Research, 16*(2), 620–641.

Dorsala, M. R., Sastry, V. N., & Chapram, S. (2021). Blockchain-based solutions for cloud computing: A survey. *Journal of Network and Computer Applications, 196*, 103246.

Ghode, D. J., Yadav, V., Jain, R., & Soni, G. (2023). Exploring the integration of blockchain technology into supply chain: Challenges and performance. *Business Process Management Journal, 29*(1), 223–239.

Henderson, S. G., & Nelson, B. L. (2006). *Handbooks in operations research and management science: Simulation*. Elsevier.

Ivanov, D., Tang, C. S., Dolgui, A., Battini, D., & Das, A. (2021). Researchers' perspectives on Industry 4.0: Multidisciplinary analysis and opportunities for operations management. *International Journal of Production Research, 59*(7), 2055–2078.

Khati, P., Shrestha, A. K., & Vassileva, J. (2023). Student certificate sharing system using blockchain and NFTs. In *International Congress on Blockchain and Applications* (pp. 61–70). Springer.

Laaper, S., Fitzgerald, J., Quasney, E., Yeh, W., & Basir, M., et al. (2017). Using blockchain to drive supply chain innovation. Retrieved January 15, 2023 from https://www2.deloitte.com/content/dam/Deloitte/us/Documents/process-and-operations/us-blockchain-to-drive-supply-chain-innovation.pdf

Li, D., Han, D., Xia, B., Weng, T.-H., Castiglione, A., & Li, K.-C. (2022). Fabric-GC: A blockchain-based Gantt chart system for cross-organizational project management. arXiv preprint arXiv:2207.09249.

Nakamoto, S. (2008). Bitcoin: A peer-to-peer electronic cash system. *Decentralized Business Review*.

Oktriono, K., Kusumaningtyas, A. W., & Prakosa, G. H., et al. (2021). The influence of blockchain technology factors on the four aspects of organizational behavior. In *2021 IEEE 7th International Conference on Computing, Engineering and Design (ICCED)* (pp. 1–6). IEEE.

Petlee. (2017). Woman cons Amazon of Rs 70 lakh, arrested. The Times of India, 2017. Retrieved January 20, 2023.

Ruso (2018). Walmart is getting suppliers to put food on the blockchain. Cryptocurrencies. Retrieved January 20, 2023.

Vilas-Boas, J. L., Rodrigues, J. J., & Alberti, A. M. (2023). Convergence of distributed ledger technologies with digital twins, IoT, and AI for fresh food logistics: Challenges and opportunities. *Journal of Industrial Information Integration, 31*, 100393.

Wood, G., et al. (2014). Ethereum: A secure decentralized generalized transaction ledger. *Ethereum Yellow Paper, 151*(2014), 1–32.

Yli-Huumo, J., Ko, D., Choi, S., Park, S., & Smolander, K. (2016). Where is current research on blockchain technology? A systematic review. *PLoS One, 11*(10), e0163477.

Zhou, X., Zhu, Q., & Xu, Z. (2022). The mediating role of supply chain quality management for traceability and performance improvement: Evidence among Chinese food firms. *International Journal of Production Economics, 254*, 108630.

Zirar, A. (2023). Blockchain and human resource management: Emerging themes and research agenda. https://doi.org/10.21203/rs.3.rs-3368951/v1

The Effect of Consolidation, Agile, DevOps, and Cloud on Outsourcing Decisions in the Financial Sector: A Morphogenetic Change Case Study

Josef Langerman

1 Introduction

Outsourcing (and the related fields of offshoring and insourcing) have been important business strategies since the early 1990s, and they continue to be significant (Bals et al., 2016; Cabral et al., 2013; Oshri et al., 2023). Outsourcing refers to moving internal activities outside the company, and offshoring refers to the geographical dimension of where to perform such activities (Bals et al., 2016). Other studies suggest that managers are reconsidering their previous outsourcing decisions, causing them to revoke some of these (Bjørn et al., 2019; Cabral et al., 2013; Dibbern & Hirschheim, 2020).

In this case study, we investigate the IT outsourcing (ITO) and insourcing decisions of one of the largest banks in Africa over the last decade, and how causal factors like consolidation, Agile, DevOps, large-scale cloud migrations, and socio-economic factors, contributed to these decisions. For simplicity, we will refer to this bank as Drakensberg Bank.

In general, the operating model of the bank in the case study followed a traditional plan, build, and run paradigm (Agarwal et al., 2013; Urbach & Ahlemann, 2019), which was popular during the early 2010s. The thinking of this paradigm was largely that of a factory that produces software products or systems. This model was the result of a consolidation phase across the bank.

Plan, build, and run paradigms (sometimes called build, operate, and transfer) emphasise the independence of the IT value chain, which requires independent planning and control. It is monitored by specialists who communicate with (usually internal) customers via clearly defined interfaces. This facilitates the outsourcing

J. Langerman (✉)
Applied Information Systems, University of Johannesburg, Auckland Park, South Africa
e-mail: josefl@uj.ac.za

F. P. García Márquez et al. (eds.), *Outsourcing*, International Series in Operations Research & Management Science 370, https://doi.org/10.1007/978-3-031-95393-4_5

of portions of the value chain, thereby making the IT department at least partially replaceable. The central goals are cost efficiency, reliability, and high-quality processes (Agarwal et al., 2013; Levy, 1996).

This operating model was primarily characterised by handoffs from the plan function to the different build areas, and then passing on to the run organisation. Based on cost, quality, and skills concerns, different parts of this production line were outsourced. The largest outsourcing decision for this organisation was around software testing.

In a traditional outsourcing relationship (like the one described above), an IT team throws a project over a wall to a vendor, and the vendor then, in turn, completes their tasks and throws the project back. This arrangement works very well for companies that use the waterfall methodology for development. But does this arrangement work in an agile work environment that demands interdisciplinary teams to work closely together; where information gets shared; problems are solved quickly; and team members work as equals (Himmelreich et al., 2019)?

During this time, Agile development was gaining traction. With the advent of cloud computing, DevOps as a methodology started to gain more prominence. Agile development, broadly characterised by the Agile Manifesto, has as its main tenets.

(Fowler et al., 2001; Lowell, 2023):

- Individuals and interactions over processes and tools.
- Working software over comprehensive documentation.
- Customer collaboration over contract negotiation.
- Responding to change over following a plan.

DevOps, in turn, focuses on breaking down the barriers between the "build" team and that of the "run" organisation (Battina, 2020; Düllmann et al., 2018; Khattak et al., 2023; Skelton & Pais, 2019). A key feature of DevOps is automation—from the time you build software up to the deployment of said software in production. This breaks down any barriers or handoffs between teams. DevOps has reduced deployment time, which means products could be delivered to customers far quicker. Agile, in general, and DevOps, in particular, is seen as a change in organisational culture rather than just a set of tools and techniques (Khattak et al., 2023; Kim et al., 2021).

As part of this ethos, Drakensberg implemented a well-co-ordinated effort regarding culture transformation in this case study. Part of the cultural transformation involved the empowerment of teams, the focus on flow, and the breakdown, even elimination, of silos, which was congruent with their shift to Agile and DevOps.

In a sense, this was counter to the outsourcing of, especially, the testing function, as this meant that there were handoffs with the same Agile team. Based on this, the management decided to insource all development activities.

With the advent of the cloud, the Drakensberg Bank decided to migrate all its infrastructure to the cloud. While the previous outsourcing engagements were mostly labour-related, the cloud migration was focused on infrastructure. The

DevOps work that had been done previously enabled the bank to move to the cloud far more easily than had it not been done.

Another aspect of outsourcing that plays a role in ITO decisions is the socio-economic reality of the operating environment. In this case study, the bank operates in South Africa. South Africa has one of the highest unemployment rates in the world (Davey, 2023; Langerman & Leung, 2023; Pasara & Garidzirai, 2020) and simultaneously one of the most sophisticated financial systems (BankSeta, 2019). Based on this, there is a constant need for access to skills, balanced with a society that is against outsourcing.

With the exception of a teaching case study by Langerman and Leung (2023), very little knowledge of this topic is available. With this study, we therefore intend to contribute to the published knowledge on the drivers of outsourcing decisions in the South African context.

As an exploratory study, this chapter aims to contribute to the existing knowledge base to enable and stimulate future research around outsourcing in the South African context. More specifically, this research seeks to answer the following research questions:

R_1: What were the major factors that drove outsourcing and insourcing decisions in the South African financial context over the last 15 years?

R_2: What dynamics influenced the outsourcing and insourcing changes in the South African financial context over the last 15 years?

Because of the length of the study (15 years) and the many possible drivers of outsourcing and insourcing decisions, we chose a morphogenetic change framework that characterises all the sourcing decisions and the strategies the bank considers for the future. In morphogenetic frameworks, full significance is accorded to the timescale through which structure, culture, and agency themselves emerge, intertwine and redefine one another (Archer, 1982, 1995, 1996, 2020, 2024). It also addresses the dynamic factors in R_2. The morphogenetic phases consist of structural and cultural conditioning; social and cultural interactions; and structural and cultural elaboration, and we will use these as lenses to investigate the sourcing decisions of Drakensberg Bank (Mirani, 2013).

The contribution of this exploratory study to the current literature is a 15-year historical overview of the financial service's ITO decisions in South Africa, and the uncovering of the outsourcing and insourcing driving forces of consolidation, Agile, and DevOps, that contributed to these decisions. We also identified socio-economic factors that serve as the background to these decisions.

The paper is structured as follows. Section 2 outlines the theoretical foundations of critical realism and morphogenetic theory and why it has been chosen for this study. Section 3 outlines the research method; and then, in the spirit of critical realism, provides a thorough background of the organisation and its operating context. Section 3 closes with a description of the three major morphogenetic changes that transpired over the 15-year period. Section 4 discusses the implication of these findings, followed by the study's conclusion in Sect. 5.

2 Theoretical Foundations

In ITO, there are two main approaches that describe ITO relationships: those that describe the structures, co-ordination, and governance (Karimi-Alaghehband & Rivard, 2020), and those that focus on the enhancements of specific attributes in outcomes.

Over the last couple of decades, the literature on the subject has built up a core of best practices useful to practitioners and researchers. Mirani (2013), however, points out that, at the core, this knowledge base is founded on a somewhat deterministic, static philosophy. Despite the theory's acknowledgement of variations, it largely ignores the diversity in underlying organisational and inter-organisation mechanisms. What is needed is a more dynamic view of how these outsourcing arrangements develop over time.

2.1 Morphogenetic Change Theory

Critical realism and its specific mechanism as morphogenetic change are in contrast with the deterministic and static approaches discussed earlier. Critical realism is a philosophical system that has been positioned as an alternative to positivism and interpretivism paradigms (Lawani, 2020; Zhang, 2023). It is regarded as a philosophy about social structures and human agency, and their interaction is used as a basis for analysing complex phenomena for theorising the interplay of structure, culture, and agency. It navigates the Scylla and Charybdis of strong positivity and strong constructivism (Willis, 2023). The critical realist investigates causal powers and mechanisms that can be experienced through their ability to cause things to occur. The ability to participate in causal analysis in a given context makes critical realism valuable for analysing social problems (Frederiksen & Kringelum, 2021; Lawani, 2020). Researchers like Mukumbang (2023) feel that critical realism offers a more epistemological and ontological grounded approach than, for example, another positivist approach like pragmatism.

Morphogenesis, as advocated by Archer (1982, 1995, 2020), is a specific framework for critical realism, and it provides a systemic framework for assessing the process of organisational change. Morphogenetic theory provides a framework for understanding the interplay between human agency and social change within the context of culture and structure. In contrast to determinism, which prioritises either agency or structure, morphogenetic theory advocates a recursive relationship between these forces, emphasising their dynamic interplay in shaping phenomena. In general, the theory suggests that social structures exert a constraining influence on an individual's actions. Individuals, through reflection, have the capacity to enact transformative changes in these structures (Archer, 2020).

Archer (2024) aptly sums up morphogenesis: "the historical configurations and courses taken by social structures are morphogenetic in nature (conforming to none of the traditional analogies—mechanical, organic, linguistic or cybernetic, but are being shaped and reshaped by the interplay between their constituents, parts and persons". This means that the progression of the decisions made in a societal context are open ended and not finalistic in their elaboration.

In more concrete terms, Mirani (2013) explains morphogenesis as:

> Morphogenetic change is envisioned as a sequence of cycles, each with three, partially overlapping phases – Conditioning, Interaction, and Elaboration. A hallmark of morphogenesis is that the Interaction phase, entailing agent actions, is considered subject to being conditioned or influenced by structural and cultural properties that pre-date it. At the same time, actions are also considered emergent, in the sense that the knowledge of influencing properties cannot in any way help predict them.

Using a similar approach to Mirani's (2013) the cases under discussion for software development sourcing decisions found a progression consisting of two important decisions, where each change was characterised by a morphogenetic cycle of three phases—structural and cultural conditioning; socio-cultural interactions; and structural and cultural elaboration. In the first phase of each change cycle, structural and cultural outcomes of antecedent cycles conditioned the context as perceived by managerial actors. In the second phase, these conditioning factors interacted with the organisation's prevailing socio-cultural dynamics to influence managerial decisions and to effect change.

Critical realism is emerging as a viable alternative for conducting social science research, as it is well suited for developing causal explanations of complex phenomena (Winch, 2023; Wynn & Williams, 2012). Generally, the use of this paradigm has not been high (Heeks & Wall, 2018; Mingers, 2015; Wynn & Williams, 2012). Heeks and Wall (2018) go as far as to say that, in the field of IT for Development (IT4D), while critical realism has not been completely ignored in ICT4D, it has been almost completely ignored. We hope that the methodological choice for this case study will rectify the dearth of available literature.

3 Case Study

In this section, we discuss the case study based on one of the largest banks in South Africa and Africa. For simplicity, we will refer to this bank as Drakensberg Bank.

3.1 Methodology

The case study approach was used as it aligns with the morphogenetic approach, which focuses on structural and cultural change. Case studies work well in contexts where group behaviours, individuals, and process behaviours need to be described in their total settings; as well as the sequence of behaviours in which these behaviours occur (Hollweck, 2015).

To collect the data, detailed interviews were conducted with senior executives at Drakensberg Bank. Their job titles were Chief Technology Officer (1); Head of Testing (2); Technical Head (1); Data Analyst; and Head of Software Engineering Practices (1). These interviews were transcribed and stored on Atlas.ti. The interviews covered the period from 2008 up to 2023—so 15 years in total. The investigation period started with the 2008 financial crash. The main events that characterised the outsourcing decisions in these organisations were the outsourcing of their respective testing functions, the advent of agile methodologies, and the cloud era. All these technological and process advances had a significant effect on the outsourcing strategy of each bank.

These changes occurred against the societal backdrop of South Africa and Africa, which is characterised by widespread joblessness and poverty. In contrast, the financial sector in South Africa is considered to be highly advanced. The interplay of highly advanced financial services and joblessness and poverty is a factor that constantly mediates outsourcing decisions.

Section 3.2 provides an overview of South Africa and the importance of its financial sector. Section 3.3 gives an overview of Agile, DevOps, and Cloud, as these played an important role in the Drakensberg outsourcing decisions.

These themes culminate in Sect. 3.4, in which we look at the interplay of the societal, process, and technology factors through a morphogenetic analytical lens. We show the organisational mechanisms inherent in each change cycle and the imperatives responsible for transitioning from one change cycle to the next. The discussion will use the morphogenesis phases of conditioning, interaction and elaboration. Following Mirani (2013) we will investigate the linkages between successive cycles in terms of the power of emergent outcomes from one cycle to the next.

3.2 The South African Socio-Economic Background

South Africa has one of the highest unemployment rates in the world. At over 30%, it is South Africa's biggest contemporary challenge. Unemployment, and issues such as poverty, stagnant growth, and inequality are not recent phenomena. These challenges were faced as early as the 1980s when the country had international sanctions applied to it. Unemployment and stagnant economic growth have been persistent economic problems. Even after the advent of democratic government in 1994, job creation and growth have not provided for all those willing to work: economic growth has been stagnant for almost a decade (Pasara & Garidzirai, 2020; Fig. 1).

South African financial markets are the most developed and liquid in Africa and are considered well-developed by global standards. This reflects credible and independent policymaking, a diverse economy, and strong financial institutions. Foreign exchange market turnover is among the top 20 in the world (International Monetary Fund, 2022). In terms of employment, the finance sector employs a total

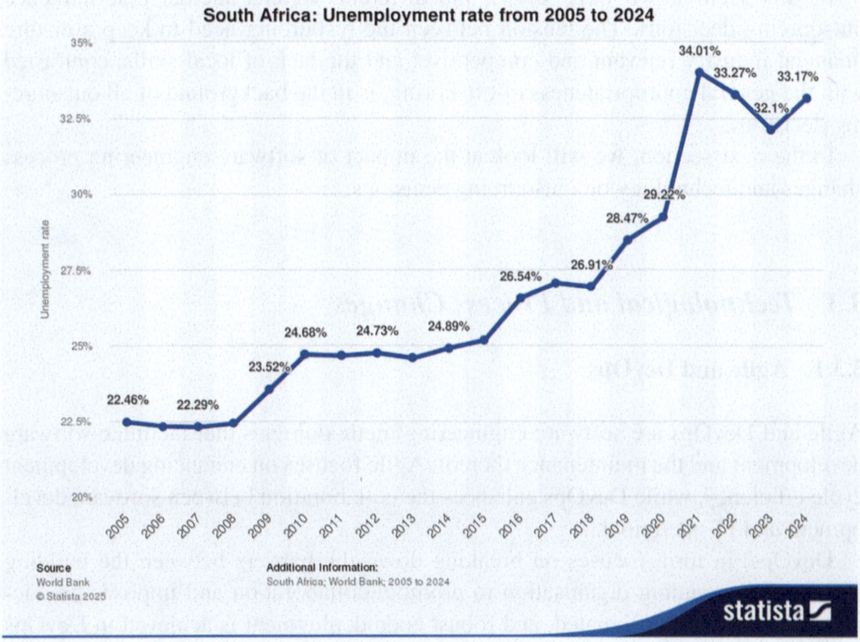

Fig. 1 South African unemployment rate from 2005 to 2024 (World Bank, 2025)

of 2.51 million employees and makes up 15% of the South African workforce (BankSeta, 2019).

The six largest banks in South Africa provide employment to over 185,000 people. Digitalisation, however, led to the closure of many branches, impacting staff numbers. In 2019, for example, Standard Bank, Absa, and Nedbank retrenched 6680 employees due to digitalisation pressures (Langerman & Leung, 2023).

The lack of skills in Africa is having a negative effect on the continent's digital transformation efforts. Four in five organisations surveyed reported some negative effect from a lack of technical skills, with 41% reporting that employees are leaving as a result of the pressures they experience due to understaffing. Other consequences include not being able to meet client needs (reported by 46%); reduced capacity for innovation (53%); and losing customers to competitors (60%) (SAP, 2023).

Against this backdrop of high unemployment, it is understandable that the sentiment from South African society is against outsourcing. As Davey (2023) notes in a South African newspaper: "An astounding 74% of South Africa's youth is unemployed, while at the same time an estimated 77,000 jobs are available, but nobody has the correct skills to do them. Add to this the fact that more than 300,000 jobs have been outsourced to employees who live overseas, and it becomes clear that addressing the skills shortage in our country, particularly in the digital sector, is key".

In this section, we have shown the different societal factors that influence outsourcing decisions. The tension between the resourcing need to keep a mature financial industry relevant and competitive, and the lack of local skills, contrasted with the general appropriateness of offshoring, is in the background of all outsourcing decisions.

In the next section, we will look at the impact of software engineering process changes and technology on outsourcing decisions.

3.3 Technological and Process Changes

3.3.1 Agile and DevOps

Agile and DevOps are software engineering methodologies that facilitate software development and the maintenance thereof. Agile focuses on enhancing development cycle efficiency, while DevOps enhances the collaboration between software development and IT operations.

DevOps, in turn, focuses on breaking down the barriers between the building team and the running organisation to promote collaboration and improve productivity. Transparent, automated, and robust code deployment is achieved in DevOps by integrating people, practices, processes, tools, and technologies (Skelton & Pais, 2019).

A key feature of DevOps is automation—from the time the software is built up to the deployment of said software in production. This breaks down any barriers or handoffs between teams. DevOps reduces deployment time, which means products can be delivered to customers far more quickly and with higher quality. The other DevOps practices are continuous development, continuous integration, testing, deployment, and monitoring on an ongoing basis.

Both Agile and DevOps are built on Lean principles for software development and delivery. In Lean thinking, eliminating waste is a key feature. DevOps achieves this by automating repetitive tasks, while Agile delivers the most valuable features first. Lean also emphasises continuous improvement, which DevOps achieves through feedback loops, and Agile achieves through retrospectives. Lean focuses on respect for people. Agile achieves this communication within self-organising teams and DevOps through the fusion of efforts of development and IT operations teams.

An important aspect of Lean is the concept of "flow". Flow means that production activities are organised as a continuous flow by eliminating discontinuities (Rodríguez et al., 2019). Flow requires that unnecessary steps and inventories are eliminated (waste). This notion finds its expression in stream-aligned agile teams. As Skelton and Pais (2019) note: "A stream-aligned team is aligned to a single, valuable stream of work like a single product or service, a set of features, or even a user journey or user persona. This team is empowered to build and deliver value quickly, safely, and (this is key) independently. There shouldn't be any hand-offs to other teams to complete parts of the work. They 'own' it from beginning to end".

The authors then note that stream-aligned teams should be the primary team-type in an organisation and that other team-types exist to reduce the burden on stream-aligned teams.

Agile, in general, and DevOps in particular, is seen as a change in organisational culture rather than just a set of tools and techniques. DevOps is a bundle of applications and cultural activities that aims to boost participation and communication (Khattak et al., 2023). One of the main barriers to DevOps' cultural transformation is the lack of collaboration and co-ordination.

Taken together, the notions of Agile, DevOps, and especially the teaming structures and cultural changes, make it hard to outsource a specific part of the development cycle as this increases handoffs and introduces process friction.

3.3.2 Cloud

During the 2010s, cloud computing emerged as a new technology and business paradigm. Cloud computing provides easy-access scaling, reliability, reconfigurability, and high performance from its resources over the Internet, without the need for complex infrastructure management by customers (Surbiryala & Rong, 2019).

The National Institute of Standards and Technology (NIST) defines Cloud computing as "a model for enabling convenient, on-demand network access to a shared pool of configurable computing resources (e.g., networks, servers, storage, applications, and services) that can be rapidly provisioned and released with minimal management effort or service provider interaction" (NIST, 2022).

There are many benefits for organisations utilising Cloud technology. In the Cloud computing paradigm, customers are able to obtain their applications and data from anywhere, thereby reducing equipment costs. Accessibility to applications and services can be delivered directly to users. As more applications move to the Cloud, servers and other computing hardware will consume less space, which reduces the need for dedicated space for data centres and server rooms. Cloud services also lessen the requirement for upfront capital to procure software and infrastructure, as services are generally consumed in a pay-as-you-go fashion (Gundu et al., 2020).

DevOps and Cloud development go hand-in-hand. Cloud computing's centralised structure offers a platform for DevOps automation. The adoption of DevOps will help with Cloud adoption in an organisation. DevOps provides the tools and processes for deploying software to the Cloud, which in turn speeds up the development process (Battina, 2020).

In general, the advent of the Cloud necessitates DevOps and, as noted earlier, DevOps works together with Agile. As corporate strategies move to the Cloud, they necessitate DevOps and Agile practices. As teaming and cultural changes lie at the heart of these methods, it is hard to outsource a specific part of the development cycle as it increases handoffs and introduces process friction. This, in turn, affects the outsourcing relationships.

3.4 *Morphogenetic Change Cycles*

3.4.1 Organisational Change Cycle 1: Consolidation

Morphogenetic Consolidation Cycle: Structural and Cultural Conditioning

Historically, Drakensberg Bank has been characterised by a business-line driven operating model that has seen very pleasing growth. Drakensberg Bank's ambition was to be the premier bank in emerging markets. In general, structural redundancies were widely accepted, with many support units duplicated across business units and geographies. Business units and geographies had their own in-house IT departments and, in many cases, their own infrastructure.

Large-scale projects were kicked off to consolidate key software and provide a consistent customer experience across the Drakensberg group. One signature programme replaced the legacy core banking systems with SAP. This caused a huge demand for resources that could not be filled in-house. Most of the resourcing was done with ad hoc contractors, with the result that processes differed and cost was generally high.

Consolidation Cycle: Socio-Cultural Interactions

These antecedent conditions cause the management to consider outsourcing options. Outsourcing, with access to offshore resources, would solve some of the problems inherent in the organisation. The cost would be lower and predictable; there would be access to resources, especially through offshore Indian vendors; and there would be one quality standard. After the 2008 financial sector crash, cost became more prominent. Around 2009, the decision was made to outsource all of the testing in the retail business unit. The next couple of years were spent managing the transition as contractors had to be let go and new processes had to be bedded down. Following the success of the retail bank's testing outsourcing, the investment bank also outsourced its testing activities, but to a different Indian offshore vendor.

A new group CIO with a strong track record in IT outsourcing was hired in 2010. Part of his agenda was a major outsourcing of the software build and run activities across the Drakensberg Group. In 2012, a proposal to this effect was tabled, but it was not approved. A couple of factors informed this decision: the risk profile of the deal; a less-than-ideal cost-benefit profile; and a general resistance to staff retrenchments, as most of the resources in this deal were permanent resources.

In the aftermath of the financial crisis of 2008 and the tightening of capital, Drakensberg Bank sharpened its strategic focus and moved from a focus on all emerging markets to only the African market.

Consolidation Cycle: Structural and Cultural Elaboration

The consolidation and outsourcing of parts of the software development lifecycle over time evolved into a "plan, build, and run" structure. Architects and strategists would plan the work; it would be handed over to a build organisation that would construct the products and services to specification, to be handed over to a run organisation that would be responsible for the day-to-day running and maintenance of the products and services. The idea was that the build and run structures could be more easily outsourced, with the planning activities kept in-house. Even though the full outsourcing of the build and run structures never fully came to fruition, the organisational structures were in place.

The cost benefits of outsourcing the testing slowly eroded, and the testing resources became more bloated over time. The handoffs from the development teams to the testing organisations created friction. Typical issues that were raised were too little automation of testing and cultural/communication differences. The friction between teams caused many offshore resources to be onshored, as the geographical, cultural, and time zone differences hampered the workflow. In essence, the goal of reducing costs by using offshore testing providers was never realised, as the resources moved to South Africa, resulting in higher costs again. Forecasting of testing demand had to be done months in advance and was not very accurate, resulting in many paid-for resources being unproductive.

3.4.2 Organisational Change Cycle 2: Agile and DevOps

Agile and DevOps: Structural and Cultural Conditioning

The previous change cycle had seen the emergence of even higher costs and a general malaise around the speed of delivery. With the amount of change in the organisation, especially the large SAP project business was unhappy with their IT counterparts and lacked capacity for new projects. A new group CIO was appointed in 2014, and an external consultancy was onboarded to facilitate a cost-reduction process.

The erosion of offshore benefits in terms of cost and the many handoffs made the cost-per-function in the organisation far higher than in comparable organisations. During this time, a new head of the build organisation was announced, and the hope was that, within the build organisation, i.e. design, construction and test, there would be far greater synergy.

The years of consolidation have helped Drakensberg Bank to standardise some form of waterfall development, and there has been a big focus on improving project management by completing PMI certifications.

Agile and DevOps: Socio-Cultural Interactions

With software development too slow and costs high, the new head of the build organisation was looking for different methodologies and ways to solve these problems. This period also saw the uptick of mobile applications and far more digitisation in the organisation. The methodologies that were in place did not deliver the benefits that were envisioned, and radical new approaches were needed.

Agile methodologies were successfully piloted as part of the online banking programme. Costs were reduced by four times per function point, and software was delivered to clients far more frequently. It was decided that Agile should be rolled out across the organisation. Agile was scaled within the build organisation using the SAFe methodology. With the focus of Agile on team culture, the organisational health index, which measures staff engagement, went up dramatically.

The development teams were organised around smaller multi-functional teams. Business involvement improved and, in general, throughput improved. Costs came down as there was less of a reliance on contractors.

Part of the issue around slow delivery was the friction of rolling out software to production. Change management processes hampered the smooth flow of code production from the cross-functional teams to the operations organisation. DevOps was chosen as an approach to remedy this situation. Programmes were put in place to build deployment pipelines, i.e. automated processes that test the code and deploy it far more smoothly to production. There was a major focus on automation, configuration management, and deployment. The focus of the cross-functional team moved from just being a build team to an ethos of: "You build it, you run it".

The advent of both Agile and DevOps eroded the rationale for an outsourced testing organisation. The organisation decided to insource all of its testing activities. As part of the Agile ethos, developers were asked to take over most of the testing activities and to automate as much of it as possible. This resulted in some immediate savings on the income statement.

The socio-economic impact and optics of outsourcing were much debated during this period. With the high unemployment rate, the attractiveness of outsourcing, especially offshoring, lost its lustre. One prominent hire during that time said she joined Drakensberg Bank because a representative of Drakensberg Bank, at an industry conference, said it was stopping outsourcing its testing functions.

It must be said that, during this time, the Indian outsourcers adapted to the general sentiment in South Africa around offshoring and set up local organisations to service large corporations like Drakensberg Bank. Many of the outsourcing contracts were also adjusted to create training programmes for South Africans and to step-up their employment of South African citizens.

Drakensberg Bank also increased their spending on training by creating focused programmes for software engineers, especially around the themes of DevOps and Agile. Leadership initiatives for highly talented technical specialists were created to try and satisfy the demand for skills.

Agile and DevOps: Structural and Cultural Elaboration

The insourcing of testing activities had some unintended consequences. The assumption that developers would take over the testing activities was flawed. The reality is that less testing took place. The overall change management around the insourcing of testing was also lacking, as each team had to handle their own testing in a way that seemed fit for them. Testing standards across the organisation were not in place, with the result that quality was inconsistent. Simple things that the outsourcers provided, like management reports, were not being produced.

A consequence was that production stability deteriorated. It should be noted that many factors contribute to production reliability, and the quality of testing is only one of these factors. The Chief Technology Officer, at that point, however, made a direct link between production stability and the maturity of testing.

The implementation of DevOps had the effect that many central service management teams got denuded as more of the deployment and service management activities moved to cross-functional development teams. An unintended consequence of this was that incident and problem management was not as effective as it could have been. This also contributed to a lack of faith by management and business in production stability and the management thereof.

It should be noted that the problems outlined above are not inherent in Agile and DevOps. Management of Drakensberg Bank concurs that the management of the insourcing was not handled well, and the management of production across various agile teams should have been handled better.

3.4.3 Organisational Change Cycle 3: Infrastructure Outsourcing

Infrastructure Outsourcing: Structural and Cultural Conditioning

After the retirement of the previous group CIO, a new group CIO was appointed. The IT strategy built on the previous change cycle but with a shift in focus to client-centricity and Cloud. Some of the signature programmes that were kicked off during this period were Application Simplification, Cloud Migration, Always On, and a Salesforce rollout.

The Always On programme resulted directly from an emerging aspect of the previous change cycle: system instability.

Some of the criticism raised against the previous change cycle was that it did not focus enough on the client engagement systems and processes. Most of the work of the last two change cycles was focused on productivity improvements or back-office upgrades. A change of focus to more client-centricity was required during the new change cycle.

Infrastructure Outsourcing: Socio-Cultural Interactions

Infrastructure outsourcing deals (IaaS) were signed with Microsoft and Amazon in 2018. The rationale for this was better cost management; faster delivery; flexible access to scale; improved productivity; better performance; and security. The strategic intent for the next decade is that the order of priority for new hosting will be public Cloud, then private Cloud and, as a last resort, on-premises. Software development will move to a "Cloud first" strategy; and all software procurement will be "Cloud first". In time, all services will migrate to the public Cloud.

The migration options presented to teams were:

- *Re-Host:* Basically, "lift and shift", means a re-hosting with no added features or benefits.
- *Re-Platform*: Moving older, not cloud-ready operating systems to the cloud, e.g. AIX to Linux.
- *Re-Purchase*: Renegotiating the pricing for locally hosted applications, to be used in the Cloud.
- *Retire*: Turning off old applications, addressed through the Simplification programme.
- *Retain*: Keeping on premise.

The move to the Cloud was planned for 5–10 years, due to the complexity of the estate. The migration strategy focuses on readiness aspects (governance, proof of concepts, security, etc.), large-scale training across the organisation, and independent assurance.

The decision to standardise on the Salesforce software and platform was an important "as a service" initiative (SaaS and PaaS). Salesforce will not only be used as a client management platform, but also as a general low-code environment.

Infrastructure Outsourcing: Structural and Cultural Elaboration

The Cloud initiative introduced new complexities which needed a change in organisational processes. As more systems and infrastructure moved to the Cloud, better billing systems needed to be put in place. Payment for services moved to the pay-as-you-go model, which was a change to the systems in place.

To implement these programmes, it was decided not to outsource any of the development and technical resources. Specialist contractors were used, and there was a drive to train all internal staff. At the height of the SaaS programme, Drakensberg Bank had the most Salesforce rangers in the world. The executive committee of the bank all completed Ranger training. The same holds for AWS and Azure. Training programmes were put in place to train and certify staff in these technologies.

As the Always On system resilience programme gained traction, it was realised that Agile and DevOps on their own were not sufficient in themselves to solve the resilience issues, and new methodologies were investigated and adopted. An example of this is the Google SRE (site reliability engineering) framework.

Infrastructure Outsourcing: Structural and Cultural Elaborations

The change cycle for infrastructure outsourcing is not complete yet, and at the time of the publication of this document, the Always On programme had just been completed. All of the training activities, the rollout of large programmes, and the implementation of Always On have not solved all of the issues they tried to address. One of the major concerns at Drakensberg Bank is its high cost of IT, compared to its peers. Outsourcing in the South African socio-economic climate is not seen, at least at this stage, as a viable solution. Teams outsource pockets of work, but no large-scale outsourcing is planned.

In-house training to create skills for SaaS and PaaS migrations is still being considered by Drakensberg as preferable to accessing skills through outsourcing.

4 Implications and Discussion

A systematic analysis of Drakensberg Bank over the last decade has highlighted three significant changes in their information technology outsourcing arrangements. As Table 1 shows, each phase consisted of an initial set of structural and cultural conditions, which interacted with the socio-cultural environment and then altered the structural and cultural environment. Following the same pattern as outlined by Mirani (2013), in each cycle, the first phase laid the foundation for change where the outcomes, many times emergent, of the previous cycle conditioned the overall decision and action context.

In the second phase, the conditioned context interacted with socio-cultural dynamics across all the system's actors. Further change occurred during the transition from the second to the third phase. This analysis is therefore helpful as it has provided a critical-realist and holistic view of the organisational changes that underpinned the evolution of Drakensberg Bank.

The use of outsourcers in the consolidation phase made sense for Drakensberg Bank. Large projects were being rolled out, and the organisation needed access to skilled resources. The outsourcing arrangements were largely around testing, so organisational structures were built to manage the outsourcing. Over time, rate attractiveness slowly eroded, and there was internal resistance to why a country with a high unemployment rate would outsource so much.

An unintended outcome of the consolidation cycle was that delivery became fragmented. New development methodologies, like Agile and DevOps, focused on cross-functional teams that prioritised the flow of work. Having a critical part of the development cycle outsourced did not help with flow, and hence, a second cycle of

Table 1 Depiction of morphogenetic cycles at Drakensberg Bank

Cycle	Structural and cultural conditioning	Socio-cultural interactions	Structural and cultural elaboration
Consolidation cycle 2008–2014	Historically, it was a period of rapid growth with no focus on cost Individual contractors make up a large portion of the workforce Federated structures across the organisation with many ad hoc processes and systemic inefficiencies Different testing teams existed in the organisation resulting in different quality standards Large-scale SAP rollout caused an unprecedented demand for testing resources	2008 financial crash caused cost pressures In-efficiencies in the testing process and increased demand for testing resources caused management to consider a testing outsource with access to offshore resources The confluence of these agendas caused the organisation to outsource testing Group CIO hired with a strong track record of outsourcing success Full-scale outsourcing of most IT functions is considered but not implemented as cost differential is not that attractive More individual area-specific outsourcing activities followed	Over time, attractiveness of rates eroded Typical plan-build-run operating models ensued. Software development is seen as a production line Having an outsourced testing organisation created many hand-offs in the software development process leading to lower efficiencies Benefits of offshore resources did not materialise Socio-economic pressure made new large-scale outsourcing deals harder
Agile and DevOps cycle 2017	Innovative processes like agile and DevOps were changing the thinking around software development with the emphasis on cross-functional teams Outsourcing in a developing country with high unemployment was frowned upon by unions and government regulations The cost advantage of outsourcing was not that attractive anymore	Testing was insourced, based on cross-functional software teams eliminating third-party and internal hand-offs Non-production environment management became insourced	Quality decreased, as not much thought was given to the governance of testing within teams Higher rates of system unreliability based on lack of quality standards resulted Cost savings ensued at the expense of quality More production issues related to poor testing emerged

Infrastructure Outsource (2019–)	In-house data centres were expensive and a slowdown in demand caused excess capacity Competitors were all considering cloud Cloud was very attractive to agile and DevOps methods as there is less centralised deployment control	Large deals were signed to migrate infrastructure to Microsoft azure and AWS (IaaS) Multi-year programmes kicked off for cloud migration New bank-wide products like salesforce were launched (SaaS & PaaS)	Increased skills demand created a need for more training. Drakensberg bank become the company in the world with the most salesforce-certified rangers. The focus stays on in-house skill development and staff augmentation through specialised contracting houses

change ensued, which focused on Agile and DevOps and reversed the outsourcing of the previous phase.

Again, as in the previous change cycle, there were some emerging issues: the erosion of quality and the concomitant increase in system outages. This was not planned for, and many improvement programmes were implemented to improve quality.

Cycle 2 also set the organisation up for the changes in Cycle 3. DevOps, focusing on automation, is a prerequisite for cloud migration. Drakensberg Bank decided to move all of its infrastructure to the cloud, which would not have been possible without the DevOps interventions of the previous cycle. Learning from their previous outsourcing engagements and the socio-economic context, Drakensberg now focuses on in-house training and skills development.

5 Limitations and Conclusion

The morphogenetic analysis employed in this study showed the evolution of Drakensberg Bank's outsourcing arrangements over the last decade. The morphogenetic analysis was helpful as it shed light on the interplays between the different factors and showed the progression of the outsourcing arrangements.

The analysis showed how the bank moved from a consolidation phase to having their outsourcing arrangements disrupted by Agile and DevOps; and then how DevOps set them up for a cloud migration.

The analysis also clarified that unintended consequences, also known as emergence, shaped outsourcing decisions. Drakensberg Bank did not know that outsourcing testing would disrupt the flow of work and that the advent of Agile to solve this problem would reverse their outsourcing decisions.

It was also unclear that, at the start of the DevOps journey, DevOps would enable the cloud journey.

We also highlighted that socio-economic factors could play a role in outsourcing decisions. The morphogenetic analysis of Drakensberg Bank showed the dynamic interplay between these factors. Agile and DevOps, together with the socio-economic situation in South Africa, resulted in an insource, but DevOps laid the foundation for an infrastructure (cloud) outsourcing. As cloud outsourcing is far less resource-intensive than labour outsourcing, this decision made sense.

These findings and methodological choices support the notion that outsourcing decisions require a deep understanding of the organisational factors that give rise to these decisions. They also answered both our research questions.

Like all conceptual research, this study has its limitations. By relying on interviews and data from one large bank in South Africa, our research is geographically limited to a developing country and to a specific industry. However, the Drakensberg Bank is the largest by assets in Africa and has operations in 18 African countries, which mitigates this limitation. The financial sector is also, as we have shown, an important driver of the South African GDP. Despite these shortcomings, we uncovered the role of consolidation, Agile, and DevOps in outsourcing decisions that should be applicable to other African countries and perhaps other industries. Nevertheless, future research should look into cases in the developed world and other geographic regions and industries. With this initial exploratory study, we hope to fuel further inquiry into outsourcing decisions based on process and technological change.

References

Agarwal, H., Bommadevara, N., & Weinberg, A. (2013). Using a plan-build-run organizational model to drive IT infrastructure objectives. *McKinsey on Business Technology, 32*.

Archer, M. S. (1982). Morphogenesis versus structuration: On combining structure and action. *The British Journal of Sociology, 33*(4), 455–483. https://doi.org/10.2307/589357

Archer, M. S. (1995). *Realist social theory: The morphogenetic approach*. Cambridge University Press.

Archer, M. S. (1996). *Culture and agency: The place of culture in social theory*. Cambridge University Press.

Archer, M. S. (2020). The morphogenetic approach; critical realism's explanatory framework approach. *Agency and Causal Explanation in Economics*, 137–150.

Archer, M. S. (2024). *Morphogenesis answers its critics*. Cambridge University Press.

Bals, L., Kirchoff, J. F., & Foerstl, K. (2016). Exploring the reshoring and insourcing decision making process: Toward an agenda for future research. *Operations Management Research, 9*(3–4), 102–116. https://doi.org/10.1007/s12063-016-0113-0

BankSeta. (2019). *BankSeta Sector Skills Plan 2020—2025*. https://www.bankseta.org.za/wp-content/uploads/2020/01/BankSeta-SSP-2020-2025.pdf

Battina, D. S. (2020). Devops, a new approach to cloud development & testing. *International Journal of Emerging Technologies and Innovative Research, 7*(8).

Bjørn, P., Søderberg, A.-M., & Krishna, S. (2019). Translocality in global software development: The dark side of global agile. *Human-Computer Interaction, 34*(2), 174–203. https://doi.org/10.1080/07370024.2017.1398092

Cabral, S., Quelin, B. V., & Maia, W. (2013). Outsourcing failure and reintegration: The influence of contractual and external factors. *Long Range Planning, 37*.

Davey, D. (2023, April 18). Addressing the skills shortage in SA will reduce youth unemployment. *The Mail & Guardian*. https://mg.co.za/partner-content/2023-04-18-addressing-the-skills-shortage-in-sa-will-reduce-youth-unemployment/

Dibbern, J., & Hirschheim, R. (2020). Introduction: Riding the waves of outsourcing change in the era of digital transformation. In R. Hirschheim, A. Heinzl, & J. Dibbern (Eds.), *Information systems outsourcing: The era of digital transformation* (pp. 1–20). Springer International Publishing. https://doi.org/10.1007/978-3-030-45819-5_1

Düllmann, T. F., Paule, C., & van Hoorn, A. (2018). Exploiting DevOps practices for dependable and secure continuous delivery pipelines. In *2018 IEEE/ACM 4th international workshop on rapid continuous software engineering (RCoSE)* (pp. 27–30).

Fowler, M., Highsmith, J., et al. (2001). The agile manifesto. *Software Development, 9*(8), 28–35.

Frederiksen, D. J., & Kringelum, L. B. (2021). Five potentials of critical realism in management and organization studies. *Journal of Critical Realism, 20*(1), 18–38. https://doi.org/10.1080/14767430.2020.1846153

Gundu, S. R., Panem, C. A., & Thimmapuram, A. (2020). Hybrid IT and multi cloud an emerging trend and improved performance in cloud computing. *SN Computer Science, 1*(5), 256. https://doi.org/10.1007/s42979-020-00277-x

Heeks, R., & Wall, P. J. (2018). Critical realism and ICT4D research. *The Electronic Journal of Information Systems in Developing Countries, 84*(6), e12051. https://doi.org/10.1002/isd2.12051
Himmelreich, H., Hildebrandt, P., Nalgirkar, R., & Bijlsma, J. (2019). When agile meets outsourcing. *URL:*https://www.bcg.com/En-Nl/Publications/2019/Agile-Meets-outsourcing.aspx. Accessed: 26.11.19.
Hollweck, T. (2015). Robert K. Yin.(2014). Case study research design and methods. *Canadian Journal of Program Evaluation, 30*(1), 108–110.
International Monetary Fund. (2022). *South Africa: Financial Sector Assessment Program (IMF Country Report No. 22/182)*. https://www.imf.org/-/media/Files/Publications/CR/2022/English/1ZAFEA2022006.ashx
Karimi-Alaghehband, F., & Rivard, S. (2020). IT outsourcing success: A dynamic capability-based model. *The Journal of Strategic Information Systems, 29*(1), 101599.
Khattak, K., Qayyum, F., Naqvi, S., Mehmood, A., & Kim, J. (2023). A systematic framework for addressing critical challenges in adopting DevOps culture in software development: A PLS-SEM perspective. *IEEE Access*, 1. https://doi.org/10.1109/ACCESS.2023.3325325
Kim, G., Humble, J., Debois, P., Willis, J., & Forsgren, N. (2021). *The DevOps handbook: How to create world-class agility, reliability, & security in technology organizations*. IT Revolution.
Langerman, J., & Leung, W. S. (2023). The effect of outsourcing and insourcing on agile and DevOps. *Journal of Information Technology Teaching Cases, 20438869231176841*. https://doi.org/10.1177/20438869231176841
Lawani, A. (2020). Critical realism: What you should know and how to apply it. *Qualitative Research Journal, 21*(3), 320–333. https://doi.org/10.1108/QRJ-08-2020-0101
Levy, S. M. (1996). *Build, operate, transfer: Paving the way for tomorrow's infrastructure*. John Wiley & Sons.
Lowell, K. R. (2023). *Leading modern technology teams in complex times: Applying the principles of the agile manifesto*. Springer Nature.
Mingers, J. (2015). Helping business schools engage with real problems: The contribution of critical realism and systems thinking. *European Journal of Operational Research, 242*(1), 316–331. https://doi.org/10.1016/j.ejor.2014.10.058
Mirani, R. (2013). A case study of morphogenetic change in long-term offshoring. *International Journal of Information Management, 33*(4), 663–673. https://doi.org/10.1016/j.ijinfomgt.2013.03.006
Mukumbang, F. C. (2023). Retroductive theorizing: A contribution of critical realism to mixed methods research. *Journal of Mixed Methods Research, 17*(1), 93–114. https://doi.org/10.1177/15586898211049847
NIST. (2022, May 12). *NIST Cloud Computing Programme*. https://www.nist.gov/programs-projects/nist-cloud-computing-program-nccp
Oshri, I., Kotlarsky, J., & Willcocks, L. P. (2023). *The handbook of global outsourcing and offshoring* (4th ed.). Palgrave Macmillan UK. https://books.google.co.za/books?id=X7LIDAAAQBAJ
Pasara, M. T., & Garidzirai, R. (2020). Causality effects among gross capital formation, unemployment and economic growth in South Africa. *Economies, 8*(2), 26.
Rodríguez, P., Mäntylä, M., Oivo, M., Lwakatare, L. E., Seppänen, P., & Kuvaja, P. (2019). Advances in using agile and lean processes for software development. In *Advances in computers* (Vol. 113, pp. 135–224). Elsevier. https://doi.org/10.1016/bs.adcom.2018.03.014
SAP. (2023). *SAP research reveals top tech skills challenges for African organisations*. SAP Africa News Center. https://news.sap.com/africa/2023/03/sap-research-reveals-top-tech-skills-challenges-for-african-organisations/
Skelton, M., & Pais, M. (2019). *Team topologies: Organizing business and technology teams for fast flow*. IT Revolution.
Surbiryala, J., & Rong, C. (2019). Cloud computing: History and overview. In *2019 IEEE cloud summit* (pp. 1–7). https://doi.org/10.1109/CloudSummit47114.2019.00007

Urbach, N., & Ahlemann, F. (2019). Development and operation are not decisive: IT management follows the "innovate-design-transform" paradigm. In N. Urbach & F. Ahlemann (Eds.), *IT Management in the Digital age: A roadmap for the IT department of the future* (pp. 41–48). Springer International Publishing. https://doi.org/10.1007/978-3-319-96187-3_4

Willis, M. E. H. (2023). Critical realism and qualitative research in psychology. *Qualitative Research in Psychology, 20*(2), 265–288. https://doi.org/10.1080/14780887.2022.2157782

Winch, G. M. (2023). From duality to dualism in complex project organizing: Structuration and morphogenetic theory. In *Research handbook on complex project organizing* (pp. 148–157). Edward Elgar Publishing. https://www.elgaronline.com/edcollchap/book/9781800880283/book-part-9781800880283-25.xml

World Bank. (March 24, 2025). South Africa: Unemployment rate from 2005 to 2024 [Graph]. *In Statista*. Retrieved June 24, 2025, from https://www.statista.com/statistics/370516/unemployment-rate-in-south-africa/

Wynn & Williams. (2012). Principles for conducting critical realist case study research in information systems. *MIS Quarterly, 36*(3), 787. https://doi.org/10.2307/41703481

Zhang, T. (2023). Critical realism: A critical evaluation. *Social Epistemology, 37*(1), 15–29. https://doi.org/10.1080/02691728.2022.2080127

Outsourcing and Precarity: The Case of Road Freight Transport

Pétronille Rème-Harnay

1 Introduction

Since the 1980s, firms have stepped up their restructuring strategies, particularly in order to transfer their workforce management responsibilities to other parties. Outsourcing is one such strategy. When outsourcing concerns the core business itself, as is often the case in the textile or technology production sectors, it often takes the form of relocation from northern developed to southern developing countries. Differences in working conditions (particularly working hours and wages) between these countries can help to minimize production costs (Berlinski, 2008; Flecker & Meil, 2010; Hale & Wills, 2005). In situations where the activity entails locally provided services, such as freight transport services, relocation is impossible. In these cases, outsourcing is implemented with local companies. This raises questions about how much is saved by firms that outsource (referred to as principals or lead firms), insofar as there are no a priori differences in wages or working conditions. And how do these outsourcing strategies affect workers, and more specifically their working and employment conditions?

This chapter seeks to show how, within a single country with a single set of laws regulating pay and working hours, subcontracting relations often result in the fragmentation of working and employment conditions and in corresponding precarities. Our hypothesis is that precarity affects different aspects of work and reaches different levels depending on the sector and activity of the workers concerned. Sections 2 and 3 set out in detail our choice of literature on precarity. Section 2 considers the literature on differences in working and employment conditions between employees of subcontractors and employees of principals, to show how

P. Rème-Harnay (✉)
Splott/AME, Université Gustave Eiffel, Champs sur Marne, France
e-mail: Petronille.reme-harnay@univ-eiffel.fr

F. P. García Márquez et al. (eds.), *Outsourcing*, International Series in Operations Research & Management Science 370, https://doi.org/10.1007/978-3-031-95393-4_6

outsourcing affects worker precarity. Section 3 examines more specifically the literature on the precarity associated with self-employed status.

To demonstrate this, we look at the forms of subcontracting relations between principals and subcontractors. We emphasize the importance of relations between firm (referred to as inter-firm relations) via the notion of economic dependence, drawing upon work on industrial relations (Emerson, 1962; Marchesnay, 1979).

Because of the sector's segmentation and high level of intermediation, we use the example of road freight transport to highlight different types of outsourcing, some more partnership-based and balanced, others that generate a high degree of subcontractor dependence. This sector thus allows us to explore in detail the links between outsourcing, economic dependence, and precarity.

Drawing on a number of field surveys conducted in France and on data from trade journals, we identify three main organizations of the road transport industry (found in most of European countries) corresponding to different scales of freight movement: long-haul freight transport, parcel delivery services, platform-based food delivery. For each of these segments, we attempt to analyze the nature of the subcontracting relations, the reasons for outsourcing, and the ways in which it is implemented (Sect. 3). In particular, we detail the role played by the structure of the market concerned, by inter-firm relations and by the economic context in determining the form taken by subcontracting relations. We then compare the levels of inter-firm of economic dependence in these three sectors, and the types of precarity associated with them (Sect. 5).

2 Outsourcing and Differences in Working Conditions for Employees of Principals and of Subcontractors

Two types of literature focus on the effects of outsourcing on workers. On the one hand, economists have mainly considered these effects through quantitative analysis of databases. Drawing upon work on global value chains (GVC), Feenstra and Hanson (1996) use data from the National Bureau of Economic Research, and in particular US foreign trade data, to show a correlation between international outsourcing and the rise of unemployment among low-skilled workers in outsourcing countries. As domestic firms relocate non-skill-intensive activities abroad, this encourages the employment of more skilled labor in domestic industries. International subcontracting thus accounted for between 31% and 51% of the increase in demand for skilled labor in the USA over the period 1972–1990, particularly in textiles, electronics and consumer goods (toys, sports equipment, etc.). In these sectors, unemployment rose and wages fell for low-skilled workers.

Algava and Amira (2011) carried out statistical analyses of the working conditions of subcontractor employees. Drawing upon the 2006–2007 "Organisational Change and Computerisation" survey (initiated by The French National Institute of Statistics and Economic Studies INSEE on behalf of the Ministry of Labor), which recorded the perceptions of both company managers and employees, they compared employment and working conditions in lead companies and in subcontracting firms, demonstrating that conditions in the latter are less favorable. In particular, they showed that the work of employees of subcontracting firms is more prescriptive (objectives, orders, instructions, quality processes) and more supervised, that they are more often blue-collar workers, are more likely to be called for night and weekend work, have to work more overtime, suffer more work-related accidents and have a higher probability of losing their jobs.

Perraudin et al. (2014) analyzed the French Ministry of Labor's REPONSE (Industrial Relations and Company Negotiations) survey. They identified differences in working conditions depending on the employer's status in the outsourcing chain. Average hourly wages are higher at the top of the chain for firms that are purely principals, and fall further down the chain for firms that act as both principals and subcontractors, and even more so for pure subcontractors, especially if their activity is heavily dependent on outsourcing. One explanation lies in the difference in the type of workforce employed, with the most highly qualified workers found mainly in businesses at the front of the outsourcing chain. As a result, "execution work, mostly involving manual labor" is carried out to a greater extent by subcontractors (Perraudin et al., 2014, p. 128).

A second, more qualitative line of research seeks to show the consequences of outsourcing for a particular sector. These studies are usually produced by sociologists and focus more on health effects.

Armelle Gorgeu and René Matthieu looked at the changes in the car industry since the oil crises of 1973 and 1979. In order to face up to international competition and apply new quality standards, carmakers have outsourced the manufacture of components to Tier 1 suppliers, generally owned by large foreign groups, who in turn outsource to Tier 2 suppliers, and so on. Ardenti et al. (2010) showed that working conditions at subcontractor sites are worse because carmaker plants have introduced "significant improvements" that subcontracting firms have not had the resources to implement. In addition, jobs in subcontractor plants are less secure. The main emphasis is placed on the consequences of outsourcing for subcontractor employees in terms of arduous work and industrial accidents. Carmakers prefer to delegate the most taxing activities to their subcontractors and demand greater productivity gains from them than from their own factories (Gorgeu & Mathieu, 2015).

In a similar vein, Thébaud-Mony (2011) offered a critical analysis of outsourcing in the nuclear industry and its consequences for the health of workers assigned to maintenance tasks in radioactive areas. She showed that subcontracted workers are more exposed to ionizing radiation than others. Subcontracted labor accounted for 80% of total radiation exposure in French nuclear plants. She linked these outcomes with the lack of monitoring of the radiation doses to which subcontracted workers are exposed. All nuclear industry workers must be monitored to remain below the radiation exposure threshold, but subcontracted workers move from reactor to reactor around the country without any real follow-up. In contrast, the exposure of employees of EDF, the lead company, is closely monitored. Lastly, she showed that the dangerous nature of subcontractor status is linked with poor working conditions and contracts that offer little protection.

However, very little work has been done on transport in particular, perhaps because categories are more blurred in this sector than elsewhere. For example, Moore and Newsome show that in the UK, precariousness affects all categories, employees and non-employees alike, within a group or a smaller company (Moore & Newsome, 2018). Chan (2023) highlights the fact that in China, even state-owned companies no longer offer the same protection to delivery drivers. Rème-Harnay (2023) introduces several clues showing, however, that in the French case, precariousness decreases with the size of the company and its position in the chain of actors.

Whether quantitative or qualitative, studies of the effects of outsourcing on workers show a differential in working or employment conditions, with the most precarious workers being invariably employees of subcontracting firms.

3 Nature of the Subcontracting Relations in Three Transport Organizations

We introduce here a breakdown between three segments of the road transport industry that highlights three types of outsourcing, so that we can later show the associated precarity.

3.1 Outsourcing of Long-Distance Transport and Management of a Customer Portfolio

Long-distance transport is transport that is run on a national or international scale. It encompasses refrigerated transport, sawn timber, livestock, and heavy or oversized products—carried in containers or in bulk—as well as tankers, car carriers and waste trucks. In this sub-segment of road freight transport, the market is structured by a multitude of small firms. The latest French company survey (INSEE ESANE)[1] reveals a sector dominated by very small firms with fewer than nine employees (Table 1). These make up 76% of the sector, while companies with more than 50 employees account for only 5%. This segmentation is likely to foster outsourcing by large firms to smaller ones.

In long-distance transport, carriers sign regular contracts with shippers or freight forwarders, which enables them to organize their routes in advance. However, these contracts rarely include return loads to the departure point. To avoid empty runs and/or to optimize the use of lorry capacity, carriers must therefore look elsewhere

[1] https://www.insee.fr/fr/statistiques/4654487.

Table 1 Firms according to numbers of employees in 2017

Activity	Size	31/12/2017
Inter-urban road transport	0–9 employees	11,792
	0 employees	*6873*
	1–9 employees	*4919*
	10–49 employees	2811
	50 employees and over	754
	Total	15,357

Source: ESANE survey conducted by INSEE

than their regular customer base for return loads. This is where the subcontracting relationship may begin. To find return freight, carriers can rely either on transport networks or on groupings (such as Astre, Flo, Evolutrans...). In long-distance transport, groupings are attractive to small transport firms in several ways. They make joint purchasing possible in order to obtain advantageous prices for fuel and vehicles, to bid on calls for tenders issued by major players (such as the mass retail sector), to negotiate prices and to have a network of peers to access return freight offers in return for a commission. Carriers can also use freight exchanges that connect them with freight forwarders offering freight for transport at certain prices, or nowadays digital platforms that connect carriers and shippers. When a carrier bids for a contract from another carrier or a freight forwarder on a freight exchange or as part of a grouping of carriers, it will be acting as a subcontractor. In these circumstances, outsourcing does not necessarily imply precarity for owner-drivers. Here, it is part of what is often a weekly organizational framework that usually involves irregular and short-term relationships with the principal via freight exchanges or with peers via networks.

First, the subcontracting relationship is short and does not entail continuous services for another firm but a single one-off trip. Second, the subcontractor generally works for a number of different customers over the year. Finally, the subcontractor may have specific assets that distinguish it from others. A subcontractor that has special vehicles, specific know-how and capacity to handle certain types of products, might be less easy to replace and may well be able to develop a relationship of mutual dependence with its principal.

In long-distance transport, there is another type of outsourcing in addition to return freight outsourcing: regular outsourcing contracts. Little research has been done on this form. Two recent sources nevertheless shed some light on the type of relations between principals and subcontractors in this sector.

The first is a small database covering 35 carriers (Rème-Harnay, 2022) that have worked as subcontractors over the last 15 years. It should be noted that this sample needs to be treated with caution as it not fully representative of the structure of the long-distance transport market. It is biased in favor of large businesses (only 7 had under 9 employees, 15 had between 10 and 49, and 11 over 50).[2] Yet as

[2] Some firms did not provide employee numbers.

we have seen, 58% of self-employed drivers work alone (see Table 1). For each of them, Rème-Harnay (2022) calculates the percentage of carrier activities that are undertaken as subcontractors: on average 47% (with a median of 40%) of the activities of 35 carriers in question are carried out as subcontractors, the rest is carried out directly for shippers. Moreover, the outsourcing rate is limited in this sector. In France, there is a ceiling on outsourcing. Carriers cannot outsource more than 15% of their sales (Decrees 1999–752 and 2016–1550), unless they have freight forwarder status. However, in long-distance transport, there are fewer large groups with this status that are principals, and more medium-sized companies. Furthermore, the activities of intercity carriers are always quite diversified. Only one company reports having worked with a single principal. For all these reasons, relations between principals and subcontractors in this sector often involve companies of the same size with several other partners.

Another survey conducted in 2016 sheds light on the form that outsourcing takes in this sector. In this article, Niérat (2016) shows that outsourcing enables carriers to operate more smoothly by benefiting from membership of a network. He describes outsourcing as a method of streamlining a company's overall organization. According to Niérat, one of the main difficulties facing long-distance carriers is time management. They cannot plan their schedules very far in advance. They have to be able to change them the day before or even the same day. His research focuses on what he sees as the typical case of a long-distance carrier, a firm that has regular contracts from central France, where it has its warehouse, but does not have a regular contract for return runs. The firm therefore spends time trying to find return freight "either through peers, members of the same grouping, or through freight exchanges" (Niérat, 2016), therefore operating as a subcontractor on these routes. On the other side, customers with whom the firm has regular contracts sometimes have requests that are incompatible with its schedule, for example a trip to a region not served by the carrier, an additional load for a region already served, or the need to send the load earlier than planned. In these situations, the transport operator has to find another carrier to perform the task, thus becoming the principal for another carrier. This detailed example illustrates the role of outsourcing in long-distance transport. Outsourcing is part of the general organization of the transport firms of the sector. It serves to fill empty capacity, avoid idle time, retain regular customers, cultivate networks of peers, etc. Principals do not make big profits but rather ensure that they can provide an efficient and regular haulage service.

3.2 *Outsourcing in the Parcel Delivery Sector and Cost Minimization*

The parcel delivery sector, which has grown considerably over the last 40 years because of the explosion in e-commerce, is organized very differently from the sector just described. It was created to meet demand for frequent, short-notice shipments of small parcels. It is constructed around nationwide networks of warehouses, called agencies. A network of this type requires very high financial investment, with the result that large multinational groups dominate the parcel delivery services market.

As in long-distance freight transport, it is difficult to get an idea of the level of outsourcing in this sub-sector. In France, several surveys have been carried out since 2010 in an attempt to measure it. An initial 2011 survey measured the outsourcing rate for parcels leaving delivery agencies in the Paris region. It established the number of subcontracted trucks out of the total number of outbound trucks. Out of a sample consisting of 15 agencies and 48 subcontractors, 71% of the total volume of goods leaving the agencies were subcontracted (Rème-Harnay, 2018). However, the sample of agencies and subcontractors was discussed in advance between the investigators and the parcel delivery groups, which obviously created a measurement bias.

Between 2019 and 2021, we conducted another field study on agencies in the Paris Region. We spoke to some 20 parcel delivery agency employees. Two direct questions were asked to establish an outsourcing rate, namely the total number of delivery drivers operating rounds for the agency on a daily basis, and the number of drivers employed by the group. We could thus deduce the ratio of subcontracted drivers to the total number of drivers. The findings are presented in Table 2.

The survey reveals that 90% of delivery drivers in the Paris region are subcontracted. This proportion seems to coincide with that found in many other European countries (Moore & Newsome, 2018; Haidinger, 2012). However, it is well above that found in long-distance transport. In France, the annual business surveys (EAE) (which no longer happen) showed a major difference in outsourcing between the two sectors (Table 3). Of course, these rates have evolved since 2007. Nevertheless, they reflect a gap between the proportions of revenues earned through outsourcing.

This difference can be explained by the nature of outsourcing in the parcel delivery sector. First, despite the sector's exceptional performance (its ability to move millions of items under tight deadlines), the parcel delivery groups (often multinational) that dominate it remain vulnerable. In France, they are the only segment of the road haulage sector with negative EBITDA (Earnings Before Interest, Taxes, Depreciation and Amortisation) according to the French company survey (INSEE ESANE 2013 and 2015). In addition, the legacy players have been weakened by the succession of economic crises—among the 15 major groups operating in France, two—Sernam and Mory Ducros—went bankrupt between 2012 and 2015—and are competing with new players, like the giant Amazon Logistics which appeared in 2017, whose labor management strategies circumvent national legal provisions. Furthermore, parcel delivery groups are entirely dependent on their customers (e-merchants and shippers) which are bigger because they are more concentrated. They owe their existence to the needs of these shippers. In order to bid for tenders issued by these large shippers, they must be able to deliver large numbers of parcels quickly and at competitive rates. There is fierce competition between parcel delivery groups to win these contracts.

Table 2 Outsourcing rates, 2019–2021

Parcel delivery groups or agencies	Outsourcing rate: Number of subcontractors/total number of delivery drivers working for firm
Amazon transport France	100%
Colis privé France	100%
Calberson 78	90%
Gefco France	100%
GLS France	100%
Dachser 91	90%
UPS (Charenton, Paris +92/94)	75%
DB Schenker 78	75%
DB Schenker tractions France	85%
DHL 77	100%
DHL IDF	99%
Chronopost 95	100%
Dachser 77	85%
DB Schenker 77	70%
Geodis 93	71%
Geodis 95	71%
Relais 77	100%
Dachser 95	95%
Dachser 77	96%
La Poste 95	100%
Relais 93	92%
Chronopost 78	85%
UPS 93	67%
Chronopost 92	99,93%
Geodis 94	88%

Source: Rème-Harnay (2022b)

Table 3 Sectors of the firms that outsource

	Long- distance transport	Parcel delivery sector (including express)
Average revenues per firm (M€)	1952	11,068
Outsourcing as a percentage of sales	17%	52%

Source: Rème-Harnay with EAE survey (2007) and Rème-Harnay (2022b)

Given the structure of the actors in the chain running from shippers to transport execution and the narrowness of their margins, cost reduction is extremely important for parcel delivery groups. In fact, transport between two agencies can be pooled, generating economies of scale, but urban delivery rounds are too fragmented, too costly. Replacing expensive employment contracts for these rounds with outsourcing contracts creates savings on a number of cost categories. Parcel delivery groups can thus save on employer contributions (half the gross salary), redundancy costs, employee absences (which can even be passed on to subcontractors). They also minimize costs because they can make self-employed drivers work longer hours than employees (whose working week in France is limited by law to 35 h). This organization of work also enables parcel delivery groups to reduce downtime and encourages delivery drivers to work harder—since subcontractors are paid per parcel delivered, the more they deliver, the more they earn. Furthermore, to ensure that subcontracted drivers work as required, parcel delivery groups impose heavy penalties for delays, delivery errors, forgotten scans, etc.

If we compare the two sectors just described, whereas outsourcing in long-distance haulage is part of the general organization of the businesses, serving to retain regular customers and maintain a network of peers, outsourcing in the parcel delivery sector serves as a means of reducing payroll costs while maintaining a high level of service performance.

3.3 Outsourcing by Digital Platforms and Flawed Business Model

In the platform-based delivery sector, Deliveroo and Ubereats largely dominate European markets. Here, outsourcing takes yet another form. It is not used to build partnerships with other carriers, nor to replace employees in order to save costs. It is inherent to the forms' business model from the outset. Unlike the parcel delivery services described above, Deliveroo and Ubereats have never employed salaried deliverers. Their business model is different from those described above. They operate like start-ups rather than traditional businesses. This means that they are not dependent on shippers but on investors. To raise funds, their priority is valuation, while profitability is only a secondary criterion. Their aim is to add to the company's future value (Montalban et al., 2019). This is probably the reason why these firms have never (or very rarely) been profitable. Nevertheless, having been established in Europe for more than 6 years, they need to move in the direction of greater profitability if they want to continue to raise funds, as investors are becoming more cautious over time. That is why they are looking for ways to achieve profits. But the task is not easy. These companies entered the meal delivery market by offering very cheap services to a young clientele with the goal of disrupting (in the sense of Christensen (2015)) the classic pizza and sushi delivery market. The delivery fees charged to consumers are very low (two euros in 2017, a little more today depending on mileage), but customers are not prepared to pay more. These charges do not cover delivery costs (Lebayle, 2023).

The delivery fees paid to cycle couriers have been pared to a minimum over the years. As the model continues to lose money, the platforms are hoping to increase their profits from restaurant owners by opening "dark kitchens" (food establishments that focus solely on meal delivery and do not have physical storefronts or areas for local consumption) on the outskirts of Paris. The platforms charge restaurateurs an average of 30% commission but this can rise to 40% or more for dark kitchens (Lebayle, 2023). Literature on "cloud kitchens" also emphasizes the role of online ordering systems in improving restaurants and platforms profitability (Beniwall & Mathur, 2021). Faced with such a fragile business model, outsourcing is the only organization of work likely to enable digital platforms to manage peaks in demand (lunchtime, evenings, match days, etc.) and secure a pool of workers, while promising investors future profits. If they were to switch to salaried employment, these platforms are well aware that their financial results would be too disastrous for survival. In Spain, for example, Deliveroo withdrew following the "Riders law" of August 2021.

To examine the impact of these different types of outsourcing on workers, we conducted a number of field surveys, which are described in the next section.

3.4 Research Method

The research described in this chapter draws on a number of sources. The French national surveys on employment and businesses do not contain sufficient data to analyze outsourcing in road freight transport. They tell us nothing about the relative proportions of subcontracted and salaried drivers and how these proportions have changed. Further investigations were therefore necessary. Four successive empirical studies were carried out. Two concern the parcel delivery sector (2015 survey and 2019–2021 survey), two others the digital platforms sector (2017–2018 survey and 2023 survey). To investigate the long-distance sector, we relied on interviews already available in the professional literature.

The 2015 empirical study covered 67 subcontracted delivery drivers. They were interviewed directly in the streets of Paris while engaged in delivering, sorting or picking up parcels. Of these, 25 were self-employed drivers working alone, while the other 42 were either employees of subcontracting companies or headed by them. Where possible, those employed by subcontracting companies gave us the contact details of their bosses, who were then interviewed in 18 additional short interviews. The aim was to build dependence indicators. Questions about economic dependence were asked before any other information about the company.

The 2019–2021 empirical study aimed to measure outsourcing in the parcel delivery agencies. Interviews were conducted with 20 employees, and where possible, visits were made to their offices. These employees of parcel delivery agencies in the Paris region worked in so-called "dispatch" offices, which determine the proportion of salaried delivery drivers and subcontractors. Two direct questions were asked to establish the ratio, namely the total number of delivery drivers carrying out delivery rounds for the agency on a daily basis, and the number of drivers directly employed by the agency.

In the 2017–2018 empirical study, interviews were conducted with 125 couriers working mainly in Paris and Lyon for Deliveroo, Foodora, Ubereats, Stuart, Foodchery, Popchef, and Frichti, including 103 on bicycles and 22 on scooters, when they were waiting for orders. We used the same questionnaire as in 2015, focusing on economic dependence. From this sample, a few calculations show that the average age of bike couriers was 27 (24.8 for scooter riders), that they worked on average (and median) 30 h a week (34 for scooters) and declared average gross monthly earnings of 1524 euros (1725 for scooter couriers), which suggests an average hourly rate of 11.4 euros.

The same process was used in 2023 for a new field study with 104 platform couriers. Many digital platforms have disappeared. The couriers worked exclusively with Deliveroo and Ubereats. During this last field study, we realized that the bike couriers were older and worked much longer hours than those in the previous survey. Their average age was 29, and they worked an average of 55 h a week. Their economic and social situations also seemed less favorable, and few of them spoke French. To take this change into account, we considered dependence in a more subjective way, as a blocking factor in the life trajectories of delivery drivers: lack of papers, language barrier, lack of qualifications, etc.

4 Outsourcing and the Precarity of Self-employed Workers

Among subcontracted workers, much of the literature on precarious work focuses on those who work in a self-employed capacity rather than as permanent employees (particularly in situations where employees have been replaced by self-employed workers).

In his work on self-employed truck drivers, for example, Pablo Lopez Calle (2016) makes the link between the outsourcing of long-distance transport in Spain and the increased vulnerability of self-employed Spanish drivers, as well as the deterioration in their living and working conditions. In particular, he emphasizes their "self-exploitation" through the "intensification of work" that truck drivers are forced to undertake in order to "try to maintain their autonomy" (Lopez Calle, 2016, p. 22). In his view, self-employed drivers achieve their desired income level largely by extending their working days. In this example, self-employed status leads to a deterioration in working conditions.

In a fairly similar domain, Moore and Newsome, (2018) look at the connection between outsourcing and self-employed delivery drivers in the United Kingdom. In particular, they highlight the role played by employers in organizing precarity by putting their directly employed workers in competition with owners-drivers and even, more recently, with home-based couriers (i.e., nonprofessional drivers doing part-time delivery work for additional income). In the end, this competition undermines all delivery drivers. It helps to maintain precarious working conditions, in particular low wages and long working hours, by exerting pressure on direct employees, who are more easily dismissed than in France. This creates a three-way division between delivery drivers, in which the precarization of the bottom group increases precarity for those above.

Also working on home-based couriers and more generally on digital platform workers, the sociologists Schor et al. (2020) reach similar conclusions, focusing on the concepts of dependence and independence. They argue, for example, that self-employed workers are totally dependent on a platform when they earn their living by working with it full-time, but are independent when they do so only occasionally. In this case, the link between dependence and precarity is almost mechanical. "We find that when platform income is supplemental (i.e., the provider has multiple sources of income), satisfaction is higher, autonomy is greater, hourly wages are generally higher and conditions are better. By contrast, those who are dependent on the platform to fund basic living expenses express more dissatisfaction and experience more precarity" (Schor et al., 2020, p. 835). Dependence is immediately associated with precarity. In considering economic dependence, these analyses by Schor et al. (2020) bring the dualization between standard (employee) and nonstandard (self-employed) contracts back to the forefront, associating precarity to the latter.

In these analyses, the link between dependence and precarity is significant. However, though it appears self-evident, it demands closer examination. It implies that certain workers are economically completely independent from their employers and hence able to avoid precarity. In so doing, it overlooks the many situations of codependence or interdependence that characterize more horizontal situations. To analyze inter-firm dependence in greater depth, we can draw on another body of literature with a more economics focus—the analysis of industrial relations since the 1970s. Seeking to introduce the notion of power into inter-firm relations, this literature proposes theoretical indicators of the level of economic dependence, on the assumption that it is always present but at different levels. However, authors in this tradition do not directly apply these indicators empirically and do not link them with work or employment.

Following from that literature, this chapter contends that self-employed or independent status is not necessarily synonymous with precarity. In our approach, there is no question of considering that there are legally self-employed workers who are strictly economically independent or strictly dependent. Following Emerson (1962) and his successors, we consider that all businesses (including one-person businesses such as owner-drivers or digital platform workers) depend on other businesses to survive (bankers, shareholders, customers, suppliers, etc.) but to varying degrees. Inter-firm dependence is therefore omnipresent. There are no non-dependent deliverers.

Moreover, in examining how dependence affects worker precarity, this chapter adopts a stance close to that of Neilson and Rositer (2008) and Moore and Newsome, (2018), who view precarity "as the norm." More precisely, we follow Paugam who identifies two aspects of precarity, based on a long survey of the French population. The most widely accepted meaning of the term is employment precarity, which expresses the discontinuous nature of employment. This is, in particular, associated with a high rate of unemployment which represents a perpetual threat (Castel, 2003; Gallie et al., 2017). Work precarity is defined more subjectively as a denial of value and rewarding ("reconnaissance"), often reflected in a deterioration in working conditions and in a decline in interest in terms of the content and remuneration of the work (Paugam, 2007).

In this chapter, we will consider several types of workers, according to their employment status (employee or self-employed) and type of employer: workers directly employed by the principal, self-employed owner-drivers, the self-employed owners of small subcontracting firms and the workers employed by such firms. For these different categories, we will examine the impact of outsourcing on the two types of precarity identified. This precarity varies according to inter-firm dependence which itself varies according to economic context, market structure, and company size.

In the upcoming sections, we will present different situations for subcontractors of three types of road freight transport organization, before comparing the degrees of dependence between subcontractors and principals and the associated precarity.

5 From Outsourcing to Precarity: The Role of Economic Dependence

We have detailed the organization of three transport sub-sectors. These three types of organization entail different relationships between the principals (long-distance intermediary companies, parcel delivery groups, digital platforms) and their subcontractors. Our aim here is to analyze these relationships in terms of economic dependence.

To do this, we draw on the two bodies of literature mentioned in Sect. 3, which allow us to link dependence and precarity. For Schor et al. (2020), dependence is defined in opposition to independence (self-employment) in the employment relationship, as the inverse of worker emancipation. They show that when independent (self-employed) workers are dependent on a principal for their survival, they experience more precarity (Schor et al., 2020, p. 835). The second literature introduces theoretical indicators of the level of dependence between firms (Emerson, 1962; Jacobs, 1974; Thompson, 1967; Marchesnay, 1979; Grand, 1997). For these authors, the aim was to reintroduce power relations into the analysis of inter-firm relations hitherto dominated by the analysis of property rights (Alchian & Demsetz, 1973) or transaction costs (Williamson, 1991).

Here we combine these two perspectives in order to incorporate independent workers into the analysis of inter-firm relations, and conversely to reintegrate the organization of work into the analysis of inter-firm relations.

From the first literature we draw the link between precarity and dependence. From the second, we draw four theoretical dependence indicators.

5.1 Indicators of Inter-Firm Economic Dependence

Theoretical indicators of economic dependence were constructed by Emerson's successors in the 1970s, primarily to analyze customer/supplier relationships (Rème-Harnay, 2020a). This is why we have sought to adapt them for the analysis of subcontracting relationships in freight transport, with the aim of establishing levels of dependence for the three sub-sectors identified. As these indicators had remained strictly theoretical in this literature, we have adapted them for our empirical analysis.

The first indicator identified in this literature is substitutability, defined by the sociologist Thompson (1967) as the existence of alternatives for a company to access the resources it needs. In the case of subcontracting relationships, this indicator loses its meaning, since it is not by replacing its main contractor with another, but by increasing the number of contractors it works with, that a subcontractor can reduce its dependence on its main contractor. We are therefore inclined to set this indicator aside for our field study.

The second dependence indicator, considered by Marchesnay (1979) as the main measure of a level of dependence (p. 711), is the concentration of trade flows between two firms. It is the most easily quantifiable and commonly used index for estimating economic dependence. It can be measured by calculating the percentage of revenue one firm generates with its main client (principal). This criterion has also been used to characterize the dependent self-employed in Germany and Spain (Rème-Harnay, 2020a).

Defined by Jacobs (1974), the third indicator—essentiality—is a measure of the level of dependence defined as follows: a situation of economic dependence exists when the severance of commercial relations between the supplier and the distributor could jeopardize the latter's continued activity. The aim is to demonstrate, by means of an indicator, the extent to which the principal is essential to the subcontractor's survival. In our case, the indicator is calculated by counting the number of principals with which a subcontractor is able to contract.

In his thesis on outsourcing in the transport sector, Lionel Grand (1997, p. 140) proposes a fourth criterion, which he calls "general dependence," constructed to analyze subcontracting relationships and defined as the necessity of the presence of an intermediary (end customer, principal, supplier, etc.) in order to carry out an activity. It only makes sense in situations where intermediation is very salient, as in the road freight sector. For the fieldwork, one of the questions the subcontractors were asked concerned their ability to access shippers without going through a parcel delivery group.

Once these theoretical indicators had been set, we conducted several surveys with subcontractors, asking targeted questions to estimate and compare the indicators.

In 2015, we surveyed 67 subcontractors of parcel delivery groups during their deliveries in the Paris region (Rème-Harnay, 2018), asking them about their main principals, the number of principals they worked with, their concentration of trade. In 2018, we surveyed 127 independent subcontractors of digital platforms in major French metropolitan areas (Rème-Harnay, 2020b), asking them similar questions.

Table 4 Comparison of dependence rates

Sectors	Number of subcontractors surveyed	General dependence: proportion of subcontractors able to operate without an intermediary	Percentage of subcontractors generating revenues with a single principal	Concentration of trade flows with one principal: average rate of sales with the main principal	Essentiality: average number of principals
Parcel delivery sector 2015	67	9%	52%	78%	2.6
Long distance transport (2006–2021)	35	53%	2.8%		
Digital platform 2018	127	5% have another main job	78%	95%	1.3

Source: Rème-Harnay (2022b)

We continued this survey in 2023, but with a greater focus on delivery driver profiles. For long-haul carriers, we draw on the database of 35 carriers described in Sect. 3.1 (Rème-Harnay, 2022). The questions asked were not the same, so the results are only partial. Nevertheless, we can attempt to compare the dependences of subcontractors in these three sub-sectors.

Although not all calculations are possible with the long-distance database, there does seem to be a clear difference in level of dependence. If we compare the dependence indicators available to us for the parcel delivery sector, digital platforms and long-distance transport, we can observe (Table 4) that economic dependence is systematically greater for digital platform couriers than for delivery drivers, and higher for both categories than for long-distance drivers.

To complete the comparison, we propose to compare dependence scores by constructing a composite indicator (Table 5). The first three components come from the indicators constructed previously (general dependence, essentiality, and concentration of exchange flows). These are the primary criteria. To make the comparison more precise, we selected a number of additional factors which, in the course of our investigations, seemed to us to play a role in this dependence: firm size—if the self-employed worker works alone, it is more difficult for them to diversify their customers; activity perimeter—urban/long-distance; use of a heavy or light vehicle—the use of a small vehicle makes the self-employed worker captive to a certain type of transport; type of operators involved—as we have seen, working for an intermediate-sized firm makes relations more partnership-based than working for a group; and the time dimension of the transport plan—the existence of hazards encourages the rapid recruitment of subcontractors with no regular relationships.

Table 5 Inter-firm dependence score linked to transport activity

Level 1 criteria	
The subcontractor work only as subcontractor	0.2 points
The subcontractor can work directly with shippers	0.1 point
The subcontractor has a single principal	0.3 points
The subcontractor has two principals	0.2 points
The subcontractor has more than two principals	0.1 point
The subcontractor generates more than 75% of sales with their main principal	0.3 points
The subcontractor generates more than 50% of sales with their main principal	0.2 points
The subcontractor generates less than 50% of sales with their main principal	0.1 point
The subcontractor works alone	0.3 points
The subcontractor has one employee	2 points
The subcontractor has several employees	0.1 point
Level 2 criteria: Transport-related factors aggravating dependence	
The subcontractor works in the urban transport sector	2 points
The subcontractor works in the long-distance transport sector	0.1 point
The subcontractor owns only one or more light commercial vehicles	2 points
The subcontractor owns at least one heavy goods vehicle.	0.1 point
The subcontractor's principal is a freight forwarder	0.2 points
The subcontractor's principal is a small firm	0.1 point
The principal only plans a few hours ahead	0.3 points
The principal draws up a daily transport plan	0.2 points
The principal draws up a weekly or near-weekly transport schedule	1 point

Source: Rème-Harnay (2022b)

According to this composite dependence indicator, the average score for independent delivery drivers in the parcel delivery survey sector is 15.5 out of 20.[3] It is difficult to assess it as precisely for the long-haul sector as we do not have as much data. Nevertheless, we can establish an average dependence score of between 8 and 11 out of 20. Two-wheeled couriers have an average score of 20 out of 20, which is significantly higher than for the sample of delivery drivers or truck drivers.

This difference in the composite indicator value confirms that levels of dependence differ according to the activity profiles of the drivers. It also illustrates the role played by the type of transport organization considered: the scope of transport, the speed and predictability of delivery. It also suggests that being a self-employed worker for a platform is likely to be a situation of greater vulnerability.

5.2 From Inter-Firm Dependence to Worker Precarity

So far, we have discussed the dependence experienced by the self-employed in the three freight transport sub-sectors. These self-employed workers are either owners of small subcontracted firms or owner-drivers working solo. In this section we focus on how this dependence is reflected in terms of precarity for four categories of workers according to their status and employer: first, self-employed workers working alone (owner-drivers) who account for 100% of platform delivery drivers, 50% of subcontracted courier delivery drivers in the Paris region (according to the hauliers' register held by the Paris Regional Direction of Transport DRIEA) and 44% of long-distance road haulage drivers; second, in the case of parcel delivery drivers and long-distance transport, self-employed small business owners who are themselves drivers. Their employees, "in the same boat as their boss" (Perraudin et al., 2014, p. 70), make up the third category of workers analyzed here, while the fourth and final category consists of workers directly employed by transport groups.

To analyze the links between dependence and precarity, we cross-reference these categories of workers with the type of work organization in the sector and the type of precarity. In so doing, we follow Paugam's distinction between employment precarity and work precarity.

5.2.1 Employment Precarity and Protection from Job Loss According to Worker Status

Dependence indicators show that dependence is much higher in the digital platform sector than in the parcel delivery and long-distance sectors. Self-employed platform-based workers are characterized by the highest dependence on their principals. Does this mean that their employment precarity is greater? There are several indications

[3] Twenty represents the maximum number of points possible.

to that effect. The first form of precarity we address is linked to the risk of losing one's job.

Of the four categories of workers identified above, those best protected from job loss are group employees, in three different ways. First, they work for a group, which is less likely to go bankrupt than a very small company. The 2017 French Employment survey confirms this to some extent, showing that the length of service of delivery drivers working for companies with over 500 employees is almost 11 years. In addition to this first form of job security, group employees are protected by labor law, which regulates and limits dismissal procedures. In France, for example, dismissal is an expensive process for employers. First, they must provide valid and genuine reasons for making an employee redundant (some, such as paternity, maternity, illness, discrimination and the right to strike, are excluded) and the employee must be called for an explanatory interview. In addition, the employee may be eligible for severance pay. An employee with more than 8 months in service is entitled to compensation which cannot be less than a quarter of a month's pay per year of service for the first 10 years or a third of a month's pay per year of service from the 11th year onwards.

As salaried workers, group employees may also be entitled to financial benefits if they become unemployed. In France, for example, the daily unemployment benefit is 57% of the reference daily wage. It cannot be less than €31.59 or more than €274.80 gross per day.

This category of worker is unfortunately rare in the freight transport sector. In the platform delivery sector, no delivery drivers are employed by the platform. In the parcel delivery sector, according to our field study (presented in Sect. 3.4), they account for 10% of delivery drivers in the Paris region. It is more difficult to establish this figure for long-distance transport, but the subcontracting rates in this sector suggest that it is much higher.

As for the second category of workers, employees of small subcontractors, they not have the protection afforded by working for a large company but, as employees, they do enjoy the regulatory and economic protections associated with their employment contracts. Once again, cycle couriers working for platforms are not represented in this category. However, in the parcel delivery and long-distance sectors, many employees work for these small companies. The 2017 French Employment survey shows that the vast majority of these employees are recruited on permanent contracts: in 2017, 71.2% had a full-time permanent contract and 18.4%, a part-time permanent contract. However, the 2017 Employment Survey shows that the median job tenure (length of service) of salaried delivery workers in these small firms is between 2 and 3 years (Rème-Harnay, 2023). Because of the lifespan of their firms, salaried delivery drivers, although on permanent contracts, are likely to lose their jobs frequently, making permanent contracts precarious. They share their employer's vulnerability. It is thus largely because the subcontracting firm is dependent on its principal that precarity is so high for its employees, despite their permanent contracts.

Unlike these two first categories of employed workers, the next two categories of self-employed workers (owners of subcontracting firms and owner-drivers) are not protected from contract termination and unemployment. A self-employed worker's contract can be terminated without specific grounds and without compensation.

In the 2015 sample, subcontractors in the Paris region had an average of 6.7 employees and the failure rate of companies of this size was around 5% (data reconstructed from the Ellisphere institute (Madjarian, 2016) and the *Score3* website), i.e., more than twice the French national average. DRIEA has assessed the average lifespan of subcontractor businesses at around 4 years (DRIEA interview, 2015). Bankruptcies are therefore numerous and frequent for small subcontracting firms.

Small business owners generally have strategies for anticipating bankruptcy. In our surveys, we first observed that the size of the firm affects the precarity of its employer and employees through the role it plays in economic dependence. As has been seen above, in order for a subcontractor to acquire more customers and become less dependent on its main principal, it must be able to recruit drivers. An increase in size therefore plays a key role in reducing dependence and through this the risk of bankruptcy.

Solo self-employed workers are the most vulnerable. They cannot diversify their customer base by working for several principals at the same time. They are the category for which strategies to reduce economic dependence are the most complex to implement. Some choose to work with a large, well-known group, even if it means being highly dependent on it, in the hope of protecting themselves from precarity. However, this strategy has limitations. Among the causes of bankruptcy cited by owner-drivers, the behavior of the principal is at the top of the list. Often, when a new branch manager is recruited in the parcel delivery sector, he or she decides to renegotiate the subcontracting contracts, which become less attractive for the subcontractors. In other cases, contract terms may be altered during the course of the contract, despite undertakings made at the outset: for example, volumes may ultimately be lower than expected, or the subcontractor is forced to invest personally in new equipment. It is also quite simple to terminate the contract after a period of notice. Nevertheless, our analysis of the career paths of self-employed delivery drivers shows that, after going out of business, they most often set up a new business in the freight sector.

In the case of digital platforms, breaking contracts is even easier. Digital management makes it possible to limit the downsides of traditional outsourcing, eliminating rigidities in order to reduce costs and manage peaks in activity. The rules of the standard subcontracting contract can be circumvented. To terminate the contract, the platform simply prevents delivery drivers from accessing the application, without giving any reason. Nevertheless, the representatives of courier collectives we met identified several reasons for the platform's breach of contract: involvement in strike action; the platform's facial recognition software, which sometimes wrongly excludes certain couriers; not conforming to the platform's interests (refusing to deliver in areas inconvenient to the courier, refusing to undertake long, unprofitable delivery runs, etc.). In our 2023 survey, a number of platform couriers explained that they could no longer work with a platform from which they had been deregistered.

5.2.2 Employment Precarity and Job Profiles

On the workers' side, precarity also depends on the more macroeconomic characteristics of employment in the sub-sector in question and on being able to hold a second job. In other words, some workers are more or less dependent than others, according to their ability to find an alternative paid activity.

In the long-haul sector, the precarity of lorry drivers is limited and there are fewer self-employed drivers. Their trajectories are more stable, partly because of the shortage of truck drivers that has affected Europe in recent years: "There is a shortage of more than three million truck drivers worldwide, and this figure is set to double over the next five years," according to the International Road Transport Union (IRU, 2022). In a survey on temporary work in transport carried out in 2020, Rème-Harnay (2022b) shows that truck drivers generally move from one transport company to another without spending time out of work, always aiming for better working conditions (sometimes the gamble of changing employers is unsuccessful in this regard).

In the parcel delivery sector, trajectories are less stable. The profiles of the bosses and employees of small subcontracting companies are fairly heterogeneous, but what they have in common is a low level of qualification. These companies are often set up by former tradespeople who already own a truck, or former employees wanting to move on. However, since 2015, particularly with the development of the major transport group A.,[4] it has been common for companies to be set up and people recruited without any qualifications or experience in transport. For them, making deliveries is more difficult because working conditions have deteriorated. Their lack of experience makes their rounds much longer and discourages them more quickly. The delivery drivers who work in A.'s subcontracting cascade are those with the most precarious employment conditions. Company A. is a parcel delivery firm and subsidiary of the e-commerce group of the same name, France's leading e-commerce operator. It receives 37,808,000 visitors to its website per month, which is equivalent to 55% of the population, while France's second largest e-commerce retailer is far behind with 27,879,000 visitors per month (FEVAD, 2023). Created in 2017 as a new parcel delivery company A. has set up a dedicated production structure. Instead of outsourcing directly to small subcontractors, the company uses intermediate subcontractors, i.e., mid-sized local companies specializing in local transport. These companies adopt A.'s processes and, in turn, impose them on their own end subcontractors. The intermediary thus plays the role of a manager on behalf of firm A., recruiting, monitoring and signing contracts with the end subcontractors. Firm A. dispenses with delivery drivers who fail to meet the volume targets for the daily shift or received poor ratings from recipients. Their employers either have to lay these drivers off or find work for them with another parcel delivery group, which would require other principals. This is reflected in the following excerpt from an interview with the director of an intermediate subcontracting company:

[4] To preserve our sources, we have chosen to anonymize company names.

> I let about ten of my thirty drivers go every week (...). You need to understand that every week I call at least two owners of subcontracting firms and tell them that such-and-such delivery driver they employ has to go [and this] is solely because A. suspects they are incompetent. In other words, A. (. . .) just says 'tell so-and-so not to bother coming in tomorrow'. So, in a way, an A. contract lands you in a load of trouble. (Interview, 2018)

By using these intermediate subcontractors, firm A. places several levels between its brand (the e-tailer) and the drivers, thus limiting the risk of reclassification lawsuits from independent to employed status.

Whilst between 2017 and 2018, the profile of platform couriers partially resembled that of A.'s operatives (men lacking experience or qualifications, but physically robust, from rundown impoverished suburbs and often with immigrant backgrounds), in 2023 that profile has largely changed. In our 2023 survey on the Paris region, 77% were undocumented workers from Africa and Asia, bearing in mind that the survey was carried out under the same conditions and in the same places as in 2017. Between 2017 and 2018, we met a large number of platform couriers who had just received notification of a change in pricing or a breach of contract. For them, this change came overnight, and almost all of them found themselves in complex circumstances with no alternative in mind. Some took up former odd jobs, others tried to find a contract with a small delivery company, others left for another platform (usually switching from Deliveroo to Ubereats). Only those who already had another parallel paid activity were protected, i.e., 8% of the sample. Our 2023 survey shows that for the large majority of undocumented migrants in the Paris region, this conversion is even more difficult. Most have already been through the physical ordeal of working on a construction site, and are struggling to find a place elsewhere where the language barrier or lack of papers is not a problem. The restaurant industry seems to be the sector most inclined to recruit them.

5.2.3 Work Precarity: Deterioration in Working Conditions

Employment precarity of employment, linked to the ease of breaking contracts and the availability of an already precarious workforce, is compounded by work precarity, as described by Paugam (2007). There are differences in the work and working conditions assigned to subcontracted workers and to group employees, to the detriment of the former.

The sector most affected by this discrepancy is the parcel delivery sector. Our 2015 survey shows that groups employees worked 35 h a week, whereas subcontracted workers worked an average of 10 h more. Remuneration is also calculated differently. Whereas employees were paid by the hour, self-employed delivery drivers were paid for each parcel they delivered, between €1.5 and €3. Furthermore, whereas under an employment contract the employer has to pay employees for leave of absence when this is justified, the subcontractors received no wages if they were absent. Their pay was also reduced by a series of penalties, ranging from 10 to 150 euros, in the event of late or defective deliveries. Although their income is lower than that of group employees because of these penalties, delivery drivers at least have a more or less fixed income. This is not the case for platform couriers. Their income is variable and not guaranteed. Firstly, the pay set by the platform (which has been steadily decreasing since 2017) is based on coefficients that are opaque to the couriers, preventing them from building strategies to earn more. Secondly, the number of deliveries in a day depends on the number of orders and the number of couriers present. In other words, couriers cannot predict their earnings from 1 day to the next, from 1 month to the next. These differences in working conditions between employees of groups and self-employed workers are largely to the detriment of the latter, as the economic dependence of these workers is no longer offset by the economic protection afforded to salaried employees.

5.2.4 Work Precarity: Loss of Meaning and Autonomy for All Delivery Drivers

The way that transport groups distance themselves from the execution of transport operations contributed to the development of surveillance and control mechanisms for so-called independent workers, and to the standardization of the tasks entrusted to them. The freedom and autonomy typically associated with the figure of the truck driver (Cholez, 2001) are thus sharply challenged by these new forms of work organization.

Whatever sector they work in, delivery drivers often speak of a loss of meaning and autonomy in their work. Dedicated freight transport vehicles are increasingly tracked, like parcels and delivery drivers, by means of software applications, smartphones, and scanners. In addition to generating incentives and directives, all these devices are also a means of surveillance, reducing the autonomy of delivery drivers. In the parcel delivery sector, for example, if a truck is parked too long, the driver gets a call from the principal. In firm A.'s chain, if the number of parcels delivered by a driver does not decrease quickly enough during the round, the driver receives a call from the intermediate subcontractor.

In long-distance transport, according to Roisin Joncquière (2023), equipment has been modernized and includes on-board logistics and route optimization software: “Whereas the profession used to be a strong symbol of worker autonomy, in contrast to factory workers working in enclosed spaces under management supervision, the end of the 20th century saw a great loss of autonomy for drivers, whose work is now strictly controlled by both the state and employers” (Roisin Joncquière, 2023). She quotes a truck driver: “Your boss sees what you’re doing, if you’re stopped, if you’re driving, he sees everything you’re doing. It’s like having the boss sitting next to you in the truck” (interview of a long-distance driver on April 17, 2020 by (Roisin Joncquière, 2023)).

In the parcel delivery chain, the drivers, who previously had regular rounds on which they learned by experience how to plan a route according to the availability of the recipients and to finish early, now have different sectors every week. They are less and less able to draw on this experience and their specific skills, i.e., hazard management. Moreover, they are required to follow a preset route produced by the principal's software. They no longer have any decisions to make. On the contrary, greater priority is assigned to routine tasks. Recording procedures are central and a source of penalties:

> you have to repeat the same things: obligatory signature, stamp for the professionals. If that is missing, pay is deducted, if the time of delivery and the name of the receiver are missing, it is deducted... Finally, there are procedures, always procedures . . . and deductions on every round. (Interview with a self-employed driver, 2022)

Platform delivery drivers also have very limited autonomy, waiting for messages from the algorithm and unable to influence the number of orders, the type of route or the weather. However, they still have a certain amount of autonomy in their choice of vehicle (bike, scooter, electric bike, etc.) and in the choice of their starting area. For two-wheeled couriers working for platforms, the approach to the work depends on the worker's profile. In 2017 and 2018, couriers who were students, young people with qualifications in transition, or athletes, appreciated this kind of work, which was experienced as combining physical activity and a "casual job." They preferred this outdoor work to working in an office, a kitchen or indoor premises. For low-skilled delivery drivers, this work was sometimes seen as more pleasant than jobs with a strict hierarchy. With the platforms, couriers had the impression of no longer having "a boss on their back." The 2023 survey shows a different picture. The platforms have gradually reduced pay, which no longer compensates for the arduous nature of the work. Similarly, working hours have risen considerably, from 30 to 51 hours a week. Undocumented couriers find meaning in their work, not least because they have had much harder jobs in the construction industry, where they were not always paid. However, tougher working and employment conditions are steadily undermining their motivation.

Gradually, with the massive spread of outsourcing and the development of control and surveillance procedures, all delivery drivers are affected by a loss of autonomy and meaning.

6 Conclusion

For these three production organizations, long-haul freight transport, parcel delivery services, platform-based food delivery, different forms of outsourcing can be identified. In long-distance transport, outsourcing can be occasional or regular and associated with a weekly schedule. It involves entities of fairly similar size. This means that dependence is lower than in other sectors. The structural shortage of long-haul drivers adds to this organizational factor. Workers in this sector are more likely to be salaried, and therefore less vulnerable to precarity.

In the parcel delivery sector, outsourcing is the process of replacing employees with subcontractors in order to save costs. This logic leads principals to set up restrictive systems to manage these subcontractors, who are highly dependent on their principals. The latter decide on volumes, working hours, the follow-up to contracts and the type of vehicles to be used. They allow small employers to hire, but they can also decide to reduce volumes, even if it means putting them out of business. As a result, their employees' permanent contracts become no more than precarious permanent contracts.

As for platform workers, they are dependent because they work full-time for these platforms and have no alternatives due to language barriers and lack of papers. While working conditions may be more favorable than in other jobs, such as construction, they enjoy none of the protections of other groups.

Through these examples, we hope to have shown that the link between outsourcing and precarity is not uniform. It varies according to the dependence relations between firms involved in outsourcing and to market conditions. There seems to be a direct link between dependence and precarity. Salaried status does little to alleviate this precarity. The link is less clear with respect to precarity of employment. In long-distance transport, where subcontractors can work with a number of principals and there is a shortage of truck drivers, their dependence on their principals is lower. Truck driver precarity is therefore limited, employee's incomes are above average for blue-collar workers (Employment survey, 2017) and periods of inactivity are very limited (idem). By contrast, urban delivery drivers are more interchangeable and subcontracted to save costs. Given the small number of principals in the market and the pool of available subcontractors, the balance of power is tilted in favor of principals, and subcontractors experience numerous breaches of contract.

There also seems to be a strong link between dependence and work precarity: outsourcing leads to a deterioration in working conditions for former employees who have become self-employed (as in the case of parcel delivery drivers). In this sector, tasks are unevenly distributed between employees and subcontracted workers. Moreover, it seems that a lack of alternatives induces platform delivery drivers to accept poorer working conditions, with low pay and long hours. Nevertheless, the loss of meaning and autonomy at work seems to affect all sectors and all workers, whatever their status and dependence. Precarity, understood as a loss of meaning and autonomy at work, is thus more difficult to relate to economic dependence.

References

Alchian, A., & Demsetz, H. (1973). The property rights paradigm. *Journal of Economic History, 33*(1), 16–27.

Algava, E., & Amira, S. (2011). Sous-traitance: des conditions de travail plus difficiles chez les preneurs d'ordres. *Dares Analyse, 11*.

Ardenti, R., Mathieu, R., & Gorgeu, A. (2010). Caractère soutenable du travail et trajectoires ouvrières: études de cas dans la filière automobile et les industries agroalimentaires. *Sociétés contemporaines, 78*(2), 87–113.

Beniwall, T., & Mathur, V. K. (2021). Cloud kitchen: A profitable venture. *International Advanced Research Journal in Science, Engineering and Technology, 8*(10).

Berlinski, S. (2008). Wages and contracting out: Does the law of one price hold? *British Journal of Industrial Relations, 46*(1), 59–75.

Castel, R. (2003). *From manual workers to wage Laborers: Transformation of the social question*. Transactions.

Chan, J. (2023). Buy with 1-click: Independent contracting and migrant Workers in China's last-mile parcel delivery. *The Asia-Pacific Journal, 21*(2), 1–18.

Cholez, C. (2001). *Une culture de la mobilité: trajectoires et rôles professionnels des chauffeurs-livreurs de messagerie et fret express*. Université François Rabelais.

Christensen, C. M. (2015). *The Innovator's Dilemma: When New Technologies Cause Great Firms to Fail*. Harvard Business Review Press.

EAE survey. (2007). Annual industry survey. EAE industry. https://www.insee.fr/en/metadonnees/source/serie/s1021

Emerson, R. (1962). Power-dependence relations. *American Sociological Review, 27*(1), 31–41.

Feenstra, R., & Hanson, G. (1996). Globalization, outsourcing, and wage inequality. *American Economic Review, 86*(2), 240–245.

Flecker, J., & Meil, P. (2010). Organisational restructuring and emerging service value chains: Implications for work and employment. *Work, Employment and Society, 24*(4), 680–698.

French e-commerce federation (FEVAD). (2023). *E-commerce in France, key figures*. https://www.calameo.com/read/00713514555800f19ece5

Gallie, D., Felstead, A., Green, F., & Inanc, H. (2017). The hidden face of job insecurtity. *Work, Employment and Society, 31*(1), 36–53.

Gorgeu, A., & Mathieu, R. (2015). Le travail ouvrier à l'épreuve des restructurations dans les usines de la filière automobile. In R. Bouchareb & M. Thibault (Eds.), *Des restructurations du travail à l'accompagnement vers l'emploi*. Editions Septentrion.

Grand, L. (1997). *Les relations de sous-traitance dans le secteur des transports routiers de marchandises*. PHD Thesis, University Lyon 2.

Haidinger, B. (2012). *On the Move in Global Delivery Chains: Labour Relations and Working Conditions in the Parcel Delivery Industries of Austria, Germany, the Czech Republic and Hungary*, Vienna, Forba.

Hale, A., & Wills, J. (2005). *Threads of labour: Garment industry supply chains from the workers' perspective*. Blackwell.

IRU, (2022). The truck driver profession in Europe, https://www.iru.org/resources/iru-library/iru-intelligence-briefing-truck-driver-profession-europe-access-and-attractiveness-executive-summary

Jacobs, D. (1974). Dependency and vulnerability: An exchange approach to the control of organizations. *Administrative Science Quarterly, 19*(1), 45–59.

Lebayle, S. (2023). *Economie de plateformes et mutations productives: Le rôle des plateformes de livraison dans la branche de la restauration*, PHD Thesis, University Paris Nord.

Lopez Calle, P. (2016). L'autoexploitation au volant : les camionneurs indépendants espagnols, *La nouvelle revue du travail* 8, https://journals.openedition.org/nrt//2725?lang=en

Madjarian, A. (2016). Défaillances d'entreprises: un seuil incompressible en 2016. *L'Officiel des transporteurs, 2842*.

Marchesnay, M. (1979). La dépendance des firmes individuelles: un essai d'analyse et d'application dans leurs relations d'échange avec les groupes. *Economie et Sociétés. Sciences de Gestion, 1*, 697–736.

Montalban, M., Frigant, V., & Jullien, B. (2019). Platform economy as a new form of capitalism: A Régulationist research programm. *Cambridge Journal of Economics, 43*(4), 805–824. https://doi.org/10.1093/cje/bez017

Moore, S., & Newsome, K. (2018). Paying for free delivery: Dependent self-employment, a measure of precarity in parcel delivery. *Work, Employment, Society, 32*(3), 475–492.

Neilson, B., & Rositer, N. (2008). Precarity as a political concept or fordism as exception. *Theory, Culture and Society, 25*(7–8), 51–72.

Niérat, P. (2016). Les conditions d'exploitation dans le transport de marchandises. In C. Blanquart, P. Niérat, & P. Rème-Harnay (Eds.), *Rapport final Transports routier de marchandises*. MEDDE.

Paugam, S. (2007). *Le salarié de la précarité*. PUF.

Perraudin, C., Petit, H., Thévenot, N., Tinel, B., & Valentin, J. (2014). *Les rapports de force au cœur des relations de sous-traitance: conséquences sur les relations de travail, working paper*. Centre d'économie de la Sorbonne.
Rème-Harnay, P. (2018). Parcours de sous-traitants économiquement dépendants: l'exemple de la messagerie urbaine. *La Revue de l'Ires, 93*(3), 79–104.
Rème-Harnay, P. (2020a). Dépendance économique dans les relations de sous-traitance : quels critères ? Le cas des chauffeurs-livreurs de la messagerie. *Droit et société, 104*(1), 189–209.
Rème-Harnay, P. (2020b). Comment les plateformes numériques accroissent la dépendance dans les relations de sous-traitance : Le cas de la livraison à vélo. *Revue Française de Socio Economie, 2*(25), 175–198.
Rème-Harnay, P. (2022). Regulating outsourcing in urban freight : Should it be limited to the last mile? *Research in Transportation Business & Management, 45*(Part A), 100833.
Rème-Harnay, P. (2022b). *La sous-traitance dans les transports routiers de marchandises : Une approche sous l'angle de la dépendance économique, Habilitation à diriger des recherches en Economie*. CNAM.
Rème-Harnay, P. (2023). Precarity and subcontracting relationships: The case of parcel delivery drivers in France. *Work, Employment, Society*.
Roisin Joncquière, M. (2023). *Tu dis ça parce que tu vas à l'étranger. Nous, on est ici, ça a moins d'intérêt. Rapports au travail et styles de vie des conducteurs grands routiers, "City and work" seminar*. University Gustave Eiffel.
Schor, J., Attwood-Charles, W., Cansoy, M., Ladegaard, I., & Wengronowitz, R. (2020). Dependence and precarity in the platform economy. *Theory and Society, 49*(5), 833–861.
Thébaud-Mony, A., Levenstein, C., Forrant, R., & Wooding, J. (2011). *Nuclear servitude. Subcontracting and health in the French civil nuclear industry*. Routledge.
Thompson, J. D. (1967). *Organizations in action: Social science bases of administrative theory*. McGraw-Hill.
Williamson, O. E. (1991). Comparative economic organization: The analysis of discrete structural alternatives. *Administrative Science Quarterly, 36*, 269–296.

Does Fiscal Condition Affect Outsourcing in Italian Municipalities?

Veronica Allegrini and Fabio Monteduro

1 Introduction

In recent decades, the public sector has increasingly turned to outsourcing, transitioning from directly providing public services to overseeing their delivery (Breul, 2010).

During the final decades of the previous century, there was a growing emphasis on privatizing public services, following the principles of New Public Management. By mirroring the private sector and integrating certain management strategies and tools, this movement aimed to boost efficiency and effectiveness in the public sector (Hood, 1991; Osborne, 1993). The use of decentralized patterns of service delivery was one of the main trends (Rhodes, 1994). This trend included a dispersal of functions from the central government to regional and local governments or autonomous agencies, bringing them nearer to citizens while still being part of the government (Torres & Pina, 2002), and the externalization of local service provision. Outsourcing, as a form of externalization, enables the downsizing of the administration maintaining control of core activities. It involves the external provision of a public service by a private or an in-house company, but the public sector has the responsibility for satisfying public needs and for reporting on resources spent and performance attained (Grossi & Mussari, 2008; Monteduro & Allegrini, 2020).

V. Allegrini (✉) · F. Monteduro
University of Rome Tor Vergata, Rome, Italy
e-mail: veronica.allegrini@uniroma2.it; fabio.monteduro@uniroma2.it

F. P. García Márquez et al. (eds.), *Outsourcing*, International Series in Operations Research & Management Science 370, https://doi.org/10.1007/978-3-031-95393-4_7

Consequently, studies on the drivers of outsourcing by municipalities appeared in the literature. The main claim is that outsourcing policies are driven by cost savings, considering outsourcing as a low-cost and more efficient choice then the direct delivery. Therefore, most studies on the determinants of outsourcing included the fiscal condition of the municipality as an explanatory variable, expecting that outsourcing is the preferred strategy of municipalities under fiscal stress. Nevertheless, the findings of the empirical studies are not univocal. A large part of the literature has suggested that fiscal stress conducts to more outsourcing, while others found no evidence to support the hypothesis (Zhang et al., 2018). Interestingly, some studies conducted in European countries found evidence of a negative relationship between fiscal stress and outsourcing (Bel & Fageda, 2017). As Boyne (1998) explained, fiscal stress may increase outsourcing if the local government wants to use outsourcing for cost savings and if perceives that outsourcing will allow to deliver the service at a lower cost. Otherwise, outsourcing requires broad capabilities, resources and experience (Warner & Hebdon, 2001) and may be considered as a "*politics of good times*", that is a policy to implement when public expenditure can be easily increased rather than a tool to solve local government economic problems (Bhatti et al., 2009; Pallesen, 2004). Some authors also suggest that outsourcing might be used to provide enhancements or additions to non-core services when slack resources are available (Ya Ni & Bretschneider, 2007).

The findings of previous literature suggest that outsourcing of public services is influenced by contingent factors. Also, the relationship between the fiscal condition of the municipality and outsourcing policy may be contingent on some attributes of the organizational environment. The assumption of the contingency approach is that organizations will select the best organizational solution, given the characteristics of the specific context in which they operate. Therefore, the development of contextual and country-specific research provides useful insights to better understand the phenomenon as a whole.

The present chapter aims to address the issue of the relationship between fiscal condition and outsourcing in the context of the Italian municipalities, answering to the following research question: Is outsourcing of public services facilitated by the fiscal condition of the municipalities? The chapter presents the results of an empirical analysis carried out on all the Italian municipalities. The analysis showed that outsourcing has a positive relationship with fiscal autonomy and a negative relationship with municipal debt. Therefore, the findings suggest that in Italian municipalities outsourcing may be seen as a "*politics of good times*" in line with other studies recently conducted in the European context.

The remainder of the chapter is structured as follows. The next section reviews the literature on the determinants of local services outsourcing. Sections 3 and 4 discuss the theoretical framework of the study and describe outsourcing policies in the context of Italian municipalities. Section 5 presents variables and data collection. Section 6 describes data analysis and results. The final section sets out the conclusion.

2 The Determinants of Outsourcing by Local Governments

Literature on the determinants of outsourcing has been extensive in the last few decades, with the first studies dating back to the 1980s. The origin of outsourcing coincided with the development of a contractual and neoliberal vision of the firm and the transformation of the firm from an integrated model into a new form marked by disintegration (Weinstein, 2012). During the last decades, several theoretical perspectives have been used to explain outsourcing. For a comprehensive review is it possible to see Gilley et al. (2017). This paragraph just includes an overview of the main. One of the most used, both in private management and in public management studies, is the transaction cost theory, proposed by Coase (1937) and advanced by Williamson (1975). According to that theory, the "make or by choices" in the firm strategy are based on the minimum costs, considering both production and transaction costs. Therefore, outsourcing strategies are determined by cost savings. In the field of public management, the theory of Public Choice assumes that if politicians and bureaucrats monopolize public service delivery, the consequence is inefficiency. Therefore, the remedy is competition in the market, which provides lower costs and more efficiency (Bel & Fageda, 2007). Another approach used to explain outsourcing is the resource-based view. Barney (1991) assumed that the distribution of strategic resources among firms is heterogeneous and remains stable over time. Given the resource scarcity, the decision to outsource depends on which resources are available internally and which resources must be acquired from outside (Gilley et al., 2017). It is possible to notice that all the mentioned theoretical approaches linked outsourcing to cost reduction. Likewise, fiscal condition is the concept most used in the previous quantitative empirical studies of factors explaining local services outsourcing. Despite diversity in the theoretical approaches used to explain the determinants of local services outsourcing, the fiscal condition of local governments is steadily included in the empirical models (Zhang et al., 2018). However, the relationship between fiscal conditions and outsourcing is still under discussion. The major claim is that outsourcing policies are driven by cost savings, considering outsourcing as a low-cost and efficient way to deliver public services respect to the direct delivery. Therefore, most studies expect that outsourcing is the preferred strategy of local governments under fiscal stress. Bel and Fageda (2007) found that the positive influence of fiscal stress on externalization was frequently verified by the early studies of the U.S.A., those where data was collected in the 1980s. Recent studies on the U.S.A. presented mixed results and fiscal stress appeared as a significant determinant only in a few cases. As an example, Zhang et al. (2018) provided evidence that fiscal stress in U.S. municipalities involves an increase in outsourcing, particularly where there are several external providers of the services.

In recent years, the research on the relationship between the fiscal condition of local governments and the decision to outsource local services has widespread also in Europe. In the European context, the evidence from the quantitative empirical studies is also mixed. Some studies showed a positive effect of fiscal stress on outsourcing. This is the case of Geys and Sørensen (2016), whose main findings indicated that financial strains are associated with more outsourcing in Norwegian local governments. On the same line, according to Schoute et al. (2018), Dutch municipalities experiencing higher levels of financial stress tend to be more inclined to outsource services to private companies. In Spain, Zafra-Gómez et al. (2014) showed that outsourcing and inter-municipal cooperation are the most chosen by councils in case of financial crisis, especially in response to negative cash flow, insufficient transfers, debts, or budget deficit. Interestingly, some studies conducted in European countries found evidence of a negative relationship between fiscal stress and outsourcing. Among these, Pallesen (2004) showed that when the Danish municipalities are fiscally stressed, the level of contracting out is reduced. In the Danish context, Bhatti et al. (2009) and Foged and Aaskoven (2017) also found that the level of outsourcing is not the result of fiscal stress or economic scarcity; on the contrary, it is more likely in rich municipalities. Dijkgraaf et al. (2003) found evidence that the wealth of local government reduces the likelihood of outsourcing in Dutch municipalities. The only study finding the same evidence in the U.S. context was from Greene (2002), who gave evidence of higher levels of contracting out in wealthier local governments than in poorer and more fiscally stressed ones.

To reconcile these different findings, it is worth mentioning the explanation from Boyne (1998), who clarified that fiscal stress may results in the increasing of outsourcing if the local government choose outsourcing for cost savings and if recognizes that outsourcing will allow to deliver the service at a lower cost. Otherwise, outsourcing requires broad capabilities, resources, and experience (Warner & Hebdon, 2001) and may be seen as a "*politics of good times*" (Bhatti et al., 2009, p. 127). Some authors even suggest that outsourcing might be used to provide enhancements or additions to non-core services when slack resources are available (Ya Ni & Bretschneider, 2007).

Even though the fiscal condition is the most studied driver of local services outsourcing, Bel and Fageda (2007, 2017) in their literature reviews found also other variables considered by previous studies and grouped them into economic and political.

The political variables attain to the political process and ideological attitudes. According to the authors, politicians in a democratic setting are primarily driven by two motivations: the desire to win elections and secure government positions, and their ideological preferences. Hence, the choice to outsource local service provision could rely on the presence of groups with a specific interest in a certain delivery method and political beliefs (Bel & Fageda, 2007). Studies that analyse the interest groups' influence mainly consider public employees and the income of households, as a proxy of the wealth of the municipality. The assumption is that public employees and their unions are interested in the direct delivery of services by the municipalities. On the contrary, high-income households should prefer externalization. Regarding ideology, right-wing parties are generally linked to more business values and are positively associated with the privatization or outsourcing of public services.

On these issues, Miralles (2008) found that the group-of-interest factor, in terms of industrial water consumers, has importance for local water services in the Catalonian municipalities. O'Toole Jr and Meier (2004) found that a large number of bureaucrats among public employees, with respect to production workers, is associated with more outsourcing in Texas school districts. Interestingly, the authors found a reciprocal causation between the two variables. Bhatti et al. (2009) discovered a correlation between the quantity of public workers and outsourcing, suggesting that public employees may band together to impede outsourcing due to their own interests. Furthermore, the study revealed that increased numbers of administrative professionals lead to an increase in outsourcing, emphasizing the importance of competencies and skills. Service outsourcing might also appeal to administrative professionals due to their professional inclinations. Dijkgraaf et al. (2003) studied waste collection services in Dutch municipalities. They found evidence that the interest group variable, that is the number of public employees, raises the probability of public provision. Similarly, an increase in income within a municipality appears to decrease the likelihood of public provision, although the calculated coefficient is not statistically significant. Political ideology appears to have little impact on the choice of provision. Similarly, Bel and Miralles (2003) observed that the choice to outsource urban solid waste collection in Catalonia was driven more by practical considerations rather than ideological beliefs. On the contrary, Walls et al. (2005), analysing local waste collection and recycling services among U.S. municipalities, found that the voter ideology variable plays a role in the decisions to use public or private provision of services. Mohr et al. (2010) and Rodrigues et al. (2012) both found that household income positively influences service externalization by local municipalities, respectively in the U.S.A. and Portugal. Mohr et al. (2010) found that also ideology matters.

The economic determinants studied in the previous literature, besides fiscal condition, attain to economic efficiency. The subject of economic efficiency is related to costs and is generally operationalized using the population size as an explanatory variable. Bel and Fageda (2007) claimed that the size of the population or the level of service demand are frequently considered when examining the impact of economies of scale on the decision to outsource local services. Previous research demonstrated an inverse correlation between population size and the choice to contract out local services. According to Bel and Fageda (2017), recent studies consistently show that externalization is more prevalent in larger municipalities due to their stronger contracting capabilities, which allow them to manage transaction costs associated with external production more effectively. On this issue, Sundell and Lapuente (2012) found that population size has a notable and positive impact on outsourcing choices, backing the notion that a municipality's administrative capability, believed to increase with population, aids in contracting. Therefore, economies of scale do not seem to be a significant factor. Bel and Miralles (2003) found an inverse-U shaped relationship between population size and the choice to outsource urban solid waste collection in Spain. The authors pointed out that small municipalities with low population sizes do not benefit much from cutting inefficiencies, but they do encounter high transaction costs when outsourcing services. Therefore, outsourcing is less likely in those municipalities. With a growing population, transaction costs decrease in proportion while expected benefits increase, leading municipalities to be more inclined to outsource. Nevertheless, economies of scale could be depleted once a specific population threshold is reached. In the same way, extremely large municipalities may have the ability to implement internal reforms when it comes to directly providing the service.

3 A Contingency Approach

The findings of the literature reviewed in the previous paragraph suggest that outsourcing of public services is influenced by contingent factors. Also, the relationship between the fiscal condition of the municipalities and the decision to outsource local services seems to be modelled by some other attributes of organizational environments. Different theoretical approaches have been used to explain this relationship. Nevertheless, the review of previous empirical studies in the preceding paragraph shows that most of the literature has implicitly followed a contingency approach, even when not clearly spelled out (Gilley et al., 2017).

The term "*contingency theory*" was coined by Lawrence and Lorsch (1967). Galbraith (1973, p. 2) asserted that contingency theory is based on two assumptions: there is no one optimal way to organize; and different organizational methods vary in effectiveness. The initial assumption contradicts the traditional beliefs of administrative theorists who try to establish universal principles for organizations across different eras and locations (Scott, 2003). The second assumption implies that it is possible to observe a wide range of effective organizations, but their differences are not random: organizational context makes a difference (Galbraith, 1973). Hence, according to the contingency theory paradigm, the optimal organizational structure depends on the characteristics of the organizational environment (Scott, 2003). As a result, organizations will naturally opt for the most appropriate organizational solution that aligns with the specific context of their operations. Lawrence (1993) even provides a list of factors that contingency theorists considered important, including organizational size, geography, individual predispositions of participants, resource dependency, and national differences.

The adoption of a contingency approach to explain the drivers of outsourcing in different contexts (see for example: Damanpour et al., 2022; Farneti & Young, 2008; O'Flynn, 2019) is based on the assumption that the decision to select a portfolio of service delivery choices is contingent on both environmental and organizational factors.

The present chapter aims to investigate the relationship between the fiscal condition and the decision to outsource local services in Italian municipalities, keeping some other factors under control. Under the contingency approach, the development of more contextual and country-specific research provides useful insights to better understand the phenomenon as a whole, without the aim of generalizing the results.

4 The Italian Context

The analysis in the current chapter was conducted within the framework of Italian municipalities. In recent decades, Italy has implemented reforms in the public sector. These reforms encompass a variety of changes, such as the transfer of authority and duties from the central government to the regional, provincial, and municipal levels. Italy operates with a high level of decentralization, where municipalities play a key role in providing services to residents (Ongaro & Valotti, 2008). Italian public administrations have had to embrace private sector managerial principles and tools to implement these reforms, particularly for managing and providing public services. Italian public administrations have increasingly turned to outsourcing as a means to improve efficiency, effectiveness, and economy by moving away from direct service provisions. Outsourcing strategies differ across the various levels of government in Italy—central, regional, and local. In the central (ministries and other central agencies and non-economic bodies) and regional governments (regions and regional autonomous bodies), outsourcing is widespread and used for internal and non-core activities or services that support primary functions. These services encompass IT, administrative, and logistical support. Within local governments, such as provinces and municipalities, outsourcing plays a crucial role in strategic planning. It is utilized for both internal functions and non-core services, as well as for delivering local public services to residents (Argento et al., 2010). Local governments are responsible for arranging and delivering public services within their jurisdictions, such as water supply, waste management, public transportation, road upkeep, educational programmes for children, and support services for residents in need. Italian municipalities are usually more inclined to contract out either whole service packages or significant parts of them to private businesses or non-profit providers (Mussari, 2006). Outsourcing is particularly relevant for local social and cultural services (Argento et al., 2010).

Italian municipalities generate revenue primarily through their own taxes and fees, as well as through transfers from higher levels of government, particularly the central government. Municipalities in Italy are empowered to make changes to their tax rates, with some restrictions, which can result in either higher or lower tax revenues (Bucci et al., 2022).

5 Variables and Data Collection

The dependent variable of the analysis was the degree of outsourcing in service delivery (*outsourcing*).

Detailed data on the revenues and expenditures of all public Italian organizations was collected from the Information System on the Operations of Public Bodies, an open-source database. The composition of municipalities' expenditures can be found in this database, which is managed by the State General Accounting

Department in collaboration with the Bank of Italy and ISTAT. We examined the expenses of each municipality in obtaining services from external entities through contracts. This data was utilized to assess the extent of outsourcing in service provision. The study only focused on services provided to the local community. The contracts for internal operations, including maintenance, cleaning, and security services, were left out. The independent variable was determined by calculating the percentage of spending on service contracts in relation to the overall expenditure of the municipality. The application of this percentage allows for the normalization of outsourcing rates across municipalities, as opposed to using the actual expenditure amount for service contracts. Data were from 2021.

In the previous literature there is no widely accepted indicator of fiscal condition. There are numerous ways to assess that, and some authors suggest that the concept requires multiple measures (Hendrick, 2006; Plata-Díaz et al., 2014). In line with this suggestion, we decided to use two different measures of the municipal fiscal condition:

- Fiscal autonomy degree (*fiscal_autonomy*): Fiscal autonomy relates to the ability of the municipality to raise revenues through municipal taxes and is measured as the ratio of current municipal tributary revenues to the total current revenues. This indicator can range from 0 (absence of fiscal autonomy) to 1 (maximum fiscal autonomy). The degree of fiscal autonomy is generally used by central institutions to measure the taxation effort of the local government and captures how a municipality is independent from contributions and transfers from the central government. High values of the indicator indicate a low fiscal stress in the municipality. Low values of the indicator indicate a high fiscal stress.
- Incidence of expenditure on loan repayment on the total expenditures (*loan_expanditures*): Such a variable represents a proxy of the debt, that is also included as a measure of fiscal stress (Zhang et al., 2018). The higher the incidence of expenditure on loan repayment, the higher the fiscal stress in the municipality.

The data source for *fiscal_autonomy* and *loan_expanditures* variables was the ISTAT, which computes such indicators annually. Data was from 2020. One of the main shortcomings of previous studies identified by Bel and Fageda (2007, 2017) is that the production form in year x is associated with the value y of some explanatory variables in that same year. The authors stated that those studies analyse the correlation between the production form and explanatory factors in period x, that is very different from understanding why the local government made the decision to privatize in period x—n. In order to keep in consideration that comment, we decided to include a time lag between the dependent and the independent variables. Therefore, data on financial autonomy degree and incidence of expenditure on loan repayment were from 2020.

The analysis also included some control variables consistent with the previous literature:

- Incidence of current expenditure on the total expenditures (*current_exp*): Some previous studies used total municipal spending believing that outsourcing is used in the case of surplus when basic services are secured. We used the mentioned ratio to standardize the variable among the municipalities.
- Population (*population*): A common finding in previous studies is that outsourcing is more likely in larger municipalities. To normalize the variable and control its variability, we used the logarithm of the number of inhabitants, rather than the absolute value.
- Income per capita (*income_percap*): Some previous literature used the income of households to analyse the interest groups' influence. The hypothesis in those studies is that high-income households have a greater preference for privatization (Bel & Fageda, 2007).
- Geographical location (*north_it*, *centr_it*, *south_it*): We included three dummy variables for geographical location in Northern, Central, and Southern Italy. Geographical location is often used in studies on Italian municipalities as the various areas are very different in their socio-economic development.

The data source for the control variables was again the ISTAT.

The statistical population of the study was the Italian municipalities, which according to ISTAT were 7904 in 2021. The analysis of the chapter was carried out on 7745 municipalities out of 7904 due to a few missing values in the databases used to collect data.

6 Data Analysis and Results

To test the study hypothesis, we carried out a multivariate analysis using an ordinary least squares (OLS) regression model. This enabled us to understand the effects of the fiscal condition, measured by *fiscal_autonomy* and *loan_expanditures* variables, on the likelihood to outsource local services provision, keeping other variables under control.

The results of Pearson's correlation analysis are shown in Table 1. The degree of outsourcing in service delivery shows a statistically significant correlation with all the dependent and the control variables. Table 2 shows the results of the OLS regression analysis. The absence of any severe multicollinearity amongst the independent variables was confirmed by examining the variance inflation factor (VIF), which had a mean value of 1.65. The normality of the residuals was checked graphically performing a kernel density estimation compared with normal density. The methods gave no evidence of problems of non-normality of the residuals. In addition, the homoscedasticity of residuals was checked by performing the Breusch-Pagan test for heteroskedasticity. The result indicates the presence of heteroskedasticity; therefore we used robust standard errors.

Table 2 shows that there were positive and statistically significant relationships between the dependent variable (*outsourcing*) and:

Table 1 Bivariate correlations

	1	*2*	*3*	*4*	*5*	*6*	*7*	*8*	*9*
1. Outsourcing	1								
2. fiscal_autonomy	0.2570*	1							
3. loan_expanditures	−0.0701*	−0.021	1						
4. current_exp	0.5265*	0.1125*	−0.0177	1					
5. Population	0.5228*	0.1750*	−0.0147	0.3607*	1				
6. income_percap	0.0950*	0.1467*	0.0853*	0.2469*	0.0870*	1			
7. south_it	−0.0558*	−0.1709*	−0.0811*	−0.2183*	0.0237†	−0.7608*	1		
8. centr_it	0.1400*	0.0376*	−0.0911*	0.0663*	0.0791*	0.0043	−0.2425*	1	
9. north_it	−0.0674*	0.1575*	0.1462*	0.1417*	−0.1340*	0.6912*	−0.7173*	−0.3937*	1

* significant at 0.001; + significant at 0.01; † significant at 0.05 (2-tailed)

Table 2 Results of the OLS regression analysis

	Outsourcing					
Independent and control variables	*Coef.*	*Robust Std. err.*	*t*	$P > \|t\|$	*95% Conf. interval*	
fiscal_autonomy	0.079709	0.004352	18.32	0.000	0.071179	0.088239
loan_expanditures	−0.11726	0.031192	−3.76	0.000	−0.1784	−0.05611
current_exp	0.221178	0.005331	41.49	0.000	0.210727	0.231628
Population	0.021116	0.00056	37.69	0.000	0.020017	0.022214
income_percap	0.003246	0.004549	0.71	0.476	−0.00567	0.012163
south_it	0.014879	0.00262	5.68	0.000	0.009744	0.020014
centr_it	0.025435	0.002463	10.33	0.000	0.020607	0.030263
Cons	−0.25215	0.043099	−5.85	0.000	−0.33663	−0.16766
Number of obs = 7.745						
Prob > F = 0.000						
$R^2 = 0.44$						

- The fiscal autonomy degree ($p < 0.001$).
- The incidence of current expenditure on the total expenditures ($p < 0.001$).
- The population ($p < 0.001$).
- The geographical location in Central and Southern Italy with respect to the Northern ($p < 0.001$).

Table 2 also shows that there were negative and statistically significant relationships between the dependent variable (*outsourcing*) and:

- The incidence of expenditure on loan repayment on the total expenditures ($p < 0.001$).

A positive but non-statistically significant relationship was found between outsourcing and income per capita.

The results evidence that an increase in the fiscal autonomy degree and a decrease in the incidence of expenditure on loan repayment led to an increase in the level of outsourcing of municipalities. We included a one-year time lag between the dependent and the independent variables. The results are the same considering a two-year or a three-year time lag. In addition, municipalities with higher wealth seem to be more likely to provide local services through outsourcing. The decision to outsource seems also more likely as the population increases. Last, the municipalities in the Central and Southern parts of the country seem more likely to outsource local public services than the municipalities in the Northern of Italy.

7 Discussion and Conclusion

The analysis aimed to extend the current understanding of the impact of fiscal conditions on local services outsourcing offering an empirical study on all the Italian municipalities. The study has demonstrated that, among Italian municipalities, a worse fiscal condition does not lead to more outsourcing. In the model, municipalities with a higher degree of fiscal autonomy and a lower incidence of expenditure on loan repayment are found more likely to outsource local services. Especially the fiscal autonomy has a high weight in explaining outsourcing. Both variables have been used to assess the fiscal condition of the municipalities. The incidence of expenditure on loan repayment represents a proxy of the debt. The evidence was that lower debt leads to more outsourcing. The level of fiscal autonomy measures a municipality's independence from financial support from the central government. The evidence was that a higher degree of fiscal autonomy leads to more outsourcing. Fiscal autonomy relates not only to the ability of municipalities to raise revenues but also to the possibility of determining how to spend them. The fiscal condition is influenced by a gaining resource component and, in turn, influences a spending resource component. Therefore, as also some previous studies asserted, municipalities that are less dependent on central government transfer seem more likely to experiment with innovative options for service delivery (Rodrigues et al., 2012).

The evidence on the incidence of current expenditure on the total expenditures is in line with the result on financial autonomy and suggests that outsourcing positively depends on the availability of financial resources. The evidence showing that population has a significant and positive effect on outsourcing decisions further validates the notion that a municipality's administrative capability, which is often tied to its population size, helps in the contracting process (Sundell & Lapuente, 2012). Moreover, bigger municipalities possess greater contracting capabilities, enabling them to effectively manage the transaction costs linked to external production. Last, the results show that the decision to outsource local services is also contingent on the geographical context in which the municipalities are located. Ceteris paribus, municipalities located in the Central and Southern of Italy seem more likely to outsource. Studies on Italian local government often included geographical location as a control variable as significant regional differences exist in Italy across a wide range of features. Geographic location is used as a proxy for the cultural, social, political, and economic context, in turn, affecting decision-making and city policies (Anessi-Pessina et al., 2008; Bingham, 1978). However, it does not focus on explaining more detailed distinctions, particularly within the same geographical region.

The results show that, in Italian municipalities, outsourcing is a phenomenon related to financial well-being. This finding is in line with a stream of recent research in the area, according to which outsourcing can be seen as a "politics of good times" depending on the wealth, information, and experience of the politicians rather than an instrument for the fiscally strained (Warner & Hebdon, 2001; Ya

Ni & Bretschneider, 2007; Bhatti et al., 2009; Rodrigues et al., 2012). In addition, the presence of resources slack may offer the opportunity to improve service quality or provide enhancements of non-core services, which will often be undertaken by private suppliers (Ya Ni & Bretschneider, 2007).

The chapter proposed country-specific research on the impact of fiscal conditions on local services outsourcing. In the view of the contingency approach, the development of contextual and country-specific research is useful to better understand the phenomenon. Therefore, the aim of the research was not about generalizing the results but about enriching the debate on the issue. The adoption of a contingency approach is based on the assumption that the decision to outsource local public services is contingent on organizational and contextual factors. This appears to be clear watching to the contrasting results of previous research. Most of the studies carried out in the 1980s and 1990s found a positive influence of fiscal stress on the decision to outsource local public services. In a contingency view, we can make a twofold set of considerations. The 1980s and 1990s were the years of various financial crises. Public administration in OECD countries was urged by the New Public Management movement to boost efficiency and effectiveness by incorporating private sector management principles and tools. This trend fostered the externalization of public services with the promise of a low-cost and efficient alternative to the direct delivery of services. In addition, all those studies were carried out in the U.S. context. Although NPM has significantly impacted public-sector decision-making globally, NPM-inspired reforms were first implemented in English-speaking countries (Gualmini, 2008). Studies carried out later, from the 2000s to these days, rarely found a positive relationship between fiscal stress and outsourcing: studies in the U.S. context mainly found non-significant results; and studies in the European context mainly found a negative relationship. Therefore, both socio-economic and geographical context seem to have an influence in modelling the relationship between the fiscal condition of municipalities and the decision to outsource local public services. Our chapter added a piece to the study of these contingencies by analysing as first the relationship between fiscal conditions and outsourcing in the Italian context.

The study included variables from previous research. Of course, this does not mean that there are no other possible explanatory variables. Future studies on this issue could expand the range of variables to further enrich the literature on the factors influencing outsourcing.

References

Anessi-Pessina, E., Nasi, G., & Steccolini, I. (2008). Accounting reforms: Determinants of local governments' choices. *Financial Accountability & Management, 24*(3), 321–342.

Argento, D., Grossi, G., Tagesson, T., & Collin, S. O. (2010). The 'externalisation' of local public service delivery: Experience in Italy and Sweden. *International Journal of Public Policy, 5*(1), 41–56.

Barney, J. (1991). Firm resources and sustained competitive advantage. *Journal of Management, 17*(1), 99–120.
Bel, G., & Fageda, X. (2007). Why do local governments privatise public services? A survey of empirical studies. *Local Government Studies, 33*(4), 517–534.
Bel, G., & Fageda, X. (2017). What have we learnt after three decades of empirical studies on factors driving local privatization? *Local Government Studies, 43*(4), 503–511.
Bel, G., & Miralles, A. (2003). Factors influencing the privatisation of urban solid waste collection in Spain. *Urban Studies, 40*(7), 1323–1334.
Bhatti, Y., Olsen, A. L., & Pedersen, L. H. (2009). The effects of administrative professionals on contracting out. *Governance, 22*(1), 121–137.
Bingham, R. D. (1978). Innovation, bureaucracy, and public policy: A study of innovation adoption by local government. *Western Political Quarterly, 31*(2), 178–205.
Boyne, G. A. (1998). The determinants of variations in local service contracting: Garbage in, garbage out? *Urban Affairs Review, 34*(1), 150–163.
Breul, J. D. (2010). Practitioner's perspective—Improving sourcing decisions. *Public Administration Review, 70*, s193–s200.
Bucci, V., Ferrara, G., & Resce, G. (2022). *Fiscal decentralization and efficiency: Empirical evidence from Italian municipalities*. University Library of Munich.
Coase, R. H. (1937). The nature of the firm. *Economica, 4*, 386–405.
Damanpour, F., Sanchez-Henriquez, F., & Avellaneda, C. N. (2022). Environmental and organizational antecedents of plural sourcing of public services. *Public Administration Review, 82*(2), 325–337.
Dijkgraaf, E., Gradus, R. H., & Melenberg, B. (2003). Contracting out refuse collection. *Empirical Economics, 28*, 553–570.
Farneti, F., & Young, D. W. (2008). A contingency approach to managing outsourcing risk in municipalities. *Public Management Review, 10*(1), 89–99.
Foged, S. K., & Aaskoven, L. (2017). Public sector unions and privatization: Evidence from the eldercare sector in Danish municipalities. *Journal of Public Administration Research and Theory, 27*(1), 135–149.
Galbraith, J. (1973). *Designing complex organizations*. Addison-Wesley Pub. Co.
Geys, B., & Sørensen, R. J. (2016). Revenue scarcity and government outsourcing: Empirical evidence from Norwegian local governments. *Public Administration, 94*(3), 769–788.
Gilley, K. M., Rasheed, A. A., & Al-Shammari, H. (2017). Research on outsourcing: Theoretical perspectives and empirical evidence. In *Global outsourcing strategies* (pp. 41–56). Routledge.
Greene, J. D. (2002). *Cities and privatization: Prospects for the new century*. Pearson.
Grossi, G., & Mussari, R. (2008). Effects of outsourcing on performance measurement and reporting: The experience of Italian local governments. *Public Budgeting & Finance, 28*(1), 22–38.
Gualmini, E. (2008). Restructuring Weberian bureaucracy: Comparing managerial reforms in Europe and the United States. *Public Administration, 86*(1), 75–94.
Hendrick, R. (2006). The role of slack in local government finances. *Public Budgeting & Finance, 26*(1), 14–46.
Hood, C. (1991). A public management for all seasons? *Public Administration, 69*(1), 3–19.
Lawrence, P. R. (1993). The contingency approach to organization design. In R. T. Golembiewski (Ed.), *Handbook of organizational behavior*. Marcel Dekker.
Lawrence, P. R., & Lorsch, J. W. (1967). Differentiation and integration in complex organizations. *Administrative Science Quarterly*, 1–47.
Miralles, A. (2008). A duration model analysis of privatization of municipal water services. *Revista de Economía Aplicada, XVII*(50), 47–75.
Mohr, R., Deller, S. C., & Halstead, J. M. (2010). Alternative methods of service delivery in small and rural municipalities. *Public Administration Review, 70*(6), 894–905.
Monteduro, F., & Allegrini, V. (2020). How outsourcing affects the e-disclosure of performance information by local governments. *Government Information Quarterly, 37*(1), 101398.

Mussari, R. (2006). Accountability and reporting: New developments in Italian local governments. In *The governance of Services of General Interest between state, market and society* (pp. 13–33). Wissenschaftlicher Verlag.

O'Flynn, J. (2019). Rethinking relationships: Clarity, contingency, and capabilities. *Policy Design and Practice, 2*(2), 115–136.

O'Toole, L. J., Jr., & Meier, K. J. (2004). Parkinson's law and the new public management? Contracting determinants and service-quality consequences in public education. *Public Administration Review, 64*(3), 342–352.

Ongaro, E., & Valotti, G. (2008). Public management reform in Italy: Explaining the implementation gap. *International Journal of Public Sector Management, 21*(2), 174–204.

Osborne, D. (1993). Reinventing government. *Public Productivity & Management Review*, 349–356.

Pallesen, T. (2004). A political perspective on contracting out: The politics of good times. Experiences from Danish local governments. *Governance, 17*(4), 573–587.

Plata-Díaz, A. M., Zafra-Gómez, J. L., Pérez-López, G., & López-Hernández, A. M. (2014). Alternative management structures for municipal waste collection services: The influence of economic and political factors. *Waste Management, 34*(11), 1967–1976.

Rhodes, R. A. (1994). The hollowing out of the state: The changing nature of the public service in Britain. *The Political Quarterly, 65*(2), 138–151.

Rodrigues, M., Tavares, A. F., & Araújo, J. F. (2012). Municipal service delivery: The role of transaction costs in the choice between alternative governance mechanisms. *Local Government Studies, 38*(5), 615–638.

Schoute, M., Budding, T., & Gradus, R. (2018). Municipalities' choices of service delivery modes: The influence of service, political, governance, and financial characteristics. *International Public Management Journal, 21*(4), 502–532.

Scott, W. R. (2003). *Organizations: Rational, natural, and open systems* (5th ed.). Prentice Hall.

Sundell, A., & Lapuente, V. (2012). Adam smith or Machiavelli? Political incentives for contracting out local public services. *Public Choice, 153*, 469–485.

Torres, L., & Pina, V. (2002). Delivering public services—Mechanisms and consequences: Changes in public service delivery in the EU countries. *Public Money and Management, 22*(4), 41–48.

Walls, M., Macauley, M., & Anderson, S. (2005). Private markets, contracts, and government provision: What explains the organization of local waste and recycling markets? *Urban Affairs Review, 40*(5), 590–613.

Warner, M., & Hebdon, R. (2001). Local government restructuring: Privatization and its alternatives. *Journal of Policy Analysis and Management: The Journal of the Association for Public Policy Analysis and Management, 20*(2), 315–336.

Weinstein, O. (2012). Firm, property and governance: From Berle and means to the agency theory, and beyond. *Accounting, Economics, and Law, 2*(2), 2.

Williamson, O. E. (1975). *Markets and hierarchies: Analysis and antitrust implications*. Free press.

Ya Ni, A., & Bretschneider, S. (2007). The decision to contract out: A study of contracting for E-government Services in State Governments. *Public Administration Review, 67*(3), 531–544.

Zafra-Gómez, J. L., Pedauga, L. E., Plata-Díaz, A. M., & López-Hernández, A. M. (2014). Do local authorities use NPM delivery forms to overcome problems of fiscal stress? *Spanish Journal of Finance and Accounting/Revista Española de Financiación y Contabilidad, 43*(1), 21–46.

Zhang, Z., Gibson, B., & Schafer, J. G. (2018). Reexamining the relationship between fiscal stress and outsourcing. *Public Performance & Management Review, 41*(1), 22–46.

Outsourcing War and Security: Rational and Justifications

Ori Swed

1 Introduction

Outsourcing is a common practice in the business world. It offers organizations greater flexibility (Bahli & Rivard, 2005), foster innovation (Nieto & Rodríguez, 2011), compensate for organizational deficiencies and limitations (Ghamat et al., 2018), increase access to expertise (Lacity & Willcocks, 1995), among other things. Its most prized function is that it permits organizations to reduce costs and increase efficiency in a process that is directly linked to profit. Yet, in the context of security, defense, and war making it can often be counterproductive. Security is an odd commodity that operates under a slightly different rationale; a rationale that challenges our understanding of the relative advantage of outsourcing. Security is indeed governed by market forces and logic. Reducing costs matters. At the same time, it introduces the different rationale of national security that can null cost-efficacy concerns. Every outsourcing has potential disadvantages (Somjai, 2017), in the case of national security, those can be lethal. States would not outsource their national security to others. In this study, we intend to stress the difference between outsourcing security and war making from standard outsourcing while explaining the motivations behind this trend.

Research on outsourcing war making and security has been focusing on the political, legal, moral, and military dimensions of this trend. Researchers focuses on the political implications of outsourcing security, discussing challenges for sovereignty (Maogoto, 2006; Petersohn, 2010), public opinion and that industry (Ramirez & Wood, 2019), and the meaning of outsourcing sacrifice (Taussig-Rubbo, 2009). Legal studies focused on the legality of using actors that can be framed as

O. Swed (✉)
Department of Sociology, Anthropology, and Social Work, Texas Tech University, Lubbock, TX, USA
e-mail: Ori.Swed@ttu.edu

F. P. García Márquez et al. (eds.), *Outsourcing*, International Series in Operations Research & Management Science 370, https://doi.org/10.1007/978-3-031-95393-4_8

mercenaries (Cameron, 2006; Salzman, 2007), questions on accountability (Bina, 2004; Chapman, 2010; Minow, 2004) and concerns on impunity (Leander, 2010; Rothe & Ross, 2010). Those discussions were linked to debates of morality of outsourcing war (Machairas, 2014; Pattison, 2014) and of the link between contractors and human rights violations (Del Prado, 2011). A bulk of studies explored military-related questions, looking at efficacy (Dunigan, 2011; Petersohn, 2013, 2017) and integration (Schaub Jr, 2016; Singer, 2007). When using economics or management methods and approaches in studies, it's been done mostly to support the other themes (political, legal, moral, and military). For example, the discussion on market forces was framed to promote arguments on human rights and morality, looking at worker's exploitation or "occupation for hire" (Simons, 2004; Swed & Burland, 2022). This study takes a step back and explains the difference between traditional outsourcing and outsourcing within the security realm.

The paper is structured as follows, it opens with a review of the practice of outsourcing and its advantages. We continue with reviewing the scope of outsourcing in the field of security and war making. Next, we engage in discussions on outsourcing those services and the motivations behind them. We conclude by explaining the unique challenges and implications of outsourcing security and war.

2 Explaining Outsourcing

The practice of outsourcing has become increasingly prevalent in the global economy, where organizations seek to leverage specialized skills, access cost advantages, and steer complex regulatory environments. A 2023 Research and Markets report estimates the 2022 global outsourcing market as over $620 billion, about the size of the Argentinian economy and larger than the Swedish or Norwegian economies (Research and Markets, 2022). Outsourcing refers to companies' strategic decision to delegate specific functions or processes to external providers, frequently located in different geographic locations. Organizations use outsourcing to enhance efficiency, reduce costs, and optimize resources. This practice encompasses a spectrum of activities, ranging from information technology services to customer support, manufacturing, and others. Essentially, it allows organizations to use external contractors to take over any specific function in the organization's operation to reduce cost and attain greater efficacy.

Outsourcing offers meaningful advantages for organizations. It can compensate for capacities deficit (Ghamat et al., 2018), addresses niche expertise (Bahli & Rivard, 2005), assist with innovation (Nieto & Rodríguez, 2011), decrease labor costs (Cheng et al., 2021), and offering flexibility (Lacity & Willcocks, 1995) among many other advantages. Yet, the primary advantage is cost reduction (Maskell et al., 2007) and increased efficacy (Magelssen et al., 2015; Picazo-Tadeo & Reig-Martínez, 2006). Outsourcing allows organizations to capitalize on the wage differentials and operational efficiencies offered by external service providers. One example, it is cheaper for Nike or Walmart to move its factories to Bangladesh, where the educated and skilled workforce costs significantly less than in Western countries (Banjo, 2014).

By leveraging the specialized expertise of outsourcing partners, companies can access a pool of skilled professionals without incurring the expenses associated with in-house training and development (Tanriverdi et al., 2007). Furthermore, the development of in-house specialized skills is extremely costly to maintain. Often, it is more economical to work with a contractor that specializes in specific skills rather than developing and maintaining those within the organization. For instance, instead of developing in-house accounting capabilities, many medium and small-size business companies purchase accounting services and products from expert companies in the field (Cahyaningtyas & Ningtyas, 2020; Everaert et al., 2010). They do not eliminate their finance department, but they do not need it to invest in high-end skills that are difficult to develop and hard to sustain. Outsourcing facilitates a more agile response to fluctuating business demands, enabling firms to scale their operations up or down swiftly in alignment with market dynamics. The global distribution of labor allows organizations, especially international corporations, to operate on a 24/7 basis, fostering continuous workflow and responsiveness to customer needs (Ritzer & Lair, 2007).

Identifying this trend, scholarship has extensively engaged with different trends and domains of outsourcing. Discussing the outsourcing of jobs, Lu et al. (2021) explored the effects of the move from in-house production to outsourcing, using sub-contractors, on companies' decision-making. Viswanathan et al. (2021) examined the outsourcing of manufacturing, showing that it intensifies market competition. Zhu et al. (2017) studied the relationship between outsourcing logistics and related management. Another body of work explores the social implications of the trend. Dube and Kaplan (2010) discuss the wage penalty associated with outsourcing, namely the reduction of individual wages domestically. Lair (2012) stresses the problem of accountability in cases of outsourcing.

3 The Different Logic of Security Markets

Yet, this entire discussion on outsourcing has been focusing on markets where the principal rationale behind every action is profit. Every company strives to maximize profit. Even if it is not the only driving factor in the organization's decision-making process, it is most definitely the dominating one. Frequently, the pathway for profit goes through increased cost-efficiency calculation. This means reducing costs while maintaining a similar or better quality of a product/service.[1] Under that type of rationale, an increase in cost-efficacy will categorically increase profit. It makes

[1] Those are often linked to an increase in work productivity, which inevitably leads to increase in profit.

sense to offshore services, workforce, and core or peripheral functions to save money, since this is the main objective of those actors.

Alas, in the market for force (Avant, 2005) the rationale is more complicated. When security is the commodity (Krahmann, 2008), cost efficiency is very important, yet it is not the main driver of every action. When the commodity is products and services that offer security, the expected outcome is not profit or reduced cost, it is security. Security is a collective good that has been outsourced. Despite treating security as a commodity, outsourcing is expected to de facto provide a public good. Cheap costs that might reduce security and put people at risk will come in contradiction to the required outcome. It means that even if economically sound, the outsourcing of critical national security services to private or external actors will counter the security logic. For instance, the US armed forces would not outsource their nuclear capabilities to a Chinese company, even if all assessments and calculations show that it would dramatically reduce costs and increase efficacy. The threat of losing access to critical weapon systems or revealing military secrets to a rival country nulls the argument for cost-efficacy, rendering it irrelevant.

National security or war-related functions are critical to governments. Often, the successful delivery of those can be linked to the survivability of a regime, to people's way of life and their liberties, and economic stability. For instance, in 2023, the inability of the Niger government to provide security in its fights against local rebels and terrorist groups led to military defeats, civilian casualties, and ended in a military coup (Ajala, 2023; Nsaibia, 2023). The military government reshaped existing geopolitical alliances, propelled the country into a perpetuate state of war, and severely harmed civilians' freedom and liberties (HRW, 2023). Indeed, the consequences of a security failure can be dire. None of those correspond with the calculations within the business and corporate realm.

Beyond the special nature of this commodity, outsourcing plays out differently in the governmental sphere. Governmental outsourcing does end with cost considerations. Governments engage in outsourcing with the broader goal of improving public service delivery, and promoting quality of life within the community and local businesses. Moreover, the level of accountability the government experiences is significantly different than companies. Unlike the limited oversight and transparency companies enjoy, governmental organizations are burdened with multiple levels and mechanisms of oversight. When outsourcing, the public sector is required to provide explanations and justifications. Government agencies need to navigate a specific, and often intricate regulatory landscape that includes procurement laws, public accountability standards, and adherence to ethical and societal considerations. The complex nature of government outsourcing demands meticulous consideration of the impact on citizens, communities, and societal welfare. That impact could be waste of public resources, dangerous to public safety, disruptive to public order, or come in contradiction to the community and constitutions' aspirations.

4 When Does the State Outsource Security

Due to the potential high risk, sometimes even existential, historically modern states preferred not to outsource military and security functions. Those included even the most mundane functions, such as housing and cleaning, given that security agencies identify those as potential points of entry for hostile elements (Cybersecurity Advisory, 2022). Thus, almost every aspect of national security operations, from cleaning bases, feeding soldiers, transporting fuel, establishing communication, and IT services has been traditionally performed in-house. By doing so, states were able to create a layer of protected isolation for the entities and people involved in those operations. A layer that is harder to penetrate or exploit.

Nonetheless, we do see today the exceeding outsourcing of military and security functions (Mahoney et al., 2022; Singer, 2017; Swed & Burland, 2020; Wither, 2020). States do use contractors for training their own forces or foreign armies (Singer, 2017: 119), they run logistics operations (Kinsey, 2009), they man security checkpoints (Havkin, 2011), used for border control and addressing illegal immigration challenges (Davitti, 2019), or provide VIP security protection in conflict areas. All those are functions historically conducted by the military. Outsourcing security and war-related functions became commonplace across the world (Swed & Burland, 2020), creating a fusion between contractors and security forces. This begs the question of when does the state outsource security?

The most prominent reason for the increase in the security outsourcing trend is the legitimacy this practice gained during the Iraq and Afghanistan wars. Those conflicts signaled a shift in the image of security providers, turning them from mercenaries, greedy criminals, into contractors, service providers. The international perception of the industry has been very negative for a long period of time. Instances such as the 1977 Bennin Affair (Taulbee & Head, 1993), the heavy mercenary's involvement in the Comoros in the 1980s (Arnold, 1999), and Sandline International's dubious coup attempt in Papua New Guinea in 1997 (Ebbeck, 1998), bolstered an image of criminals and soldiers for fortune that destabilize the international system. Other interventions in the 1990s, though considered more successful, were either concealed (such as Military Professional Resources and Kellogg Brown & Root involvement in Bosnia) or received a forceful pushback by the international community (such as the Executive Outcome's involvement in Sierra Leone) (Avant, 2004). Yet, the American need for additional personnel due to its commitment to two wars simultaneously in Iraq and Afghanistan brought the Private Military and Security (PMSC) industry to the mainstream. Contractors were able to fill the personnel gap the military could not while avoiding the alternative of national draft (Avant, 2013). With that legitimacy, the floodgates were open. During the surge, which included the massive increase of US soldiers in Iraq, the number of contractors surpassed those numbers (Swed & Crosbie, 2017) (see Fig. 1).

With legitimacy, other aspects of outsourcing security and war making were explored. The discussion on cost-efficacy gained momentum focusing at first on the decreased cost of contractors in comparison to soldiers due to reduced fringe

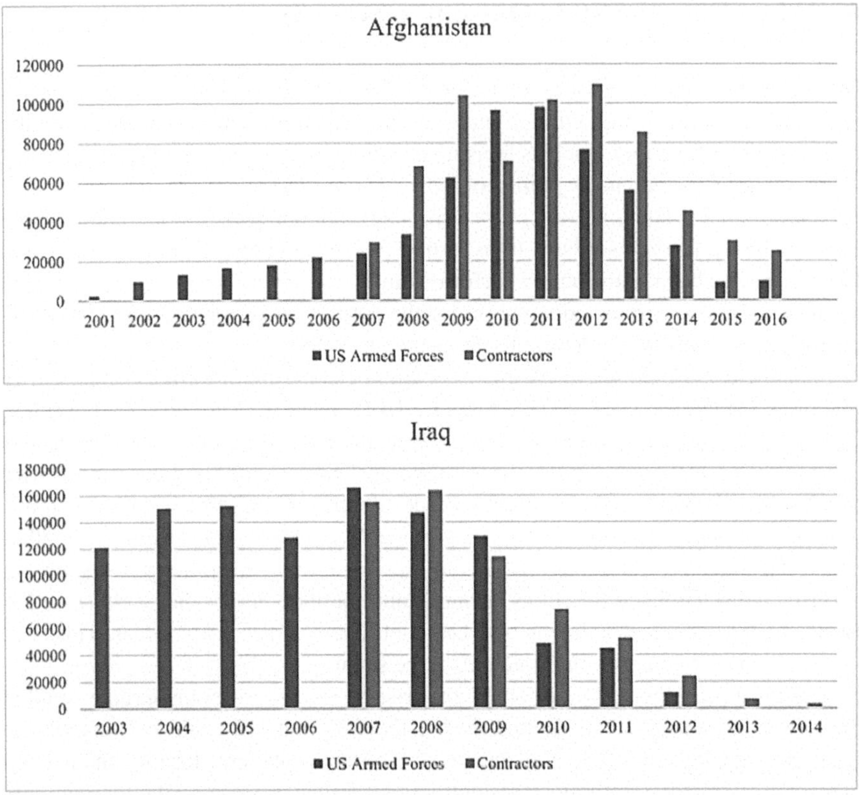

Fig. 1 US forces and contractors in Afghanistan and Iraq 2001–2016. *Figures are taken from Swed and Crosbie (2017)

costs, among them training, insurance, rehabilitation, and recovery (Brayton, 2002; MacDonald, 2010). Later, it moved towards offshoring services and functions, replacing Western contractors with cheaper labor from the global south (Eichler, 2014; Li, 2015). Similar to other types of outsourcing, the reliance on a cheaper workforce contributes to cost reduction. Chisholm (2014) illustrates how the Nepalese contractors in Iraq received lower salaries and worse work conditions compared to their Western counterparts. A great portion of the offshoring takes place within the areas of conflict, with locals joining as contractors. For instance, Isenberg (2008, p. 96) explains that most of the contractors in Iraq during the war were Iraqis. Kinsey and Patterson (2012, p. 64) explain that about 75% of the contractor workforce in Afghanistan during the war has been local Afghanis (78,430 contractors).

Cost-efficacy calculations can play out differently across different armies and countries. One of the cardinal factors in those calculations is access to skills and specializations. The modern battlefield and dimension of security threats demand the development of a comprehensive and holistic array of specialized capabilities. For instance, counterterrorism or cyber threats require substantially different skills and capacities than those developed for conventional warfare. To master and obtain those different skills the armed forces are required to have access to specialized knowledge and skills as well as to have the resources to develop and maintain them. Those are often not easily accessible and demand significant investment. For instance, an army that wishes to acquire air reconnaissance capabilities will be required to build or purchase the relevant platforms, have the ability to train personnel and operators in running and maintaining those platforms, develop or secure replacement parts and logistical chains, and create specialized doctrine and operation manuals. Each of those steps is demanding and costly. Most nations cannot obtain those types of skills and capabilities. Those sorts of skills and specialization are hard to gain. For example, only a handful of nations have the ability to execute an armed maneuver or to deploy missions from naval platforms. Consequently, a shortcut to gaining those capabilities is outsourcing. Instead of massive investments in developing and owning those skills, states can buy the relevant skillset from contractors. For example, struggling in its fight against Jihadi insurgents, Nigeria used the services of the company Special Tasks, Training, Equipment and Protection Ltd. (STTEP) (Kinsey & Krieg, 2021). STTEP offered specialized capabilities in counterinsurgency operations, skills the Nigerian armed forces did not possess.

Another unique attribute of outsourcing security and military functions is the ability to distance international and domestic critique and to shift blame from the employer to the contractors. Using contractors instead of soldiers can divert the political implications of problematic incidents or controversial activities from the national discourse into the market framework. Namely, transforming an event of war crimes or human rights violations into corporate misconduct and bad performance. By shifting blame and responsibility to the contractors or the company, the employer can clear itself of blame. An example of that is the 2007 Nisour Square incident. A detail of Blackwater, a company offering VIP protection services in Iraq during the war, panicked and opened fire while running a mission at the center of the city of Baghdad. The incident ended with 37 casualties, all Iraqi bystanders (Glanz & Rubin, 2007). The incident was highly publicized and brought international critique and raised concerns on the US operation in Iraq. Yet, the political pressure shifted from the US government, which contracted Blackwater and initiated the war, into the company (Tiefer, 2009; Whitten, 2012). Turning into the subject of critique, Blackwater faced substantial damage to its brand and reputation, forcing the company to reconstruct itself under a different name (AP, 2009).

Another iteration of the same quality is the *plausible deniability*. States that prefer not to be associated with actions that are controversial or hold political risk, use contractors. Unlike the Blackwater case, where the government's association with the company has been clear, in instances of plausible deniability the employer claims that the actions of the contractors are not related to the employer; done not with their consent or knowledge. An example of that is the Russian reliance on the Wagner Group in Syria (Sukhankin, 2019). Explaining that mercenaryism is illegal according to Russian law, Russia denied any official connection with the contractors. This distancing came in handy during an explosive incident that took place in 2018. The incident, also known as the Battle of Khasham, included the ground assault of Syrian forces backed by Wagner operatives against a contingent of American soldiers and SDF fighters. The battle ended with a defeat and many casualties for the Syrian and Wagner forces (Rondeaux, 2019). Surprisingly, the incident did not deteriorate into a political scandal and was not interpreted as an act of aggression between Russia and the USA. The plausible deniability Russia developed around its contractors in the region allowed the Kremlin to save face and the USA to look aside. The plausible deniability dismantled a geopolitical bomb.

5 The Unintended Implications of Outsourcing Security and Military Functions

Outsourcing war and security functions generates an odd situation where the state shares part of its ultimate power, its ability to use coercive violence. Moreover, it shares it with corporate actors. Weber defined the state through its ability to use violence. He described the state as the entity with the legitimate monopoly of the means of violence within a territory (1978[1922]). By giving up that type of power the state effectively becomes less of a state, less of a sovereign. At the same time, the private actors gain significant authority that is regularly reserved for the state. For instance, security guards in state prisons or detention camps control every aspect of the lives of the prisoners. A company that is contracted to assist with counterterrorism surveillance may get access to private correspondence of civilians. Contractors that run checkpoints in a conflict area gain the capacity to detain individuals and even the right to use deadly force against others. Those faculties are categorically different than other types of authorities and capacities companies have.

With that level of power and influence, the issue of oversight surfaces. The state enjoys the legitimacy of using coercive violence since it is empowered by the people of the state. It acts on their behalf and for the collective good. As such, the state holds oversight mechanisms and checks and balances to ensure that it does not abuse this power. However, when the state outsources some of those functions to the private sector, the level of supervision and accountability diminishes. Swed and Crosbie (2017) discuss the lack of oversight we have about that market for force, stressing how little we know about it, its workforce, and its operations. Private actors are less transparent than government bodies. Furthermore, they fall outside of governmental oversight mechanisms. This gap is even worse in conflict areas where the law is often unclear, the rule of law is ineffective, and sovereignty is diminished. Swed and Materne (2022) explain how outsourcing in conflict areas leads to decreased oversight and an increase likelihood of fraud and misconduct. Companies are for-profit entities. They are not invested in or designed to cater for the public good. A company that profits from providing security functions in a conflict area may be invested in the continuation of the conditions that lead to insecurity.

Several studies and reports showcase problematic practices of private military and security companies, ranging from war profiteering to misconduct. Petersohn (2014) asserts that the participation of mercenaries and private military and security contractors in civil wars exacerbates the severity of hostilities in the conflict. Similarly, Lees and Petersohn (2023) show that the deployment of private military and security contractors in armed conflict increases its severity. Beyond severity, several studies point out the connection between human rights abuse and the deployment of contractors. Addressing the prevalence of contractors associated with human rights abuse, Radziszewski (2023) explores potential explanations for why some companies would be less likely to commit human rights abuse than others. In this study she suggests that the company's CEO's military background, or the lack of, are strong indicators for company associated human rights abuse. Rothe and Ross (2010) highlight the criminal dimension of contractors' work in conflict areas, looking at overcharging, lack of services, account irregularities, and illegal trading. Higate (2012) examines issues with labor rights, looking at hazing practices among contractors. Problems with labor rights within that industry were also mentioned by Li (2015). Li tackles the exploitation of third country nationals in the industry; workers with precarious legal status who are tasked with dangerous and challenging jobs.

The main fear of outsourcing the ability to use coercive violence and ancillary functions is in the creation of a threat from within to the state. A threat of a potentially armed and trained group with an oppositionary political agenda. Authoritative regimes and centralized regimes have demonstrated the greatest concerns for this possibility. In Russia, mercenaryism has been considered illegal. Article 279 in the Russian Criminal Code prohibits the "recruitment, training and financing" of mercenaries. Transgression is punished by incarceration for over 12 years (Krupskiy, 2023). This means that every paramilitary contingent in Russia is linked to a government approval and function. The government has to control all armed organizations. Therefore, any private military contracting has been associated with government officials. Groups like Wagner, Redut, Slavonic Corps, and others are in fact government proxies. Those concerns materialized in the 2023 Wagner rebellion (Bhangal, 2023). Due to political disagreements between the Wagner leadership and some political factions in the Kremlin, armed Wagner continents left their battle stations in Ukraine and invaded Russia. They took over some cities and eliminated any state attempt to stop their armed column on its way to Moscow (Marten, 2023). The rebellion ended with political agreements. Yet, in the aftermath, the Wagner leadership was assassinated, and the group was dismantled and absorbed into other security units. In China, the government legalized private security companies in 2009, while maintaining private military companies illegal (Markusen, 2022). Those companies that operate domestically are unarmed. At the same time, China allowed armed companies to offer services abroad, mostly in support of the country's economic and geopolitical interests (Yuan, 2022). The threat of marriage politics with the capability to use security measures is relevant also to democratic countries. Concerns about the influence and access of Erik Prince, a central figure in the industry, with the Trump administration, raised concerns regarding war profiteering (Cole, 2019). In the Czech Republic in 2010, a private security corporation, White Lion (ABL)/Mark2 Corporation, took over a minor political party. Bureš (2014) describes the episode and its associated scandals, one of them including spying on rival politicians and their families.

6 Conclusion

To summarize, within the context of security and war making, outsourcing is driven by different rationales. Outsourcing in that domain involves unique challenges and conditions that shape this practice. This chapter discusses the points of similarity and differences between traditional and security outsourcing. It also presents the trend of outsourcing within those subfields.

Outsourcing security has become an integral part of existing security architecture and apparatuses. What started as a problematic engagement grew over a period of 20 years into an international norm. Contractors and their services are today an essential part of many countries' security and military planning. Identifying this trend, scholars point out the embeddedness of private entities in state security and military operations and functions. Embeddedness to the degree that it makes it hard to distinguish one from the other (Leander, 2010). The market for force and its fluid and flexible nature has been described as security assemblages, referring to complex structures of skills, actors, expertise, technologies, and practices that fuse together the private and the state (Abrahamsen & Williams, 2009, 2011). Those new structures and relationships introduce new challenges and risks. States as well as the international community are still adjusting and learning the potential implications and solutions for this trend.

References

Abrahamsen, R., & Williams, M. C. (2009). Security beyond the state: Global security assemblages in international politics. *International Political Sociology, 3*(1), 1–17.

Abrahamsen, R., & Williams, M. C. (2011). Security privatization and global security assemblages. *The Brown Journal of World Affairs, 18*(1), 171–180.

Ajala, O. (2023). What caused the coup in Niger? An expert outlines three driving factors. *The Conversation*. July, 31. https://theconversation.com/what-caused-the-coup-in-niger-an-expert-outlines-three-driving-factors-210721

AP. (2009). Blackwater Changes Its Name to Xe. *New York Times*. February, 13. https://www.nytimes.com/2009/02/14/us/14blackwater.html

Arnold, G. (1999). Island destabilization: Comoros, Seychelles, Denard. In *Mercenaries: The scourge of the third world* (pp. 56–64). Palgrave Macmillan UK.

Avant, D. (2004). The privatization of security and change in the control of force. *International Studies Perspectives, 5*(2), 153–157.

Avant, D. (2005). *The market for force: The consequences of privatizing security*. Cambridge University Press.

Avant, D. (2013). The mobilization of private forces after 9/11: Ad hoc response to inadequate planning. *How, 9*(11), 209–231.

Bahli, B., & Rivard, S. (2005). Validating measures of information technology outsourcing risk factors. *Omega, 33*(2), 175–187.

Banjo, S. (2014). Inside Nike's Struggle to Balance Cost and Worker Safety in Bangladesh. *The Wall Street Journal*. April, 14. https://www.wsj.com/articles/inside-nikes-struggle-to-balance-cost-and-worker-safety-in-bangladesh-1398133855

Bhangal, S. (2023). The Wagner Rebellion and the Stability of the Russian State. *The Wilson Center*. September, 21. https://www.wilsoncenter.org/blog-post/wagner-rebellion-and-stability-russian-state

Bina, M. W. (2004). Private military contractor liability and accountability after Abu Ghraib. *Journal of Marshall Law Review, 38*, 1237.

Brayton, S. (2002). Outsourcing war: Mercenaries and the privatization of peacekeeping. *Journal of International Affairs*, 303–329.

Bureš, O. (2014). Private security companies in The Czech Republic: Rearticulating the security field and transforming politics. *Security Dialogue, 45*(1), 81–98.

Cahyaningtyas, F., & Ningtyas, M. N. (2020). The use of outsourced accounting service and its impact on SMEs performance. *JABE (Journal of Accounting and Business Education), 4*(2), 79–97.

Cameron, L. (2006). Private military companies: Their status under international humanitarian law and its impact on their regulation. *International Review of the Red Cross, 88*(863), 573–598.

Chapman, K. J. (2010). The untouchables: Private military contractors' criminal accountability under the UCMJ. *Vanderbilt Law Review, 63*, 1047.

Cheng, W. J., Riezman, R., & Wang, P. (2021). The dynamics of outsourcing: From labor cost-saving to preference-based outsourcing. *International Journal of Economic Theory, 17*(1), 57–73.

Chisholm, A. (2014). The silenced and indispensable: Gurkhas in private military security companies. *International Feminist Journal of Politics, 16*(1), 26–47.

Cole, M. (2019). The Complete Mercenary. *The Intercept*. May, 3. https://theintercept.com/2019/05/03/erik-prince-trump-uae-project-veritas/

Cybersecurity Advisory. (2022). Russian State-Sponsored Cyber Actors Target Cleared Defense Contractor Networks to Obtain Sensitive U.S. Defense Information and Technology. *Cybersecurity & Infrastructure Security Agency*. February, 16.

Davitti, D. (2019). The rise of private military and security companies in European Union migration policies: Implications under the UNGPs. *Business and Human Rights Journal, 4*(1), 33–53.

Del Prado, J. L. G. (2011). Impact on human rights of a new non-state actor: Private military and security companies. *The Brown Journal of World Affairs, 18*(1), 151–169.

Dube, A., & Kaplan, E. (2010). Does outsourcing reduce wages in the low-wage service occupations? Evidence from janitors and guards. *ILR Review, 63*(2), 287–306.

Dunigan, M. (2011). *Victory for hire: Private security companies' impact on military effectiveness*. Stanford University Press.

Ebbeck, G. (1998). Mercenaries and the'sandline affair'[this article examines the position of the mercenary soldier within the framework of the rules of international humanitarian law (IHL)]. *Australian Defence Force Journal, 133*, 5–23.

Eichler, M. (2014). Citizenship and the contracting out of military work: From national conscription to globalized recruitment. *Citizenship Studies, 18*(6–7), 600–614.

Everaert, P., Sarens, G., & Rommel, J. (2010). Using transaction cost economics to explain outsourcing of accounting. *Small Business Economics, 35*, 93–112.

Ghamat, S., Pun, H., & Yan, X. (2018). Optimal outsourcing strategies when capacity is limited. *Decision Sciences, 49*(5), 958–991.

Glanz, J., & Rubin, A. (2007). From Errand to Fatal Shot to Hail of Fire to 17 Deaths. *New York Times*. October, 3. https://www.nytimes.com/2007/10/03/world/middleeast/03firefight.html

Havkin, S. (2011). The reform of Israeli checkpoints: Outsourcing, commodification, and redeployment of the state. *Les Études du CERI, 174*, 1–39.

Higate, P. (2012). Drinking vodka from THE 'butt-crack' MEN, masculinities and fratriarchy in the private militarized security company. *International Feminist Journal of Politics, 14*(4), 450–469.

HRW. (2023). Niger: Rights at Risk Since Military Coup. *Human Rights Watch*. July, 27. https://www.hrw.org/news/2023/07/27/niger-rights-risk-military-coup

Isenberg, D. (2008). *Shadow force: Private security contractors in Iraq*. Bloomsbury Publishing USA.

Kinsey, C. (2009). *Private contractors and the reconstruction of Iraq: Transforming military logistics*. Routledge.

Kinsey, C., & Krieg, A. (2021). Assembling a force to defeat boko haram: How Nigeria integrated the market into its counterinsurgency strategy. *Defense & Security Analysis, 37*(2), 232–249.

Kinsey, C., & Patterson, M. H. (Eds.). (2012). *Contractors and war: The transformation of United States' expeditionary operations*. Stanford University Press.

Krahmann, E. (2008). Security: Collective good or commodity? *European Journal of International Relations, 14*(3), 379–404.

Krupskiy, M. (2023). Impunity over Wagner mutiny signals further degradation of rule of law in Russia. *The Conversation*. July, 17. https://theconversation.com/impunity-over-wagner-mutiny-signals-further-degradation-of-rule-of-law-in-russia-208703

Lacity, M. C., & Willcocks, L. P. (1995). IT outsourcing: Maximize flexibility and control. *Harvard Business Review, 73*(3), 84–93.

Lair, C. D. (2012). Outsourcing and the contracting of responsibility. *Sociological Inquiry, 82*(4), 557–577.

Leander, A. (2010). The paradoxical impunity of private military companies: Authority and the limits to legal accountability. *Security Dialogue, 41*(5), 467–490.

Lees, N., & Petersohn, U. (2023). To escalate, or not to escalate? Private military and security companies and conflict severity. *Studies in Conflict & Terrorism, 46*(12), 2622–2645.

Li, D. (2015). Offshoring the army: Migrant workers and the US military. *UCLA Law Review, 62*, 123.

Lu, L., Zhang, L., & Ou, J. (2021). In-house production and outsourcing under different discount schemes on the total outsourcing cost. *Annals of Operations Research, 298*, 361–374.

MacDonald, P. (2010). *Economics of military outsourcing* (Doctoral dissertation, University of York).

Machairas, D. (2014). The ethical implications of the use of private military force: Regulatable or irreconcilable? *Journal of Military Ethics, 13*(1), 49–69.

Magelssen, C., Sanchez, F., & Damanpour, F. (2015). Learning from outsourcing: The effects of outsourcing strategy on organizational efficiency. In Academy of management proceedings (2015, 1, p. 17468). : Academy of Management.

Mahoney, C. W., Tkach, B. K., & Rethmeyer, C. J. (2022). Defense contractors, private equity firms, and US national security. *Journal of Global Security Studies, 7*(4), ogac018.

Maogoto, J. N. (2006). Subcontracting sovereignty: Commodification of military force and fragmentation of state authority. *Brown Journal of World Affairs, 13*, 147.

Markusen, M. (2022). *A stealth industry: The quiet expansion of Chinese private security companies*. Center for Strategic and International Studies.

Marten, K. (2023). Whither Wagner? The consequences of Prigozhin's mutiny and demise. *Survival, 65*(5), 45–64.

Maskell, P., Pedersen, T., Petersen, B., & Dick-Nielsen, J. (2007). Learning paths to offshore outsourcing: From cost reduction to knowledge seeking. *Industry and Innovation, 14*(3), 239–257.

Minow, M. (2004). Outsourcing power: How privatizing military efforts challenges accountability, professionalism, democracy. *Boston College Law Review, 46*, 989.

Nieto, M. J., & Rodríguez, A. (2011). Offshoring of R&D: Looking abroad to improve innovation performance. *Journal of International Business Studies, 42*, 345–361.

Nsaibia, H. (2023). Fact sheet: Military Coup in Niger. *ACLED*. August, 3. https://acleddata.com/2023/08/03/fact-sheet-military-coup-in-niger/

Pattison, J. (2014). *The morality of private war: The challenge of private military and security companies*. Oxford University Press.

Petersohn, U. (2010). Sovereignty and privatizing the military: An institutional explanation. *Contemporary Security Policy, 31*(3), 531–552.

Petersohn, U. (2013). The effectiveness of contracted coalitions: Private security contractors in Iraq. *Armed Forces & Society, 39*(3), 467–488.

Petersohn, U. (2014). The impact of mercenaries and private military and security companies on civil war severity between 1946 and 2002. *International Interactions, 40*(2), 191–215.

Petersohn, U. (2017). Private military and security companies (PMSCs), military effectiveness, and conflict severity in weak states, 1990–2007. *Journal of Conflict Resolution, 61*(5), 1046–1072.

Picazo-Tadeo, A. J., & Reig-Martínez, E. (2006). Outsourcing and efficiency: The case of Spanish citrus farming. *Agricultural Economics, 35*(2), 213–222.

Radziszewski, E. (2023). Private military and security companies and human rights abuses: The impact of CEOs' military background. *Conflict Management and Peace Science, 07388942231155396*.

Ramirez, M. D., & Wood, R. M. (2019). Public attitudes toward private military companies: Insights from principal–agent theory. *Journal of Conflict Resolution, 63*(6), 1433–1459.

Research and Markets. (2022). Global Outsourcing Services Market—Forecasts from 2022 to 2027. *Research and Markets*. https://www.researchandmarkets.com/reports/5649238/global-outsourcing-services-market-forecasts

Ritzer, G., & Lair, C. (2007). Outsourcing: Globalization and beyond. In *The Blackwell companion to globalization* (pp. 307–329). Blackwell.

Rondeaux, C. (2019). *Decoding the Wagner group: Analyzing the role of private military security contractors in Russian proxy warfare*. New America.

Rothe, D. L., & Ross, J. I. (2010). Private military contractors, crime, and the terrain of unaccountability. *Justice Quarterly, 27*(4), 593–617.

Salzman, Z. (2007). Private military contractors and the taint of a mercenary reputation. *New York University Journal of International Law and Politics, 40*, 853.

Schaub, G., Jr. (2016). *Brothers in arms?: Identity, military professionals and armed contractors. Private military and security contractors: Controlling the corporate warrior*. Rowman and Littlefield.

Simons, D. (2004). Occupation for hire: Private military companies and their role in Iraq. *The RUSI Journal, 149*(3), 68–71.

Singer, P. W. (2007). *Can't win with'em, can't go to war without'em: Private military contractors and counterinsurgency*. Brookings Institution.

Singer, P. W. (2017). *Corporate warriors: The rise of the privatized military industry*. Cornell University Press.

Somjai, S. (2017). Advantages and disadvantages of outsourcing. *The Business and Management Review, 9*(1), 157–160.

Sukhankin, S. (2019). Russian pmcs in the Syrian civil war: from Slavonic Corps to Wagner Group and beyond. *Jamestown Foundation"[online], 18*.

Swed, O., & Burland, D. (2020). The global expansion of PMSCs: Trends, opportunities, and risks. *The Working Group on the use of mercenaries as a means of violating human rights and impeding the exercise of the rights of peoples to selfdetermination*.

Swed, O., & Burland, D. (2022). Contractors in Iraq: Exploited class or exclusive Club? *Armed Forces & Society, 48*(1), 3–24.

Swed, O., & Crosbie, T. (2017). Private security and military contractors: A troubling oversight. *Sociology Compass, 11*(11), e12512.

Swed, O., & Materne, A. (2022). No accounting for bad contracting: Private military and security contracts and ineffective regulation in conflict areas. *Studies in Comparative International Development*, 1–27.

Tanriverdi, H., Konana, P., & Ge, L. (2007). The choice of sourcing mechanisms for business processes. *Information Systems Research, 18*(3), 280–299.

Taulbee, J. L., & Head, D. A. (1993). Mercenary commando coup operations: Theory versus practice. *The Journal of Strategic Studies, 16*(1), 109–121.

Taussig-Rubbo, M. (2009). Outsourcing sacrifice: The labor of private military contractors. *Yale Journal of Law and Humanities, 21*, 101.

Tiefer, C. (2009). No more Nisour squares: Legal control of private security contractors in Iraq and after. *Oregan Law Review, 88*, 745.

Viswanathan, M., Mukherji, P., Narasimhan, O., & Chandy, R. (2021). The performance impact of core-component outsourcing: Insights from the LCD TV industry. *Journal of Marketing Research, 58*(4), 801–826.

Whitten, J. H. (2012). They're getting away with murder: How the international criminal court can prosecute US private security contractors for the Nisour Square tragedy and why it should. *Washington University Global Studies Law Review, 11*, 503.

Wither, J. K. (2020). Outsourcing warfare: Proxy forces in contemporary armed conflicts. *Security and Defence Quarterly, 31*(4), 17–34.

Yuan, J. (2022). China's private security companies and the protection of Chinese economic interests abroad. *Small Wars & Insurgencies, 33*(1–2), 173–195.

Zhu, W., Ng, S. C., Wang, Z., & Zhao, X. (2017). The role of outsourcing management process in improving the effectiveness of logistics outsourcing. *International Journal of Production Economics, 188*, 29–40.

The Role of Management Accounting in Outsourcing Projects: An Illustrative Case Study

Mirghani N. Ahmed

1 Introduction

Over the past three decades, there has been growing interest in the opportunities presented by interorganizational networks and strategic alliances (Lamming, 1993; Ring & Van de Ven, 1994; Harland, 1996; Berry et al., 2000; Das & Teng, 2001; Meira et al., 2010). Organizations increasingly recognize that these collaborative relationships can offer significant benefits, including enhanced productivity and reduced overhead costs (Coad & Cullen, 2006; Smith et al., 2005), access to suppliers' expertise (Aman et al., 2012), improved knowledge and innovation (Ambos et al., 2021), better product quality (Langfield-Smith & Smith, 2003), risk sharing (Das & Teng, 2001), and strengthened market position and competitiveness (Ding et al., 2010; Munjal et al., 2019).

While these relationships offer economic organizations alternative forms of organizing activities, they also introduce various risks and challenges, such as potential opportunistic behavior from partners, loss of control, lack of partner compatibility, inadequate governance, and the complexity of managing ongoing relationship between the client and the vendor (Dekker et al., 2018; Langfield-Smith, 2008; Langfield-Smith & Smith, 2003; Van der Meer-Kooistra & Vosselman, 2000; Williamson, 1985). The adverse consequences of interorganizational relationships have also been widely discussed in economics and management literature. Various theoretical frameworks and perspectives have been proposed to address these issues, including motivation and incentive contracting models in agency theory (Jensen & Meckling, 1976), institutional forms for transaction governance, and

M. N. Ahmed (✉)
Department of Accounting and Finance, KFUPM Business School, King Fahd University of Petroleum and Minerals, Dhahran, Saudi Arabia
e-mail: mnahmed@kfupm.edu.sa

F. P. García Márquez et al. (eds.), *Outsourcing*, International Series in Operations Research & Management Science 370, https://doi.org/10.1007/978-3-031-95393-4_9

trust-based models derived from neo-institutional economics and organizational theory (Williamson, 1985).

Among strategic relationships, outsourcing stands out for its significant growth in size and popularity, drawing considerable interest in industrial and business practices (Berry et al., 2000; Das & Teng, 2001; Dekker, 2008; Langfield-Smith & Smith, 2003; Smith et al., 2005). Since the early 1990s, it has become common practice across various organizations, spanning the public and private sectors, service, and manufacturing industries. Its application has expanded beyond manufacturing and core business activities (Aman et al., 2012), now encompassing traditional in-house administrative and management functions as well (Rodríguez & Nieto, 2015).

Outsourcing involves the transfer or delegation of an organization's internal business processes, production factors, and related decision-making to an external supplier or service provider (Drinta, 1994). This arrangement enables the organization to receive services that fulfill specific business functions and integrate seamlessly into its overall operations. Generally, organizations choose to outsource functions that are not central to their core activities, including accounting, payroll, logistics, cleaning, catering, training, maintenance, and information technology (Chalos, 1995; Datar & Rajan, 2017). The primary goal of outsourcing is to enable organizations to concentrate their resources on key areas or functions of value-added capability, or core competencies, thus enhancing organizational flexibility (Datar & Rajan, 2017; Smith et al., 2005). However, there is a growing trend where companies are considering outsourcing for some of their core processes or functions, such as design and manufacturing. In such cases, outsourcing becomes strategic, serving as a tool that contributes to the long-term success of the enterprise. It is also important to differentiate between offshoring and offshore outsourcing. Offshoring refers to the relocation of work from a firm's home country to a subsidiary located in another country (Langfield-Smith & Smith, 2003). In contrast, offshore outsourcing involves contracting activities or services to third-party vendors situated in countries different from the client firm's home country.

While the topic has a focal interest across many academic disciplines, e.g., industrial dynamics, institutional economics, information technology, operations management, marketing, purchasing, and logistics (Meira et al., 2010), it has also attracted the attention of management accounting researchers and practitioners (Seal et al., 1999; Langfield-Smith & Smith, 2003; Smith et al., 2005; Brandau & Hoffjan, 2010; Dekker et al., 2018). Managing outsourcing like any other interorganizational relations, means managing and coordinating across traditional functional areas within the firm and managing interaction and interdependence external to the firm with both suppliers and customers (Berry et al., 2000; Dekker, 2016; Partridge & Perren, 1994). Outsourcing involves several characteristics that often necessitate information and decision support from management accounting (Brandau & Hoffjan, 2010; Seal et al., 1999). Management accounting typically addresses challenges such as managing complex information flows, supporting resource allocation, handling high levels of risk and uncertainty in decision-making, evaluating network performance, and addressing cost management issues (Dekker, 2016; Dent, 1996).

Several studies have explored the use of management accounting techniques and the roles of management accountants in different outsourcing contexts (Berry et al., 2000; Langfield-Smith & Smith, 2003; Smith et al., 2005; Nicholson et al., 2006; Brandau & Hoffjan, 2010; Dekker et al., 2018; Nielsen et al., 2015). While the findings of some of these studies clearly indicate an increasing use of management accounting and growing roles for management accountants in managing outsourcing arrangements, other studies present evidence demonstrating a lesser involvement for management accounting or management accountants working in the shadows of other experts such as supply chain managers (Brandau & Hoffjan, 2010). This chapter aims to offer further insights into the role of management accounting in strategic outsourcing decisions and management control processes, through a case study of a leading Saudi manufacturing company. The study adds to the literature that calls for investigating the contribution of the ideas and initiatives from management accounting and management accountants in the management of interorganizational relationships.

The chapter unfolds in the following manner: Sect. 2 offers a literature review that explores how management accounting influences and contributes to outsourcing decisions, examining both theoretical perspectives and practical applications. Section 3 describes the research methodology and design employed for data collection. Following this, Sect. 4 explores detailed observations and findings on how management accounting influences strategic decisions and control in the context of the three outsourcing agreements. Finally, the study concludes with a summary and suggestions for future research.

2 Literature Review

The formation of interorganizational and collaborative relationships, such as outsourcing, has presented novel challenges for management accounting and management control practices (Harland, 1996; Seal et al., 1999; Berry et al., 2000; Mouritsen et al., 2001; Dekker, 2004, 2016; Langfield-Smith & Smith, 2003; Cooper & Slagmulder, 2004; Smith et al., 2005; Meira et al., 2010). Designing management accounting systems to function effectively within an interorganizational context has not traditionally been a focal point in management accounting, primarily due to its historical inward focus (Partridge & Perren, 1994). Traditional management accounting systems and techniques have typically been tailored for internal use, neglecting considerations beyond the firm's conventional and legal boundaries. This inward focus overlooks the interconnectedness and value generated outside the firm's legal confines, thereby rendering management accounting systems and techniques ill-suited for addressing the informational needs associated with managing outsourcing functions, conducting cost analyses of the value chain, or evaluating suppliers' performance (Berry et al., 2000; Partridge & Perren, 1994). Additionally, interorganizational transactional relationships necessitate the coordination of resources and activities between cooperating parties. Unlike hierarchical organizational relationships, this coordination is not centrally organized. Instead, the parties involved must independently develop and maintain the control mechanisms required to coordinate and manage these relationships (Van der Meer-Kooistra & Vosseiman, 2006).

Traditional management accounting practices primarily focus on providing internal financial information to assist management in planning, decision-making, and control (Horngren, 1962). These practices typically involve preparing product costing reports, financial statements, budgets, and variance analyses. The main emphasis is on historical data, resulting in a rigid approach that concentrates on cost reduction and cost control. In contrast, strategic management accounting broadens this focus by incorporating nonfinancial information and a forward-looking perspective (Shank & Govindararajan, 1992). This approach analyzes both internal and external factors that affect the company's performance, such as market trends, competitor analysis, and customer preferences. By aligning financial strategies with broader organizational goals, strategic management accounting emphasizes long-term planning and value creation, moving beyond the traditional emphasis on cost reduction and cost control (Datar & Rajan, 2017; Dent, 1996; Dixon, 1998).

Even with this forward-looking perspective, several accounting researchers have acknowledged the complexities that interorganizational relationships pose for management accounting and have called for the development of the necessary skills and techniques to cope with the complex planning and monitoring information systems inherent in these evolving organizational structures (Berry et al., 2000; Bromwich & Bhimani, 1994). For instance, Bromwich and Bhimani (1994) advocate for the utilization of purchaser/supplier partnerships, suggesting that as producers, suppliers, and assemblers become increasingly integrated, accountants can introduce modified controls and management accounting techniques suitable for these alternative organizational forms. By drawing on transaction and incomplete contacts and citing Japanese business practice, Gietzman (1996) argues that interorganizational and cooperative strategies require a reexamination of accounting governance systems which were designed for hierarchical mode of governance combined with make or buy decisions which assume arms-length transactions. In a similar vein, Seal et al. (1999) identify three crucial roles for management accounting in interorganizational relationships: (1) aiding in the make-or-buy decision that can initiate a partnership; (2) contributing to the management of established partnerships; and (3) facilitating performance measurement, such as quantifying the benefits derived by each party from engaging in such contractual arrangements. Similarly, Lamminmaki (2008) highlights several strategic implications of outsourcing for management accounting. Firstly, the importance of cost relativity in outsourcing decisions emphasizes the significant role management accounting can play in determining whether to outsource. Secondly, outsourcing decisions carry long-term implications and present analytical challenges akin to those encountered in capital budgeting, a key area in management accounting. Thirdly, the development of management control systems for subcontracting imposes additional demands on management accounting and its broadening influence in terms of financial as well as nonfinancial accountability.

Empirical findings and observations from research studies investigating interorganizational practices, including outsourcing arrangements, suggest that new applications of accounting techniques and expanded roles for management accountants are emerging. For instance, Berry et al. (2000) conducted a study of interfirm supply chain and outsourcing cases within UK-based manufacturing companies, revealing various uses of management accounting. These included evaluating projects on the make-or-buy decisions for components, leading to increased outsourcing and parts redesign, as well as analyzing the total cost of ownership, benchmarking suppliers' performance, and developing cost of quality projects. Notably, the adoption of supply chain and outsourcing programs by one case company led to the establishment of a cost management group comprising a project accountant, a project engineer, and an R&D and project designer. Furthermore, Berry et al. (2000) identified a construction company that focused entirely on creating partnerships and utilized a version of the balanced scorecard to measure performance in outsourcing partnership situations. Similarly, Cooper and Slagmulder (2004) investigated outsourcing decisions within Japanese manufacturing firms and identified three interorganizational cost management techniques: functionality (balancing price and quality), interorganizational cost investigations, and concurrent cost management. These techniques are designed to address information asymmetry and improve effective cooperation and coordination. In another study focusing on outsourcing practices across various types of UK organizations—private sector companies, the National Health Service, and Local Authorities, Smith et al. (2005) concluded that organizational changes resulting from outsourcing have prompted specific alterations in management accounting systems. For instance, in a UK NHS Trust Hospital, the study uncovered the use of key performance indicators (KPIs) tailored to measure contractors' performance in areas such as cleanliness standards, response time to ad hoc requests, adherence to legislation during domestic services, and compliance with hospital policies and procedures. Nielsen et al. (2015) found in their study of outsourcing arrangements at two European companies that management accounting information and techniques play a crucial strategic role in complex and strategic decision-making, particularly in the analysis of risks and uncertainty.

Other studies have observed a broad range of management control mechanisms and practices used in managing outsourcing relationships, including market-based, bureaucratic, and trust-based patterns of control (Dekker, 2004; Langfield-Smith & Smith, 2003; Nielsen et al., 2015; Van der Meer-Kooistra & Vosselman, 2000). For example, Langfield-Smith and Smith (2003) studied the outsourcing of IT operations in an Australian electricity company and found that outcome controls (e.g., contractual rules, setting performance targets, designing a risk-reward scheme) and social controls (communication, negotiations, and conflict resolution mechanisms) along with the development of trust, played significant roles in managing the relationship. Nicholson et al.'s (2006) study of the offshore outsourcing of accounting and finance services by British and Indian vendors and client companies revealed various control mechanisms employed to minimize transaction costs at different stages and phases of the outsourcing projects. At the contact level, the study, for example, observed an emphasis on minimizing client-based search costs by obtaining references for potential vendors and scrutinizing their international accreditation standards and certifications. Additionally, companies instituted service level agreements (SLAs) with provisions for rewards and penalties for achieving target performance, contractual clauses for dispute resolution through legal and arbitration bodies, and implemented data protection clauses at the contract level. During the control stage, specific codes of conduct for offshore outsourcing were established, ensuring adequate levels of data protection and setting boundaries on the "venue" of the data. Employees were required to sign nondisclosure and confidentiality agreements, and vendors and clients agreeing on a lease-and-sale-back option to be included in the outsourcing contracts. Similar findings were reported by Söderberg et al. (2017), who studied how firms' relative capabilities impact their decisions on maintenance outsourcing governance. Based on a multiple case analysis involving four global Swedish buying firms and four service suppliers, the study revealed that the governance and control strategies adopted by buying are significantly affected by the suppliers' relative capability positions. These positions are determined by a blend of technical capabilities (such as skilled personnel, process knowledge, advanced technology, and an innovative and entrepreneurial approach) and organizational capabilities (such as process maturity). This combination sets the prerequisites for the various governance options available.

Amidst the extensive body of literature highlighting the increasing use of management accounting techniques and information in driving strategic planning, decision-making, and control within outsourcing frameworks (see Meira et al., 2010), a counter-narrative has emerged, questioning the efficacy of management accounting in facilitating the outsourcing process. One such critical perspective is illustrated by Brandau and Hoffjan (2010), who conducted a comprehensive multiple case study encompassing 14 German multinational corporations engaged in offshoring and outsourcing arrangements. Contrary to prevailing expectations, their study revealed a notably diminished involvement of management accounting in these activities. Their study revealed that in two-thirds of the responding companies, no management accountant was responsible for coordinating and monitoring offshoring activities, and there was often no perceived need for management accounting. Additionally, in some companies, the management accounting function was partially handled by the functional areas responsible for offshoring services, leading to an unclear distinction between management and management accounting. Brandau and Hoffjan (2010) attribute this phenomenon to a confluence of factors, including the presence of contractual arrangements that partially substitute for management accounting interventions, reliance on external consultants, limited collaboration between management accounting and general management, and challenges within accounting departments stemming from competency issues such as background and training. Consequently, Brandau and Hoffjan (2010) concluded that management accounting failed to furnish the needed support for strategic planning and coordination within the outsourcing arrangements scrutinized in their study.

Brandau and Hoffjan (2010) observations and conclusions align with findings from previous strategic management studies. For instance, Dixon (1998) asserts that the collection, analysis, and use of data for strategic purposes can be accomplished without necessitating the formal adoption of a strategic management accounting process. Likewise, Lord's (1996) empirical investigation indicates that components of strategic management accounting although are present in corporate practices, the pertinent information is not consistently quantified within accounting paradigms nor systematically gathered and analyzed by management accountants. Finally, Håkansson and Lind (2004) study found that managers involved in interorganizational relationships do not receive formalized accounting information about either the relationship itself or the partner company.

Against this backdrop, this chapter aims to explore the extent of management accounting's role in guiding strategic interorganizational decisions and exercising management control. The focus is on three outsourcing agreements within the supply function of a prominent Saudi manufacturing company. The next section of this chapter provides an overview of the case company and describes the research method employed for data collection.

3 Research Method and Data Collection

The company selected for this study is a manufacturer of mechanized systems. To maintain confidentiality, it will be referred to as Agro Engineering Limited. Agro enhances its product range by manufacturing gear drives, electrical switchboards, control panels, transfer switches, and control equipment. The company operates a "job shop" manufacturing process, supported by a mill that creates specialized components for constructing the frames and structures of its mechanized systems. To address Saudi Arabia's challenging weather conditions, Agro has established auxiliary plants to treat and reinforce these systems, protecting them against corrosion and potential malfunctions. Currently the company is having three major outsourcing agreements in its supply chain function: Third-Party Logistics, Offshore Purchasing, and Third-Party Manufacturing.

The research study utilizes a combination of semi-structured interviews, archival records and documentation to collect and analyze data. The interviews were conducted with the Supply Chain Director (SCD), Finance Director, a Senior Management Accountant, Vice President for Operations, Strategic Business Analyst, a logistic expert and a one staff from the Sourcing Office (See Table 1 for more details of the interviews' locations, duration, focus, and issues). Some of the questions used in the interviews were open ended and the opportunity was given to the interviewees to talk about their own involvement and personal experiences with the outsourcing projects' initiatives. The Supply Chain Director (SCD) was the focal point for interviews and a number of his subordinates assisted the author in gaining access to a number of critical documents including the projects' memoranda of understanding, Service Level Agreements (SLAs), outsourcing contract structures, Board presentations, key performance indicators (KPI's), cost reduction plans, supplier quotations, number of reports containing outsourcing programs' results.

Table 1 Interviews' focus and issues

	Location	# of meetings	Interview duration	Interviews' focus and issues
Supply chain director	Global sourcing unit (GSU)	3	3 h	• Third-party logistics, warehousing, global sourcing • Request for proposal (RFP) and (SLA) development and importance, savings calculations and the role of finance in outsourcing across the three supply chain outsourcing initiatives • Intervention by the finance director and management control
Finance director	Finance department	2	2.5 h	• Third-party logistics business case and tracking against SLA • Offshore representative office and its value proposition • Third-party manufacturing and the role of finance in strategic decision-making • Involvement of accounting and finance staff in planning and managing outsourcing projects • Decision-making process and the role of finance office in outsourcing arrangements
Vice president for operations	Corporate office	1	1 h	• The role of HR and sales and marketing in assessing the reasonableness of outsourcing initiatives and estimating savings based on projected activity • The reasons behind the focus on supply chain as a source of value
Strategic business analyst	Global sourcing unit (GSU)	1	1.5 h	• The strategic insights of the role of finance and management accountant's problem-solving tasks • The significance of China as a source of value and future market
A senior management accountant			2 h	• Financial and cost analysis for outsourcing projects and proposals • Inventory management • Monitoring the vendor's performance • Tasks related to risk analysis • Involvement in multifunctional teams
Logistics expert	Global sourcing unit (GSU)	1	1.5 h	• The importance of functional expertise • The limitations of relying on finance for financial information

The researcher also benefited from discussions, project and case presentations on outsourcing practices at Agro made by one of the company's senior staff who at the time was the company Finance Director and an MBA student in the author's university. Subsequently he became a contact person and valuable information source. Agro's website proved to be a useful source of secondary information related to the outsourcing projects such as the company's strategies and plans for improving productivity, product and service quality, cost reduction and performance via global outsourcing and supply chain arrangement initiatives. Finally, in order to validate the quality and accuracy of some of the data earlier collected, two additional field visits to the company premises were made by the researcher and discussions were held with the Supply Chain, the Finance Director and a senior management accountant. One advantage of using a case study research method is that it provides the possibility of an in-depth investigation and analysis of the subject matter of research under consideration (Scapens, 1990). In particular, it enables researchers to examine a contemporary phenomenon within its real-life context, especially when the boundaries between the phenomenon and context are not distinctly defined, using multiple sources of evidence (Yin, 2009).

4 Case Study: Results and Interpretations

4.1 Third-Party Logistics

Managing inventory in terms of logistics and warehousing were significant challenges faced Agro during the last two decades. According to the Vice President for Operations Agro's plants are highly interdependent and the company's inventory needs to be coordinated and efficiently retrieved across multiple plants which require extensive investment in logistical and warehouse management capability. Importantly, as the company continued to increase its regional and global presence by opening plants and warehouses in the United States, Europe, China, and a number of Arab countries, it needed also to optimize its supply chain for raw materials, subassemblies and finished goods at a competitive cost. According to the Global Supply Chain Director (SCD) these factors encouraged the company's executive team to establish a long-term strategic relationship with a third-party logistics partner that can provide an outsourced high-quality solution to meet logistics and warehousing requirements. Agro's prime objective behind outsourcing its logistics function was to balance the company's inventory in an optimized fashion without causing delays in shipments to local and international customers. The Global Supply Chain Director (SCD) described the initiative as:

> A rationalization of the supply chain process that in essence is being able to have the right products (balanced inventory) in the right quantities (optimized inventory), at the right place, at the right moment and at the minimal landed cost (lowest cost of ownership) to maximize company profitability and service quality.

Before engaging potential vendors through a Request for Proposal (RFP), the Supply Chain Director (SCD) justified the need for a third-party logistics and warehousing solution to the Board of Directors by demonstrating that "*current corporate spending is fragmented and not fully leveraged.*" His presentation to the board included a review of a number of cases involving duplicate shipments that could have been consolidated had there been a global information system and operating platform. Also, the SCD confirmed that the spending on supply chain did not give Agro enough leverage with international carriers, freight forwarders and providers of marine insurance. During the interview, the Vice President of Operations made the following remarks on this issue:

> Huge resources are spread across various supply chain activities such as warehousing, shipping, inventory and freight insurance without a comprehensive plan [....] they are not efficiently and effectively deployed to generate the maximum value for Agro. If the current situation continues without a change in strategy certainly the underutilized resources will lead to inefficiencies in our supply chain operations

The role of Agro's logistics expert was both essential and complementary, particularly in analyzing potential suppliers' capabilities. The discussion with the logistics expert gave us a detailed overview of the tasks assigned to him and his team. These tasks included researching suppliers' warehouse storage and transportation methods, examining their inventory control systems, scheduling product deliveries, and reviewing logistics policies and procedures. However, not all tasks could be completed as planned. Some suppliers were reluctant to be transparent, primarily due to market competition and confidentiality concerns.

Although, the contribution of management accounting was limited during the planning and justification phases of the project, it responded to several inquiries in connection with the initiative which included requests for detailed inventory records by location, the costs of outbound and inbound freight over the last several months and the credit terms offered by existing carriers. This information helped the SCD in building the case for the third-party logistics and paved the way for the management accountant to participate in the development of the RFP. Additionally, the role of management accounting was feasible in monitoring the vendor's performance. While the overall structure and tone of the RFP was set by Supply Chain, Agro's management accountants actively participated in setting the key performance indicators (KPI's) relating to the financial aspects of the vendor's scope of work. A number of financial requirements were stipulated in the RFP such as the provision of a monthly and quarterly management report in multiple currencies and the tracking of cost reduction programs relating to duty, network design and inventory holding optimization.

The supplier selection process involved detailed analyses of vendors' profiles in terms of business, quality assurance and compliance which were mainly conducted by the Supply Chain Office. Intuitively, high-quality suppliers with proven track records in generating savings for transnational organizations quoted relatively higher rates that decline in a stepped fashion based on usage. Management accountants performed cost analyses through comparative evaluation of the costs of routes and warehousing. In conjunction with quoted suppliers' rates, historical shipping and storage patterns were used to determine the overall expected cost of going into business with the shortlisted vendors. The comparison of the costs of routes easily ranked suppliers in terms of direct shipping costs, but the costs of warehousing needed to be broken down into storage, handling, stuffing and lifting. Some suppliers quoted an all-inclusive rate while others used different rates for each of the warehousing services. Based on feedback from Supply Chain, management accountants determined the frequency of use and importance of each of the warehousing services based on the expected product mix and shipping patterns which culminated in a second layer of rankings among potential vendors based on overall warehousing costs.

The Supply Chain built the cost analysis performed by the management accountant into a scorecard comparing the competing vendors across four thrusts which are corporate capabilities, inbound services, in house services and distribution. The corporate capabilities thrust measures the competing vendors' operating platforms, reporting systems and aggressiveness in offering discounts to high volume customers. The vendors' scores on the latter criterion were mainly determined by the objective evaluation of management accountants. The inbound services thrust relates to the competing vendors' capabilities in customs brokering and in leveraging international carriers and freight forwarders. Although financial in nature, the savings that may be generated from the efficiencies achieved in customs clearance by the competing vendors were estimated by the Supply Chain team. This is mainly on account of Supply Chain's in-depth knowledge of customs duty regulations across the jurisdictions in which the competing vendors operate. The in-house services thrust mainly represents management accounting's ranking of potential vendors based on warehousing costs. There were nonfinancial indicators attached to this thrust which included the vendors' potential in implementing integrated Vendor Managed Inventory (VMI) programs with back end support. The distribution thrust ranked the competing vendors based on the cost analysis of routes performed by management accountants. Lastly, the Supply Chain team added a nonfinancial indicator to the distribution thrust by comparatively assessing the vendor's network design in terms of sophistication and compatibility with business objectives.

An internationally recognized vendor was finally selected based on the four scorecard thrusts described above. This was followed by the development and implementation of a project rollout plan and the Service Level Agreement (SLA). The management accounting role was to track the direct and indirect costs of the outsourcing arrangement and assists the Supply Chain team in ascertaining the vendor's performance against the SLA. Prior year logistics costs such as freight, customs duty and warehousing are used as a baseline for determining the savings generated by the outsourcing arrangement. There were instances where costs were flexed to account for changes in shipping and storage levels from year to year.

4.2 Offshore Representative Office

Agro Engineering strategically established a Representative Office (RO) in China to streamline and strengthen the company's procurement operations. The decision to operate the purchasing function from China was a strategic move, influenced by the active engagement of Agro's competitors in the region and the concentration of qualified suppliers within China's borders. This led to the relocation of the company's purchasing and supply chain personnel from its headquarters in Riyadh, Saudi Arabia, to a permanent base in China. The Supply Chain Director (SCD) team took the lead in conceptualizing and executing this offshoring initiative. Employing a systematic approach, the SCD implemented a three-step strategy to establish the RO and transition the purchasing function into an offshore outsourcing operation.

Initially, a business case was developed to justify the need for unifying the supplier selection process across operating entities. The purchasing history for the past several years was examined to identify duplicate purchasing efforts by Agro's operating units. This led to the calculation of the buying savings that could have been generated had a Global Supply Unit (GSU) been in operation at various points in time. While the mining for data was mainly performed by Supply Chain Office, management accountants did most of the needed analysis and verification. Additionally, the potential for savings based on quantity discounts and optimal supplier selection was assessed by Supply Chain and factored into the calculations performed by management accountants. With the help of the Sales & Marketing Function, management accountants projected the buying savings per major subassembly based on a five-year strategic sales forecast.

The second phase involved matching the projected buying savings against the anticipated cash outflows associated with establishing the Global Sourcing Unit (GSU). The costs of setting up the RO in China were detailed by Supply Chain and validated by management accountants. The latter included checking the estimated asset values, salaries, benefits, and rent expenses through independent sources such as recruitment agencies and real estate brokers. The management accountants also worked with the Human Resources Function (HR) on checking the sensibility of the administrative structure proposed by Supply Chain Office. New positions were introduced into the supply chain organization, representing incremental fixed costs which had to be absorbed by the projected buying savings, such as the Supplier Development Quality Engineer, Logistics Expert and Strategic Business Analyst. Lastly, management accountants asked Supply Chain Office to extend the baseline forecasts of the RO's costs into the next 5 years taking into consideration the latest estimates of the magnitude and timing of the eventual appreciation of the Chinese currency (Renminbi) against Agro's functional currency (Saudi Riyals) and the US dollar.

Thirdly, the actual buying savings and expenses incurred by the RO were closely monitored and reported upon on a monthly basis. The Supply Chain assumed responsibility for calculating the buying savings, employing a methodology that entailed a comparative analysis of material costs per assembly between the current period and the prior year. The variances in material costs per assembly were then multiplied by the number of assemblies shipped to customers during the current period to ascertain the direct impact of the savings generated on the bottom line. Management accountants kept track of the RO's accumulated direct expenses and compared them against the accumulated buying savings and budget. After the passage of 1 year from the setup of the RO office, the SCD notified Agro's President and Finance Director (FD) that "even with the very limited shipments during the year, the RO has been able to breakeven based on the savings generated on the shipments achieved (i.e., the variances calculated against the prior year costs) versus the RO's direct expenses." Before congratulating the SCD on his achievement, the President asked the FD to check the validity of the buying savings calculations and identify their limitations. Having gone through the detail, the FD realized that the Supply Chain's claimed buying savings cannot be fully attributed to the RO in view of the recent decline in commodity price, but the fact remains that year on year comparisons are the most logical approach to calculating buying savings. The FD added that as long as the point of reference is systematically shifted from one period to the next, then Supply Chain will be forced to raise the bar ahead of every reporting period. There was also agreement within the Executive team on the RO's prime objectives which are to maintain a sourcing cost below that of the competition, leverage supplier relations, improve capabilities in purchasing, and mobilize the GSU to swiftly take advantage of opportunities in the commodities markets. Hence, the FD's comments put the use of the purchase price variance calculation into perspective and demonstrated that judging functional excellence and returns on investment involves more than just examining variances and determining their causes.

On a more technical front, management accountants adjusted Supply Chain's calculation of the purchase price variance to take account of the total purchases made during the period as opposed to only basing the calculation on the number of assemblies shipped to customers. This made Supply Chain Function realize that it is not necessary to link sales volume to the amount of savings reported because as long as purchasing activity is controlled by a purchasing budget then favorable and adverse purchase price variances should be reported in their totality and used to assess the overall effectiveness of sourcing in isolation from other functions. This conclusion is corroborated by the fact that management accountants at Agro dispose of purchase price variances in the cost of sales at the time of purchase as opposed to the time of sale.

4.3 Third-Party Manufacturing

Through its Offshore Representative Office in China, Agro built strong relationships with several reputable Chinese manufacturers. The Supply Chain Office approached one of Agro's strategic suppliers to discuss the potential for a Strategic Quality-Cost-Delivery Agreement (SQCDA). The goal was to have Chinese-sourced raw components assembled and partially processed before arriving at Agro's main manufacturing facilities in Riyadh. This approach aimed to reduce labor and transportation costs while speeding up the order-to-delivery cycle. The Supply Chain office collaborated with the management accounting function to develop a business case for this initiative. The management accounting team provided cost comparisons between the current and proposed states, focusing solely on "relevant costs," while the Supply Chain office included both financial and nonfinancial justifications, such as the permanent reduction in working capital, better resource allocation higher up the value chain, and improved access to talent.

An SQCDA was eventually finalized between Agro and its Chinese supplier, QCD. The agreement encompasses the development of tooling for component production, including sample creation and mass production. Tooling development and production are critical to the success of the manufacturing process. Under the agreement, Agro has the option to either consign tooling to QCD or allow QCD to manufacture tooling based on Agro's specifications. The SCO determined which option to pursue for each tooling item through a technical and sourcing study, supported by a costing analysis conducted by the management accountant function. The agreement safeguards Agro's drawings, technology, and intellectual property through detailed confidentiality and noncompetition clauses. Agro retains sole ownership of the tooling, and QCD is prohibited from using it for any purpose other than conducting business with Agro. A complication arose concerning the option of having QCD manufacture tooling on Agro's behalf, as the agreement initially stipulated that ownership would depend on reimbursing QCD for its direct manufacturing costs. The Finance Director challenged this, contending that "the tooling should be the property of Agroo regardless of when payment is made since Agro is the party possessing the know-how." The agreement was revised to incorporate a clause that guarantees Agro's ownership of the tooling, regardless of any future commercial disagreements or trade disputes.

The agreement contains a comprehensive list of the prices at which QCD will sell each assembly, subassembly, and sample to Agro. Additionally, the agreement specifies that the prices and production costs at QCD are to be reviewed quarterly or whenever there is a significant fluctuation in commodity prices. The management accountant supported the Supply Chain Office in establishing the thresholds for significant changes in major commodity prices that would impact Agro's overall product costs. This process involved analyzing Agro's historical cost structure and assessing the maximum and minimum cost levels of key materials as a proportion of total product costs.

To ensure the ongoing financial benefits from third-party manufacturing with QCD, Agro incorporated a rigorous cost reduction program into the agreement. Under this program, QCD is required to continuously explore and assess new technical improvements, materials, and design alternatives. QCD is incentivized with a 30% gain-sharing ratio from the cost savings achieved, which will be reviewed and validated by the management accountant. The Finance Director requested the Supply Chain Office to evaluate the reasonableness of this incentive and its prevalence in the industry. Based on their experience, the Supply Chain Director endorsed the incentive scheme and agreed to have Agro's manufacturing team visit QCD's production sites quarterly. These visits will involve conducting value analyses, reviewing production costs with the management accountant, qualifying QCD's suppliers, and ensuring the effective implementation of agreed-upon cost reduction programs and initiatives. The Supply Chain Director also stipulated that any findings from Agro's value analyses and QCD's cost reduction initiatives should be implemented once the relevant inventory items are depleted. Consequently, the management accountant is responsible for closely monitoring inventory records and confirming the start date of any cost reduction efforts.

Working capital is yet another area that was of great concern to the Finance Director and management accountant. The agreement is meant to decrease Agro's permanent working capital through extended credit terms with QCD and the consignment of a proportion of QCD's finished goods to Agro. The consigned inventory would be invoiced upon its consumption greatly shortening Agro's working capital cycle. However, the Finance Director wanted the "final bearer of the risks and returns of the consigned inventory to be defined in the agreement as QCD" to clear the agreement from being considered as an attempt to window dress Agro's balance sheet. The proposal put forth by the Finance Director was integrated into the agreement, outlining a modification in the scope of QCD's insurance coverage to encompass the inventory consigned to Agro.

Agro's third-party manufacturing arrangement with QCD is still in its infancy and its overall effectiveness and practicality is yet to be determined by the supply chain and management accounting functions. Also, this agreement must be integrated with the third-party logistics agreement to assist QCD in efficiently coordinating its supply chain and inventory needs.

5 Concluding Remarks and Directions for Future Research

The evidence presented by Agro's three outsourcing cases illustrates that the scope and role of management accounting is no longer confined to the legal boundaries of the organization (Berry et al., 2000; Dekker, 2016; Partridge & Perren, 1994; Porter, 1985; Seal et al., 1999). It also suggests that accounting has constitutional and communicative roles to play in the establishment and management of the outsourcing arrangements (Seal et al., 1999; Berry et al., 2000; Nicholson et al., 2006; Nielsen et al., 2015). The contribution of management accountants as experts and members of cross-functional teams is more evident in tasks related to developing cost comparisons between the current and proposed states, and assisting the supply chain function in setting thresholds for significant changes in major commodity prices, building the proposal for the Third-Party Logistics case, monitoring inventory record, analyzing risks, evaluating cost reduction opportunities, monitoring vendors' performance, setting the key performance indicators (KPI's) relating to the financial aspects of the vendor's scope of work.

Agro's outsourcing initiatives provided clear evidence of the important role of management accounting in guiding an organization through major transformations in business models and processes. Such guidance can be proactive as in the case of the Finance Director's risk management of Intellectual Property Rights and obligations that may arise (i.e., contingent liabilities) from third-party manufacturing, or reactive as in the case of management accounting's detailed KPIs reporting on third-party logistics. The offshore RO project involved a balanced level of guidance by management accounting where foreign exchange risks were proactively addressed and reporting routines were reactively fine-tuned in accordance with best practice.

In the Third-Party Logistics initiative, the management accountant was guided and led by Supply Chain throughout the project process. This was credited to Supply Chain's in-depth functional knowledge and appreciation of outsourcing as a source of value, which confirms the conclusions reached by Brandau and Hoffjan (2010) of the lack of evidence that management accounting is the main initiator of strategic cost reductions through outsourcing initiatives. According to Brandau and Hoffjan (2010) specialized departments such as "strategic sourcing" are needed to initiate and implement outsourcing projects, reducing the need for strategic initiation and intervention by management accounting. However, given the management accountant's response to inquiries for financial information and active participation in the Request for Proposal (RFP) process, Agro's experience with the outsourcing of Third-Party Logistics function is contrary to one of the conclusions reached by Brandau and Hoffjan (2010) that management accounting is quite often not perceived as an internal service for information support. The Supply Chain's use of financial information provided by management accountants to populate scorecards, develop KPIs and provide justification is enough evidence that management accounting is considered a valuable source of input to strategic decision-making.

Previous studies have highlighted the significant role of management accounting in the effective development of supply chain strategies and collaborative initiatives. For instance, Berry et al. (2000) found that management accountants collaborate with multidisciplinary teams, including supply chain officers, to coordinate tasks such as strategic analysis of supply chains, enhancing partnerships through supply chain management, measuring performance with the balanced scorecard, and developing open book costing, which includes profit-sharing when costs are reduced. Similarly, Carr and Ng (1995) identified the role of multifunctional teams in supply chain management, performing tasks related to value chain analysis, projects, and initiatives aimed at achieving total cost control across the entire supply chain and identifying cost reduction opportunities. The findings of the current study support Lord's (1996) assertion that elements of strategic management accounting are present in corporate practice. Additionally, they highlight the incorporation of qualitative and strategic factors into the financial and cost analysis of outsourcing decisions, as observed by Nielsen et al. (2015).

The strategic roles played by the management accountant in the development and monitoring of business strategy as defined by Simmonds (1981) were evident in the RO initiative. Environmental scanning activity through the help of independent sources such as recruitment agencies and real estate brokers and incorporating possible volatility in the value of foreign currencies into financial projections are strategic interventions on the part of management accounting. But this may also be interpreted in the context of attention directing (Datar & Rajan, 2017) where the management accountant played a controlling role. Moreover, it is difficult to ascertain whether the Finance Director's comments on the accuracy of the Supply Chain Director's comments were a mere reflection on the effectiveness of the RO initiative or a form of strategic management accounting meant to alter Agro's strategic direction. In other words, the Finance Director did not necessarily rely on a strategic management accounting process instilled by management accounting (Brandau & Hoffjan, 2010; Dixon, 1998; Håkansson & Lind, 2004) to participate in the strategic evaluation of the RO initiative, but has instead employed management controls to influence behaviors and decisions in light of corporate objectives and strategies. Brandau and Hoffjan (2010) supports the latter through comparing and contrasting management controls with management accounting, "*whereas management accounting acts as a consulting and information providing function, management control activities exert a direct influence on individuals in organizations.*" The Finance Director's seniority and high position in Agro's hierarchy support the argument that he was mainly reliant on management controls to dispose of his responsibilities, but the reclassification of management accounting' sense checking and risk management tasks from strategic management accounting to attention directing and controlling may be more of a case with semantics. The fact remains that the management accountant participated in the strategic planning process by partnering with HR and also in highlighting foreign exchange risks.

In the context of the Third-Party Manufacturing Initiative, management accounting proved to be a source of input for strategic decision-making while at the same time remaining as a follower rather than an initiator of strategic outsourcing initiative. More specifically, the management accounting's definition of the thresholds for changes in major commodity prices is a type of target cost management as defined by Mouritsen et al. (2001). What is different about this particular initiative is that management accounting, which is led by the Finance Director seemed to have a say into the approval of the project. The management accountant's risk management skills were evident from the Finance Director's concerns over the reasonableness of QCD's gain sharing incentive scheme and possible loss of intellectual property right (IPR). This coincides with some of the findings made by Brandau and Hoffjan (2010) on management accounting's high level of involvement with supplier selection and investment calculations prior to the launch of an outsourcing project. But the latter is contrasted with the management accountant's limited role once the project becomes fully operational given the naturally more prominent roles that manufacturing and supply chain functions will have to play in such a technically involved and complex task. It is not surprising that Brandau and Hoffjan (2010) believe that the coordination and information support for individual activities within complex outsourcing projects are the responsibility of the relevant specialist departments. Finally, the Finance Director's insistence on the amendment of the agreement to clear it from being considered as a window dressing arrangement contradicts the conclusions of Brandau and Hoffjan (2010) that few indications exist of the management accountant's role in controlling the credibility of outsourcing projects.

Although the strategic significance of management accounting in Agro's outsourcing initiatives is undeniable, it important to note that its applicability to other organizations may not be generalized. The evidence and interpretations presented in this case are based on a single manufacturing company, thus constraining the generalizability of the findings to a broader organizational spectrum. Expanding the research horizon across a diverse array of organizations could yield a more robust understanding of the role and contribution of management accounting and accounting information in decisions to outsource organizational functions. Another major limitation of the study is the main focus on the early phases of Agro's outsourcing projects' development. Further research is required to obtain an in-depth understanding of the outsourcing decision-making and control processes at, for example, mature phases as different governance controls may be needed (Nicholson et al., 2006; Varoutsa & Scapens, 2015). Finally, further investigation may be needed into how intraorganizational accounting techniques and routines could be adapted for use in an interorganizational context, and how these interorganizational practices might, in turn, impact the former. This involves exploring the interactions between intraorganizational and interorganizational management control and practices (Coad & Cullen, 2006; Dekker, 2016). Investigating these questions and issues can offer valuable insights into how firms adapt their accounting practices to facilitate collaboration. Furthermore, it can reveal how collaborative practices and experiences impact management accounting practices within organizations (Dekker, 2016).

Acknowledgments The author sincerely thanks the two anonymous reviewers for their constructive and valuable feedback, which significantly enhanced the chapter. Special appreciation also goes to King Fahad University of Petroleum and Minerals for their financial and logistical support.

References

Aman, A., Hamzah, N., Amiruddin, R., & Maelah, R. (2012). Transaction costs in finance and accounting offshore outsourcing: A case of Malaysia. *Strategic Outsourcing: An International Journal, 5*(1), 72–88. https://doi.org/10.1108/17538291211221960

Ambos, B., Brandi, K., Perri, A., & Scalera & Assche, A. (2021). The nature of innovation in global value chains. *Journal of World Business, 56*(2021), 1–10. https://doi.org/10.1016/J.JWB.2021.101221

Berry, A., Cullen, J., Seal, W. A., & Dunlop, A. (2000). *The consequences of inter-firm supply chains for management accounting*. CIMA.

Brandau, M., & Hoffjan, A. H. (2010). Exploring the involvement of management accounting in strategic decisions and control: The case of offshoring. *Journal of Accounting & Organizational Change, 6*(1), 72–95.

Bromwich, M., & Bhimani, A. (1994). *Management accounting: Pathways to progress*. CIMA.

Carr, C., & Ng, J. (1995). Total cost control: Nissan and its UK supplier partnerships. *Management Accounting Research, 6*(4), 347–365.

Chalos, P. (1995). Costing, control, and strategic analysis in outsourcing decisions. *Journal of Cost Management, 8*(4), 31–37.
Coad, A., & Cullen, J. (2006). Inter-organizational cost management: Towards an evolutionary perspective. *Management Accounting Research, 17*(4), 342–369.
Cooper, R., & Slagmulder, R. (2004). Inter-organizational cost management and relational context. *Accounting, Organizations and Society, 29*(1), 1–26.
Das, T. K., & Teng, B. (2001). A risk perception model of alliance structuring. *Journal of International Management, 7*(1), 1–29.
Datar, S., & Rajan, M. (2017). *Horngren's cost accounting: A managerial emphasis* (16th ed.). Pearson.
Dekker, H. C. (2004). Control of inter-organizational relationships: Evidence on appropriation concerns and coordination requirements. *Accounting, Organizations and Society, 29*(1), 27–49.
Dekker, H. C. (2008). Partner selection and governance design in inter-firm relationships. *Accounting, Organizations and Society, 33*(7/8), 915–941.
Dekker, H. C. (2016). On the boundaries between intrafirm and interfirm management accounting research. *Management Accounting Research, 31*, 86–99.
Dekker, H. C., Kawai, T., & Sakaguchi, J. (2018). Contracting abroad: A comparative analysis of contract design in host and home outsourcing relations. *Management Accounting Research, 40*, 47–61.
Dent, J. F. (1996). Global competition challenges for management accounting and control. *Management Accounting Research, 7*(2), 247–269.
Ding, R., Dekker, H., & Groot, T. (2010). An exploration of the use of interfirm cooperation and the financial manager's governance roles: Evidence from Dutch firms. *Journal of Accounting & Organizational Change, 6*(1), 9–26.
Dixon, R. (1998). Accounting for strategic management: A practical application. *Long Range Planning, 31*(2), 272–279.
Drinta, R. E. (1994). The outsourcing decision. *Management Accounting*, 56–62.
Gietzman, M. B. (1996). Incomplete contracts and the make or buy decision: Governance design and attainable flexibility. *Accounting, Organizations and Society, 21*, 611–626.
Håkansson, H., & Lind, J. (2004). Accounting and network coordination. *Accounting, Organization and Society, 29*(1), 51–72.
Harland, C. M. (1996). Supply chain management: Relationships, chains, and networks. *British Journal of Management, 7*(1), 563–580.
Horngren, T. (1962). *Cost accounting: A managerial emphasis*. Prentice Hall.
Jensen, M. C., & Meckling, W. H. (1976). Theory of the firm: Managerial behavior, agency costs and ownership structure. *Journal of Financial Economics, 3*(4), 305–360.
Lamming, R. (1993). *Beyond partnership: Strategies for innovation and lean supply*. Prentice Hall.
Lamminmaki, D. (2008). Accounting and the management of outsourcing: An empirical study in the hotel industry. *Management Accounting Research, 19*(2), 163–181. https://doi.org/10.1016/j.mar.2008.02.002
Langfield-Smith, K. (2008). The relationship between transactional characteristics, trust and risk in the startup phase of a collaborative alliance. *Management Accounting Research, 19*(4), 244–264.
Langfield-Smith, K., & Smith, D. (2003). Accounting systems and trust in outsourcing relationships. *Management Accounting Research, 14*(3), 281–307.
Lord, R. (1996). Strategic management accounting: The emperor's new clothes. *Management Accounting Research, 7*, 347–366.
Meira, J., Kartails, N., Tsamenyi, M., & Cullen, J. (2010). Management controls and inter-firm relationships: A review. *Journal of Accounting & Organizational Change, 6*(1), 149–169.
Mouritsen, J., Hansen, A., & Hansen, C. (2001). Inter-organizational controls and organizational competencies: Episodes around target cost management/functional analysis and open book accounting. *Management Accounting Research, 12*(2), 221–244.

Munjal, S., Requejo, I., & Kundu, S. (2019). Offshore outsourcing and firm performance: Moderating effects of size, growth and slack resources. *Journal of Business Research, 103*(4), 484–494.

Nicholson, B., Jones, J., & Espenlaub, S. (2006). Transaction costs and control of outsourced accounting: Case evidence from India. *Management Accounting Research, 17*(3), 238–258.

Nielsen, L., Mitchell, F., & Nørreklit, H. (2015). Management accounting and decision making: Two case studies of outsourcing. *Accounting Forum, 39*(1), 64–82. https://doi.org/10.1016/j.accfor.2014.10.005

Partridge, M., & Perren, L. (1994). *Cost analysis of the value chain: Another role for strategic management accounting* (pp. 22–28). Management Accounting.

Porter, M. E. (1985). *Competitive advantage: Creating and sustaining superior performance*. The Free Press.

Ring, P. S., & Van de Ven, A. H. (1994). Developmental processes of cooperative interorganizational relationships. *The Academy of Management Review, 19*(1), 90–118.

Rodríguez, A., & Nieto, M. (2015). Does R&D offshoring lead to SME growth? Different governance modes and the mediating role of innovation. *Strategic Management Journal, 37*(8), 1734–1753.

Scapens, R. (1990). Researching management accounting practice: The role of case study methods. *The British Accounting Review, 22*(3), 259–281.

Seal, W., Cullen, J., Dunlop, A., Berry, T., & Ahmed, M. (1999). Enacting a European supply chain: Case study on the role of management accounting. *Management Accounting Research, 10*(3), 303–322.

Shank, J. K., & Govindararajan, V. (1992). Strategic cost management and value chain. *Journal of Cost Management, 40*(5), 5–21.

Simmonds, K. (1981). Strategic management accounting. *Management Accounting, 59*(4), 26–29.

Smith, J. A., Morris, A., & Ezzamel, M. (2005). Organizational change, outsourcing and the impact on management accounting. *The British Accounting Review, 37*(4), 415–441.

Söderberg, L., Bengtsson, L., & Kaulio, M. (2017). A model for outsourcing and governing of maintenance within the process industry. *Operations Management Research, 10*, 20–32. https://doi.org/10.1007/s12063-016-0121-0

Van der Meer-Kooistra, J., & Vosselman, E. (2000). Management control of inter-firm transactional relationships: The case of industrial renovation and maintenance. *Accounting, Organization and Society, 25*(1), 51–77.

Van der Meer-Kooistra, J., & Vosselman, E. (2006). Research on management control of interfirm transactional relationship: Whence and whither. *Management Accounting Research, 17*(3), 227–237.

Varoutsa, E., & Scapens, R. W. (2015). The governance of inter-organizational relationships during different supply chain maturity phases. *Industrial Marketing Management, 46*(1), 68–82. https://doi.org/10.1016/j.indmarman.2015.01.006

Williamson, O. E. (1985). *The economic institutions of capitalism*. The Free Press.

Yin, R. K. (2009). *Case study research: Design and methods* (4th ed.). Sage.

Dr. Mirghani N. Ahmed, BSc. (Hons), MA (Econ), PhD, is an Associate Professor of Accounting at the KFUPM Business School, King Fahd University of Petroleum & Minerals, Saudi Arabia. He has previously held academic positions at the University of Manchester, Portsmouth Business School, and Sheffield Hallam University in the United Kingdom. His research focuses on cost allocation, performance management, inter-firm relationships, and their implications for management accounting theory and practice.

Modelling the Quality of Inspections by Maintenance Service Providers Based on an Opportunistic Inspection and Replacement Policy

Mônica F. Marsaro, Cristiano A. V. Cavalcante, Alexandre R. Alberti, Phil Scarf, Rodrigo S. Lopes, and Augusto J. S. Rodrigues

1 Introduction

The increasing demands for the continuity of operating systems lead to progressively shorter time-windows for maintenance activities (Wang et al., 2023). To operate safely and reliably, maintenance actions are necessary and have a direct

M. F. Marsaro
Department of Production Engineering, State University of Maranhão (UEMA), São Luís, Brazil

RANDOM - Research Group on Risk and Decision Analysis in Operations and Maintenance, UFPE, Recife, PE, Brazil

C. A. V. Cavalcante (✉) · A. R. Alberti
RANDOM - Research Group on Risk and Decision Analysis in Operations and Maintenance, UFPE, Recife, PE, Brazil

Department of Production Engineering, Federal University of Pernambuco (UFPE), Recife, Brazil
e-mail: cristiano.avcavalcante@ufpe.br

P. Scarf
RANDOM - Research Group on Risk and Decision Analysis in Operations and Maintenance, UFPE, Recife, PE, Brazil

Cardiff Business School, Cardiff University, Cardiff, UK

R. S. Lopes
RANDOM - Research Group on Risk and Decision Analysis in Operations and Maintenance, UFPE, Recife, PE, Brazil

Department of Mechanical and Production Engineering, Federal University of São João del Rei–UFSJ, São João del Rei, Minas Gerais, Brazil

A. J. S. Rodrigues
RANDOM - Research Group on Risk and Decision Analysis in Operations and Maintenance, UFPE, Recife, PE, Brazil

Technology Center, UFPE, Caruaru, PE, Brazil

F. P. García Márquez et al. (eds.), *Outsourcing*, International Series in Operations Research & Management Science 370, https://doi.org/10.1007/978-3-031-95393-4_10

impact on business performance aspects such as productivity and profitability (Alsyouf, 2007; Yuan et al., 2023). Therefore, maintainers cannot afford to waste precious opportunities for maintenance. In addition, the current manufacturing landscape is characterized by high automation, high productivity, and accelerating technological development (De Jonge et al., 2017). These create challenges for maintenance management (Chalabi et al., 2016). It is argued that integrated operation and maintenance, achieved through simultaneous monitoring and control of the system-state and production output (Robert et al., 2018; uit het Broek et al., 2020), can address the challenges related to automation and productivity. However, rapid technological development presents a significant challenge for contracting and training maintenance personnel, which, in turn, affects the quality of maintenance actions (Alberti et al., 2018).

Recent research has increasingly highlighted the importance of ensuring the quality of maintenance actions. Variations in the quality of replacement components, as well as the quality of installation services, can significantly influence system reliability. To integrate these factors into mathematical models, Scarf et al. (2009) propose a framework where components are considered to come from a heterogeneous population. This population comprises both weak and strong items, which cannot be distinguished individually. Thus, the reliability function for an item is derived from a mixture of the characteristic functions of these subpopulations.

Furthermore, the quality of inspections is a crucial factor. Inaccuracies in assessing the system's condition, such as false positives (false alarms) or false negatives, can occur (Berrade et al., 2012, 2013). Furthermore, inspections can sometimes introduce defects (Alberti et al., 2018; Scarf & Cavalcante, 2012) or contribute to failures (Flage, 2014). Maintenance strategy effectiveness can be drastically impacted by these maintenance quality aspects. Suboptimal decision-making can be a result of neglecting them.

To address the quality problem, operators can rely on the Original Equipment Manufacturer (OEM) for maintenance and spare part supplies (Berrade et al., 2012). Despite this, these contracts can be quite costly. Therefore, considering the trade-off between maintenance quality and the cost paid for it, the following question arises: *What would be the appropriate level of maintenance quality*? To answer this question, we developed a maintenance model that relies on opportunistic maintenance and investigated the different maintenance service providers to find the best cost-benefit ratio. By doing this, we aim to guide decision-making regarding maintenance quality and supplier selection, while maintaining a balance between cost and performance.

The policy and model accommodate varying skill levels, which in turn affect cost and quality across different maintenance aspects. Additionally, we simulate real-world scenarios encountered in industries where high productivity drives operators to perform maintenance opportunistically. These scenarios include contexts with high technological complexity (e.g., automated manufacturing systems) or significant risks to personnel (e.g., wind turbines, offshore production), which can impact maintenance quality.

When designing contracts for maintenance services, it's important to consider both opportunities and quality together. A large number of authors concentrate solely on one of these aspects. However, the number of studies addressing opportunistic maintenance is growing (Abdollahzadeh et al., 2016; Alotaibi et al., 2023; Cavalcante et al., 2024; Colledani et al., 2018; Ding & Tian, 2012; Shafiee et al., 2015; Song et al., 2018). This is especially relevant for systems that have significant maintenance challenges, like offshore turbines, petroleum platforms, or gas supply networks. In these circumstances, opportunistic maintenance is a smart way to maximize resources. Preventive actions are made not just based on a plan, but also on available opportunities. The challenging maintenance conditions not only offer opportunities to exploit, but they also increase the impact of quality-related problems on the system. For instance, an inspection that fails to detect a defect on a wind turbine in rough seas results in much greater waste than an inspection that can be performed at any time on an easily accessible device. Additionally, the quality of maintenance activities may be hampered by these harsh conditions. Thus, analyzing the effect of maintenance quality on system performance, as studied by some authors (Alberti et al., 2018; Berrade et al., 2012, 2013, 2015; Cavalcante et al., 2018; Scarf et al., 2009; Scarf & Cavalcante, 2012), becomes increasingly important for hard-to-access systems (HAS).

This study differs from previous approaches by introducing an analytical model that accounts for variations in inspection quality, including false positives and negatives (misclassifications), as well as different levels of replacement quality (e.g., poor installation). The primary decision criterion is the long-term cost per unit of time. Furthermore, we incorporate the mean time between operational failures (MTBOF) as an additional criterion to furnish the decision-maker with more information. This approach helps to complement the main cost-based decision criterion with reliability-related information.

The paper's structure is as follows: The following section discusses the system's intrinsic characteristics and the proposed maintenance policy. The mathematical modelling of the policy is explained in Sect. 3. In Sect. 4, a numerical application is presented, the results are discussed, and practical implications are highlighted. Finally, Sect. 5 concludes with observations.

2 System Characterization and Maintenance Policy

Table 1 presents some notations that will be used throughout this paper.

We consider a single-component system composed by a component and a socket that provide an important function while it is operational (non-failed) (Ascher & Feingold, 1984). During the operation, the system deteriorates, resulting in a defect. This state evolves to failure if no action is taken. The defective state is only detected by inspection. We consider the concept of delay-time to model the

Table 1 Notation used in equations of the model

Notation	Meaning
Δ	Time between inspections
M	Minimum number of inspections to consider an opportunity
K	Maximum number of inspections in renewal cycle
α	False positive probability
β	False negative probability
X	Time to defect arrival
H	Delay-time
Z	Time to opportunity arrival
$f_X(.)$, $F_X(.)$	For X, probability density function, accumulated distribution function
$f_H(.)$, $F_H(.)$	For H, probability density function, accumulated distribution function
$f_Z(.)$, $F_Z(.)$	For Z, probability density function, accumulated distribution function
C_i	Cost of an inspection
C_p	Cost of a preventive replacement
C_o	Cost of a preventive replacement at an opportunity
C_f	Cost of a replacement in a failure
P_n	Probability of renewing the component in a specific scenario n
C_n	Maintenance cost in a specific scenario n
L_n	Cycle length in a specific scenario n
$E_\infty(\Delta, M, K)$	Cost-rate
$MTBOF$	Mean time between operational failures

process of failure (Wang, 2012). In such a way that are three the total number of states: good (G), defective (D), and Failed (F) states. The failure prevents the system to provide its function, from the exact moment that it occurs, thus there is no doubt about it (self-announced failure). The sojourn in G and D are random variables (r.v.) denoted respectively as X and H. We consider that these r.v. are independent, and we know its density function $f_X(x)$, $f_H(h)$, respectively. As we consider the possibility of bad installation, that is a quality issue related to the replacement action that makes the component presents distinct behavior with respect to defects arrival: early defect arrival and a later, we adopt the apparatus proposed by (Scarf et al., 2009; Scarf & Cavalcante, 2012), i.e., $f_X(x)$ is a mixture of distributions: $f_X(x) = pf_1(x) + (1 - p)f_2(x)$. Therefore, p is the probability of a bad installation happens and $f_1(x)$ and $f_2(x)$ is respectively the density function related to X, if bad installation occurs and if it doesn't occur.

We also consider that system is subject to opportunities they occur in a Poisson process with rate λ_Z and time denoted as Z. Opportunities are defined by corrective or preventive maintenance required by other components that make part of the plant. At an opportunity the component under study may be replaced opportunistically. Opportunity motivation comes from any realistic scenario where some of the following particularities can be observed: high productivity, which consequently results in the encouragement of undertake maintenance at opportunity basis; the existence of maintenance quality issues due to high personnel turnover or any other reason; maintenance activities that involve certain level of difficulty, i.e., it requires a high level of skills (training), it involves hard-to-access systems (HAS), it involves risks on the execution (e.g., climbing in high altitudes). Once some of these characteristics are observed, we consider that one of the main problems that the decision-maker faces is the definition of the best supplier.

Regarding the maintenance policy, we consider an inspection-maintenance approach, wherein the system is inspected at a frequency of $1/\Delta$ up to age $K\Delta$. At age $K\Delta$, the system will be preventively replaced if it has not already been replaced. Besides the preventive replacement at $K\Delta$, the component will be replaced at the time of the ith inspection if it is found to be defective, or upon failure. If none of these events occur, it will be replaced at an opportunity arising within the interval $[M\Delta, K\Delta]$. Inspections are imperfect. A false positive occurs when the component is incorrectly identified as defective, with a probability of α. Conversely, a false negative occurs when the component is incorrectly identified as good, with a probability of β. Then, the model has three decision variables:

- Δ: Time between inspections
- M: Minimum number of inspections to consider an opportunity
- K: Maximum number of inspections in renewal cycle

3 Policy Modelling

The modelling is based on the renewal-reward theorem (Ross, 1996), developing exhaustive equations for all renewal scenarios. The construction of these scenarios encompasses all possible events in a component's life cycle, such as the occurrence of a failure, defect identification, and replacement when an opportunity arises. From these equations, it is possible to identify which scenarios are most likely, with some having higher probabilities of occurrence than others, directly impacting the optimization of decision variables.

For calculating performance measures, i.e., the cost-rate (the expected cost per unit of time in the long-run) and the Mean Time Between Operational Failure (MTBOF), formulations are developed for 13 system renewal scenarios. The descriptions and respective mathematical formulations of these scenarios are developed in the following, where $C_i(\Delta, M, K)$, $L_i(\Delta, M, K)$, and $P_i(\Delta, M, K)$, represent the expected cost, the expected length, and the probability of each renewal cycle i, for $i = 1, \ldots, 13$, respectively.

Scenario 1: System Renewal Due to Component Inspection up to $M\Delta$, Due to a True Positive

$$P_1(\Delta, M, K) = \begin{Bmatrix} \sum_{i=1}^{M} P_{1i}(\Delta, M, i) \text{ if } M \geq 1, K > M \\ \sum_{i=1}^{M-1} P_{1i}(\Delta, M, i) \text{ if } M \geq 2, K = M \end{Bmatrix},$$

$$C_1(\Delta, M, K) = \begin{Bmatrix} \sum_{i=1}^{M} \left[\left(iC_i + C_p\right) P_{1i}(\Delta, M, i)\right] \text{ if } M \geq 1, K > M \\ \sum_{i=1}^{M-1} \left[\left(iC_i + C_p\right) P_{1i}(\Delta, M, i)\right] \text{ if } M \geq 2, K = M \end{Bmatrix},$$

$$L_1(\Delta, M, K) = \begin{Bmatrix} \sum_{i=1}^{M} \left[(i\Delta) P_{1i}(\Delta, M, i)\right] \text{ if } M \geq 1, K > M \\ \sum_{i=1}^{M-1} \left[(i\Delta) P_{1i}(\Delta, M, i)\right] \text{ if } M \geq 2, K = M \end{Bmatrix},$$

where:

$$P_{1i}(\Delta, M, i) = \sum_{j=1}^{i} \left[(1-\alpha)^{j-1} \beta^{i-j} (1-\beta) \int_{(j-1)\Delta}^{j\Delta} f_X(x) \int_{i\Delta}^{\infty} f_H(h) \mathrm{d}h \mathrm{d}x \right].$$

Scenario 2: System Renewal During Inspection After $M\Delta$, Due to a True Positive

$$P_2(\Delta, M, K) = \sum_{i=M+1}^{K-1} P_{2i}(\Delta, M, K, i),$$

$$C_2(\Delta, M, K) = \sum_{i=M+1}^{K-1} \left[\left(iC_i + C_p\right) P_{2i}(\Delta, M, K, i)\right],$$

$$L_2(\Delta, M, K) = \sum_{i=M+1}^{K-1} \left[(i\Delta) P_{2i}(\Delta, M, K, i)\right],$$

where:

$$P_{2i}(\Delta, M, K, i) = \sum_{j=1}^{i} \left[(1-\alpha)^{j-1} \beta^{i-j} (1-\beta) \left[1 - F_Z((i-M)\Delta)\right] \int_{(j-1)\Delta}^{j\Delta} f_X(x) \int_{i\Delta - x}^{\infty} f_H(h) \mathrm{d}h \mathrm{d}x \right].$$

Scenario 3: System Renewal During Inspection up to $M\Delta$, Due to a False Positive

$$P_3(\Delta, M, K) = \left\{ \begin{array}{l} \sum_{i=1}^{M} P_{3i}(\Delta, M, i) \text{ if } M \geq 1, K > M \\ \sum_{i=1}^{M-1} P_{3i}(\Delta, M, i) \text{ if } M \geq 2, K = M \end{array} \right\},$$

$$C_3(\Delta, M, K) = \left\{ \begin{array}{l} \sum_{i=1}^{M} \left[\left(iC_i + C_p\right) P_{3i}(\Delta, M, i)\right] \text{ if } M \geq 1, K > M \\ \sum_{i=1}^{M-1} \left[\left(iC_i + C_p\right) P_{3i}(\Delta, M, i)\right] \text{ if } M \geq 2, K = M \end{array} \right\},$$

$$L_3(\Delta, M, K) = \left\{ \begin{array}{l} \sum_{i=1}^{M} [(i\Delta) P_{3i}(\Delta, M, i)] \text{ if } M \geq 1, K > M \\ \sum_{i=1}^{M-1} [(i\Delta) P_{3i}(\Delta, M, i)] \text{ if } M \geq 2, K = M \end{array} \right\},$$

where:
$P_{3i}(\Delta, M, i) = (1-\alpha)^{i-1}\alpha[1 - F_X(i\Delta)]$.

Scenario 4: System Renewal During Inspection After $M\Delta$, Due to a False Positive

$$P_4(\Delta, M, K) = \sum_{i=M+1}^{K-1} P_{4i}(\Delta, M, K, i),$$

$$C_4(\Delta, M, K) = \sum_{i=M+1}^{K-1} \left[\left(iC_i + C_p\right) P_{4i}(\Delta, M, K, i)\right],$$

$$L_4(\Delta, M, K) = \sum_{i=M+1}^{K-1} [(i\Delta) P_{4i}(\Delta, M, K, i)],$$

where:
$P_{4i}(\Delta, M, K, i) = (1-\alpha)^{i-1}\alpha[1 - F_Z((i-M)\Delta)][1 - F_X(i\Delta)]$.

Scenario 5: System Renewal on Failure up to $M\Delta$, After a True Negative

$$P_5(\Delta, M, K) = \sum_{i=1}^{M} P_{5i}(\Delta, M, K, i),$$

$$C_5(\Delta, M, K) = \sum_{i=1}^{M} \left[\left((i-1)C_i + C_f\right) P_{5i}(\Delta, M, K, i)\right],$$

where:

$$P_{5i}(\Delta, M, K) = (1-\alpha)^{i-1} \int_{(i-1)\Delta}^{i\Delta} f_X(x) \int_{0}^{i\Delta - x} f_H(h) \mathrm{d}h \mathrm{d}x,$$

and:

$$L_5(\Delta, M, K) = \sum_{i=1}^{M} \left[(1-\alpha)^{i-1} \int_{(i-1)\Delta}^{i\Delta} f_X(x) \int_{0}^{i\Delta - x} (x+h) f_H(h) \mathrm{d}h \mathrm{d}x \right].$$

Scenario 6: System Renewal on Failure After $M\Delta$, After a True Negative

$$P_6(\Delta, M, K) = \sum_{i=M+1}^{K} P_{6i}(\Delta, M, K, i),$$

$$C_6(\Delta, M, K) = \sum_{i=M+1}^{K} \left[\left((i-1)C_i + C_f\right) P_{6i}(\Delta, M, K, i)\right],$$

where:

$$P_{6i}(\Delta, M, K, i) = (1-\alpha)^{i-1} \int_{(i-1)\Delta}^{i\Delta} f_X(x) \int_{0}^{i\Delta - x} f_H(h)\left[1 - F_Z\left(x + h - M\Delta\right]\mathrm{d}h\mathrm{d}x,$$

and:

$$L_6(\Delta, M, K) = \sum_{i=M+1}^{K} \left[(1-\alpha)^{i-1} \int_{(i-1)\Delta}^{i\Delta} f_X(x) \int_{0}^{i\Delta - x} (x+h)\, f_H(h)\left[1 - F_Z\left(x + h - M\Delta\right]\mathrm{d}h\mathrm{d}x\right].$$

Scenario 7: System Renewal on Failure up to $M\Delta$, After a False Negative

$$P_7(\Delta, M, K) = \sum_{i=2}^{M} P_{7i}(\Delta, M, K, i),$$

$$C_7(\Delta, M, K) = \sum_{i=2}^{M} \left[\left((i-1)C_i + C_f\right) P_{7i}(\Delta, M, K, i)\right],$$

where:

$$P_{7i}(\Delta, M, K, i) = \sum_{j=1}^{i-1} \left[(1-\alpha)^{j-1}\beta^{j-j} \int_{(j-1)\Delta}^{j\Delta} f_X(x) \int_{(i-1)\Delta - x}^{i\Delta - x} f_H(h)\mathrm{d}h\mathrm{d}x\right],$$

and:

$$L_7(\Delta, M, K) = \sum_{i=2}^{M}\sum_{j=1}^{i-1} \left[(1-\alpha)^{j-1}\beta^{i-j} \int_{(j-1)\Delta}^{j\Delta} f_X(x) \int_{(i-1)\Delta - x}^{i\Delta - x} (x+h)\, f_H(h)\mathrm{d}h\mathrm{d}x\right].$$

Scenario 8: System Renewal on Failure After $M\Delta$, After a False Negative

$$P_8(\Delta, M, K) = \left\{ \begin{array}{l} \sum_{i=M+1}^{K} P_{8i}(\Delta, M, K, i) \text{ if } M \geq 1 \\ \sum_{i=M+2}^{K} P_{8i}(\Delta, M, K, i) \text{ if } M = 0 \end{array} \right\},$$

$$C_8(\Delta, M, K) = \left\{ \begin{array}{l} \sum_{i=M+1}^{K} \left[\left((i-1)C_i + C_f\right] P_{8i}(\Delta, M, K, i) \text{ if } M \geq 1 \\ \sum_{i=M+2}^{K} \left[\left((i-1)C_i + C_f\right] P_{8i}(\Delta, M, K, i) \text{ if } M = 0 \end{array} \right\},$$

where:

$$P_{8i}(\Delta, M, K, i) = \sum_{j=1}^{i-1} \left[(1-\alpha)^{j-1} \beta^{i-j} \int_{(j-1)\Delta}^{j\Delta} f_X(x) \int_{(i-1)\Delta - x}^{i\Delta - x} f_H(h) \left[1 - F_Z(x + h - M\Delta)\right] \mathrm{d}h\mathrm{d}x \right],$$

and:

$$L_8(\Delta, M, K) = \left\{ \begin{array}{l} \sum_{i=M+1}^{K} \sum_{j=1}^{i-1} \left[(1-\alpha)^{j-1} \beta^{i-j} \int_{(j-1)\Delta}^{j\Delta} f_X(x) \int_{(i-1)\Delta-x}^{i\Delta-x} (x+h) \right. \\ \quad \times f_H(h) \left[1 - F_Z(x + h - M\Delta)\right] \mathrm{d}h\mathrm{d}x] \text{ if } M \geq 1 \\ \sum_{i=M+2}^{K} \sum_{j=1}^{i-1} \left[(1-\alpha)^{j-1} \beta^{i-j} \int_{(j-1)\Delta}^{j\Delta} f_X(x) \int_{(i-1)\Delta-x}^{i\Delta-x} (x+h) \right. \\ \quad \times f_H(h) \left[1 - F_Z(x + h - M\Delta)\right] \mathrm{d}h\mathrm{d}x] \text{ if } M = 0 \end{array} \right\}.$$

Scenario 9: System Renewal on Opportunity, After a True Negative, with the Component Defective

$$P_9(\Delta, M, K) = \sum_{i=M+1}^{K} P_{9i}(\Delta, M, K, i),$$

$$C_9(\Delta, M, K) = \sum_{i=M+1}^{K} \left[\left((i-1)C_i + C_o\right)\right] P_{9i}(\Delta, M, K, i),$$

where:

$$P_{9i}(\Delta, M, K, i) = (1-\alpha)^{i-1} \int_{(i-1)\Delta}^{i\Delta} f_X(x) \int_{x-M\Delta}^{(i-M)\Delta} f_Z(z) \left[1 - F_H(M\Delta + z - x)\right] \mathrm{d}z\mathrm{d}x,$$

and:

$$L_9(\Delta, M, K) = \sum_{i=M+1}^{K} \left[(1-\alpha)^{i-1} \int_{(i-1)\Delta}^{i\Delta} f_X(x) \int_{x-M\Delta}^{(i-M)\Delta} (M\Delta + z) \times f_Z(z) \left[1 - F_H(M\Delta + z - x)\right] dz dx \right].$$

Scenario 10: System Renewal on Opportunity, After a True Negative, with the Component Good

$$P_{10}(\Delta, M, K) = \sum_{i=M+1}^{K} P_{10i}(\Delta, M, K, i),$$

$$C_{10}(\Delta, M, K) = \sum_{i=M+1}^{K} \left[((i-1) C_i + C_o)\right] P_{10i}(\Delta, M, K, i),$$

where:

$$P_{10i}(\Delta, M, K, i) = (1-\alpha)^{i-1} \int_{(i-1-M)\Delta}^{(i-M)\Delta} f_Z(z) \left[1 - F_X(M\Delta + z)\right] dz,$$

and:

$$L_{10}(\Delta, M, K) = \sum_{i=M+1}^{K} \left[(1-\alpha)^{i-1} \int_{(i-1-M)\Delta}^{(i-M)\Delta} (M\Delta + z) \times f_z(z) \left[1 - F_x(M\Delta + z)\right] dz \right]$$

Scenario 11: System Renewal on Opportunity, After a False Negative

$$P_{11}(\Delta, M, K) = \left\{ \begin{array}{l} \sum_{i=M+1}^{K} P_{11i}(\Delta, M, K, i) \text{ if } M \geq 1 \\ \sum_{i=M+2}^{K} P_{11i}(\Delta, M, K, i) \text{ if } M = 0 \end{array} \right\},$$

$$C_{11}(\Delta, M, K) = \left\{ \begin{array}{l} \sum_{i=M+1}^{K} \left[\left((i-1) C_i + C_o\right] P_{11i}(\Delta, M, K, i) \text{ if } M \geq 1 \\ \sum_{i=M+2}^{K} \left[\left((i-1) C_i + C_o\right] P_{11i}(\Delta, M, K, i) \text{ if } M = 0 \end{array} \right\},$$

where:

$$P_{11i}(\Delta, M, K, i) = \sum_{j=1}^{i-1} \left[(1-\alpha)^{j-1} \beta^{i-j} \int_{(j-1)\Delta}^{j\Delta} f_X(x) \int_{(i-1-M)\Delta}^{(i-M)\Delta} \times f_Z(z) \left[1 - F_H(M\,\Delta + z - x)\right] dh dx \right],$$

and:

$$L_{11}(\Delta, M, K) = \left\{ \begin{array}{l} \sum\limits_{i=M+1}^{K} \sum\limits_{j=1}^{i-1} \Bigg[(1-\alpha)^{j-1} \beta^{i-j} \int\limits_{(j-1)\Delta}^{j\Delta} f_X(x) \\ \quad \times \int\limits_{(i-1-M)\Delta}^{(i-M)\Delta} (M\Delta + z)\, f_Z(z) \\ \quad \times [1 - F_H(M\Delta + z - x)]\, \mathrm{d}h\mathrm{d}x \Bigg] \text{ if } M \geq 1 \\ \sum\limits_{i=M+2}^{K} \sum\limits_{j=1}^{i-1} \Bigg[(1-\alpha)^{j-1} \beta^{i-j} \int\limits_{(j-1)\Delta}^{j\Delta} f_X(x) \\ \quad \times \int\limits_{(i-1-M)\Delta}^{(i-M)\Delta} (M\Delta + z)\, f_Z(z) \\ \quad \times [1 - F_H(M\Delta + z - x)]\, \mathrm{d}h\mathrm{d}x \Bigg] \text{ if } M = 0 \end{array} \right\}.$$

Scenario 12: System Renewal at the Established End-of-Life for the Component ($K\Delta$), with the Component Defective

$$P_{12}(\Delta, M, K) = \sum_{i=1}^{K} \Bigg[(1-\alpha)^{i-1} \beta^{K-i} \Big[1 - F_Z\Big((K-M)\Delta \Big] \int\limits_{(j-1)\Delta}^{j\Delta} f_X(x) [1 - F_H(K\Delta - x)]\, \mathrm{d}x \Bigg],$$

$$C_{12}(\Delta, M, K) = \left[(K-1)\, C_i + C_p \right] P_{12}(\Delta, M, K),$$
$$L_{12}(\Delta, M, K) = (K\Delta)\, P_{12}(\Delta, M, K).$$

Scenario 13: System Renewal at the Established End-of-Life for the Component, with the Component Good

$$P_{13}(\Delta, M, K) = (1-\alpha)^{K-1} [1 - F_X(K\Delta)] \Big[1 - F_Z\Big((K-M)\Delta \Big],$$
$$C_{13}(\Delta, M, K) = \left[(K-1)\, C_i + C_p \right] P_{13}(\Delta, M, K),$$
$$L_{13}(\Delta, M, K) = (K\Delta)\, P_{13}(\Delta, M, K).$$

Thus, in order to find the optimal value for the model's decision variables, the objective is to minimize the cost-rate, given by:

$$C_\infty(\Delta, M, K) = \frac{\sum\limits_{i=1}^{13} C_i(\Delta, M, K)}{\sum\limits_{i=1}^{13} L_i(\Delta, M, K)}.$$

Furthermore, the MTBOF is calculated considering the expected cycle length and the probability of the cycle ending with a failure, which involves the probabilities of Scenarios 5, 6, 7, and 8.

$$MTBOF(\Delta, M, K) = \frac{\sum_{i=1}^{13} L_i(\Delta, M, K)}{\sum_{i=5}^{8} P_i(\Delta, M, K)}.$$

4 Numerical Application

To analyze the behavior of the proposed maintenance policy model, we evaluate the quality of inspection actions, taking into account both a local team and a specialized maintenance team. Typically, OEM (Original Equipment Manufacturer) teams demonstrate higher quality in maintenance, generally avoiding errors (misclassifications), albeit at a higher cost.

To this end, two scenarios will be analyzed:

1. Application 1: All maintenance actions are carried out by a local team, meaning the company's maintenance team performs both inspection and replacement functions. The use of this team results in lower maintenance costs, but the quality of the actions is lower.
2. Application 2: All maintenance actions are conducted by a specialized maintenance team (OEM—Original Equipment Manufacturer), with their hiring governed by contracts. Indeed, using an OEM team provides higher maintenance quality, with no errors in inspection, but the cost associated with this hiring is higher than using the local team.

The evaluation of these two distinct teams for maintenance results in different values for the parameters of inspection quality, maintenance quality, and costs (inspection, preventive, opportunistic preventive, and failure), as described below.

4.1 *Specification of the Parameters*

We use a Weibull probability distribution for the time to defect arrival, with shape parameters (b) and scale parameters (η). The population of the components is heterogeneous (week and strong components). For week components we consider $b_w = 2.5$ and $\eta_w = 0.8$, and for strong components $b_s = 3.6$ and $\eta_s = 5$. In the case where the maintenance is performed by a local team about 12% of the components are weak, and because of this a penalty of the quality in maintenance and we use $p_1 = 0.12$, and for the maintenance performed by the OEM this penalty is p_2=0.05. The unit of time is considered 1 year. For the delay-time we use an exponential distribution with parameter $\lambda_H = 1$ and we consider that the time to opportunities arrival is modelled according to a Poisson process, with mean $\lambda_Z = 2$.

Table 2 Optimal results of the applications considering some variation in the maintenance quality parameter p

		Application 1: Local team					Application 2: OEM				
Case	p	Δ	M	K	C_∞	*MTBOF*	Δ	M	K	C_∞	*MTBOF*
1	0	1.819	1	2	0.342	60.15	1.799	1	2	0.509	60.93
2	0.05	1.837	1	2	0.416	31.22	1.006	2	3	0.587	43.98
3	0.1	1.063	2	3	0.492	26.66	1.015	2	3	0.650	32.48
4	0.12	1.067	2	3	0.514	23.96	1.018	2	3	0.677	29.31
5	0.15	1.072	2	3	0.548	20.72	0.746	3	4	0.746	28.97
6	0.2	1.080	2	3	0.609	16.80	0.599	4	5	0.769	26.96

About the parameters that represents de quality of the inspection, that depends of the team of maintenance (1: Local Team; 2: OEM) is defined as: the false positive is $\alpha_1 = 0.1$ and $\alpha_2 = 0$, and the false negative is $\beta_1 = 0.2$ and $\beta_2 = 0$. This means that when the OEM performs all maintenance actions, we assume there is 100% accuracy.

The unit cost is represented by the cost of preventive replace C_p. The value of the others costs depends on the team that executes the action: C_i is the inspection cost $C_{1i} = 0.03$, $C_{2i} = 0.09$; C_f, is the failure cost, $C_{1f} = 5$, $C_{2f} = 7.5$; C_o, is the cost for replace in opportunity, $C_{1o} = 0.5$, $C_{2o} = 0.8$.

4.2 Results and Discussions

This section provides a numerical investigation to verify the effectiveness of the proposed maintenance model, followed by the analysis of the performance of the OEM and local team. Finally, sensitivity analysis is performed by plots with respect to the inspection interval.

Table 2 presents the optimal policy values, showing the decision variable values that minimize the cost-rate, with MTBOF evaluated for the two numerical applications described earlier. Different values for the parameter related to maintenance quality are presented in this table. The base case (BC) is case 4.

Based on the cost-rate, the strategy in Case 1 demonstrates the best performance for both applications, particularly due to the presence of a population consisting solely of robust components. It is noticeable that as the quality of maintenance decreases, the optimal cost-rate increases. There is a significant change in the inspection interval Δ when changes occur in M and K, as observed in the comparison between Cases 2 and 3 for Application 1, and Cases 1 and 2 for Application 2. Additionally, an abrupt decline in reliability is observed when considering a loss of maintenance quality (Cases 1 and 2), analyzed through MTBOF.

The decision on which team to choose for maintenance depends on the system's needs, balancing reliability and costs. As shown in Table 2, if the priority for the maintenance manager is to maximize reliability, opting for an OEM team is

Table 3 Some variation for the model parameters

Application	Case	α	β	p	C_p	C_i	C_f	C_o	λ_Z	Δ	M	K	C_∞	$MTBOF$
1: Local team	1	0.1	0.2	0.12	1	0.03	5	0.5	2	1.022	2	4	0.5108	24.06
	2	0.08	0.15	0.09	1.1	0.033	5.5	0.55	2	1.009	2	4	0.5088	29.79
	3	0.05	0.1	0.05	1.4	0.042	7	0.7	2	0.97	2	4	0.5593	42.24
	4	0.1	0.2	0.12	1	0.03	5	0.5	1	0.883	2	4	0.5477	23.04
	5	0.1	0.2	0.12	1	0.03	5	0.5	3	1.083	2	4	0.4980	25.11
2: OEM	6	0	0	0.05	1	0.09	7.5	0.8	2	0.997	2	3	0.5830	44.99
	7	0	0	0.05	1	0.09	7.5	0.8	1	0.919	2	3	0.6007	44.73
	8	0	0	0.05	1	0.09	7.5	0.8	3	1.012	2	3	0.5720	46.12
	9	0	0	0.05	1	0.09	13	0.8	2	0.883	2	3	0.6878	59.33
	10	0	0	0.05	1	0.09	19	0.8	2	0.597	3	4	0.7738	80.10

preferable. On the other hand, if cost savings are a primary concern, selecting the local team would be the optimal choice.

We will investigate the impacts on the optimal results of the models considering an improvement in the quality of maintenance actions by the local team, with a certain increase in maintenance cost. Table 3 presents these cases.

For the first application, where the local team undertakes all maintenance actions, the cost of preventive replacement increased, as shown in Cases 2 and 3. Consequently, other costs are also increased, with β and α decreasing. When the probabilities of inspection errors are reduced by 50% and the preventive replacement cost (C_p) is 40% more expensive, the MTBOF increases by 75.5%, while the cost rate increases by around 7%. Comparing these results with the OEM performance (Case 6), it can be noted that the MTBOF values are closer, and the cost-rate remains lower.

Maintenance costs and MTBOF are two critical indicators that have influence in the maintenance strategy. In critical equipment, a higher MTBOF results in greater safety for operation and production. It is possible to verify that the performance of the OEM team greatly improves the MTBOF. The model, proved to be sensitive to the quality of inspections, demonstrating that depending on the definition of which team will perform the inspection action, the model results in different inspection intervals, demonstrating the optimal interval according to the quality of the team.

The model was shown to be relatively insensitive to the cost of each type of maintenance activity and more significantly sensitive to changes in the quality of maintenance teams.

Figure 1 illustrates the sensitivity of maintenance effectiveness for different values of false positive and the false negative on the cost rate of inspection model.

Figure 1 illustrates that the optimal cost-rate for different values of β and α Overall, the optimal cost-rate increase with the increase of misclassification for different intervals of inspection. These observations illustrate that a more effective inspection results in a more costs. This effect was particularly more sensible when application of OEM team.

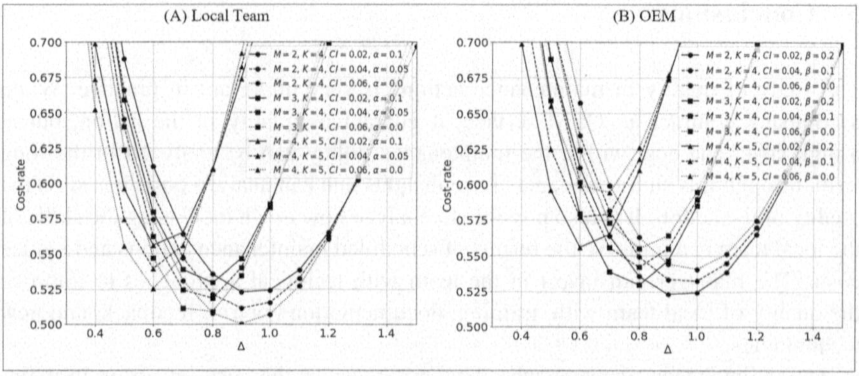

Fig. 1 Cost-rate as a function of Δ, for different values of α *(A)* and β *(B)*, and varying *M*, *K* and the cost of inspection (C_i), for $p = 0.12$, $C_f = 5$, $C_o = 0.5$. *In (A)* $\beta = 0.2$; *In (B)* $\alpha = 0.1$. Other parameters from Sect. 4.1

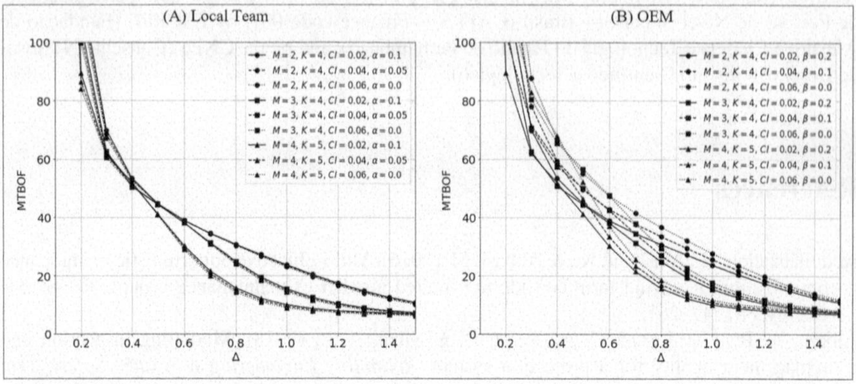

Fig. 2 MTBOF as a function of Δ, for different values of α *(A)* and β *(B)*, and varying *M*, *K* and the cost of inspection (C_i), for $p = 0.12$, $C_f = 5$, $C_o = 0.5$. *In (A)* $\beta = 0.2$; *In (B)* $\alpha = 0.1$. Other parameters from Sect. 4.1

From Fig. 2, we study variation of quality inspection in MTBOF. In practice a quality of inspection is a critical parameter that have a great impact on maintenance strategy.

From Fig. 2, a decline in inspection quality results in a reduced MTBOF, particularly as the inspection interval becomes longer. Thus, maintaining a high standard of inspection is crucial when implementing extended inspection intervals.

5 Conclusions

The study of quality in maintenance actions is very important in practice. When a company contract an OEM service, it guarantees quality in the action, but at a high cost. The cost within the maintenance policy can be analyzed in the long term, through this study, managers have insights and can analyze costs based on the quality of the action. It is also possible to analyze how much increasing the skills of the local team can improve the results of scheduled maintenance actions and reduce costs. The manager can invest in the team with technical approaches to improve the quality of local team with, training, documentation control, feedback, and new technologies.

The maintenance manager who does not consider the costs of errors in maintenance actions ends up having a distorted view of the policy being implemented. This study demonstrated technical characteristics and evaluated how the quality of inspection actions impacts the inspection policy.

Acknowledgments This study was financed in part by the Coordenação de Aperfeiçoamento de Pessoal de Nível Superior—Brasil (CAPES)—Finance code 001, by FACEPE (Fundação de Amparo à Ciência e Tecnologia do Estado de Pernambuco), and by the CNPq (Conselho Nacional de Desenvolvimento Científico e Tecnológico).

References

Abdollahzadeh, H., Atashgar, K., & Abbasi, M. (2016). Multi-objective opportunistic maintenance optimization of a wind farm considering limited number of maintenance groups. *Renewable Energy, 88*, 247–261.

Alberti, A. R., Cavalcante, C. A., Scarf, P., & Silva, A. L. (2018). Modelling inspection and replacement quality for a protection system. *Reliability Engineering & System Safety, 176*, 145–153.

Alotaibi, N. M., Scarf, P., Cavalcante, C. A., Lopes, R. S., Silva, A. L. D. O., Rodrigues, A. J. S., & Alyami, S. A. (2023). Modified-opportunistic inspection and the case of remote, groundwater well-heads. *Reliability Engineering & System Safety, 237*, 109389.

Alsyouf, I. (2007). The role of maintenance in improving companies' productivity and profitability. *International Journal of Production Economics, 105*(1), 70–78.

Berrade, M. D., Cavalcante, C. A., & Scarf, P. A. (2012). Maintenance scheduling of a protection system subject to imperfect inspection and replacement. *European Journal of Operational Research, 218*(3), 716–725.

Berrade, M. D., Scarf, P. A., & Cavalcante, C. A. (2015). Some insights into the effect of maintenance quality for a protection system. *IEEE Transactions on Reliability, 64*(2), 661–672.

Berrade, M. D., Scarf, P. A., Cavalcante, C. A. V., & Dwight, R. A. (2013). Imperfect inspection and replacement of a system with a defective state: A cost and reliability analysis. *Reliability Engineering & System Safety, 120*, 80–87.

Cavalcante, C. A. V., Scarf, P., Ribeiro, Y. R., Rodrigues, A. J. S., & Alotaibi, N. (2024). Planning maintenance when resources are limited: A study of periodic opportunistic replacement. *IMA Journal of Management Mathematics*, dpae015.

Cavalcante, C. A., Lopes, R. S., & Scarf, P. A. (2018). A general inspection and opportunistic replacement policy for one-component systems of variable quality. *European Journal of Operational Research, 266*(3), 911–919.

Chalabi, N., Dahane, M., Beldjilali, B., & Neki, A. (2016). Optimisation of preventive maintenance grouping strategy for multi-component series systems: Particle swarm based approach. *Computers & Industrial Engineering, 102*, 440–451.

Colledani, M., Magnanini, M. C., & Tolio, T. (2018). Impact of opportunistic maintenance on manufacturing system performance. *CIRP Annals, 67*(1), 499–502.

De Jonge, B., Teunter, R., & Tinga, T. (2017). The influence of practical factors on the benefits of condition-based maintenance over time-based maintenance. *Reliability Engineering & System Safety, 158*, 21–30.

Ding, F., & Tian, Z. (2012). Opportunistic maintenance for wind farms considering multi-level imperfect maintenance thresholds. *Renewable Energy, 45*, 175–182.

Flage, R. (2014). A delay time model with imperfect and failure-inducing inspections. *Reliability Engineering & System Safety, 124*, 1–12.

Robert, E., Bérenguer, C., Bouvard, K., Tedie, H., & Lesobre, R. (2018). A predictive approach to jointly schedule missions and maintenances for a deteriorating vehicle. In *Safety and reliability–safe societies in a changing world* (pp. 529–537). CRC Press.

Scarf, P. A., & Cavalcante, C. A. (2012). Modelling quality in replacement and inspection maintenance. *International Journal of Production Economics, 135*(1), 372–381.

Scarf, P. A., Cavalcante, C. A., Dwight, R. A., & Gordon, P. (2009). An age-based inspection and replacement policy for heterogeneous components. *IEEE Transactions on Reliability, 58*(4), 641–648.

Shafiee, M., Finkelstein, M., & Bérenguer, C. (2015). An opportunistic condition-based maintenance policy for offshore wind turbine blades subjected to degradation and environmental shocks. *Reliability Engineering & System Safety, 142*, 463–471.

Song, S., Li, Q., Felder, F. A., Wang, H., & Coit, D. W. (2018). Integrated optimization of offshore wind farm layout design and turbine opportunistic condition-based maintenance. *Computers & Industrial Engineering, 120*, 288–297.

uit het Broek, M. A., Teunter, R. H., de Jonge, B., Veldman, J., & Van Foreest, N. D. (2020). Condition-based production planning: Adjusting production rates to balance output and failure risk. *Manufacturing & Service Operations Management, 22*(4), 792–811.

Wang, Y., He, R., & Tian, Z. (2023). Opportunistic condition-based maintenance optimization for electrical distribution systems. *Reliability Engineering & System Safety, 236*, 109261.

Yuan, S., Reniers, G., Yang, M., & Bai, Y. (2023). Cost-effective maintenance of safety and security barriers in the chemical process industries via genetic algorithm. *Process Safety and Environmental Protection, 170*, 356–371.

Ascher, H., & Feingold, H. (1984). *Repairable systems reliability*. Marcel Dekker.

Wang, W. (2012). An overview of the recent advances in delay-time-based maintenance modelling. *Reliability Engineering & System Safety, 106*, 165–178.

Ross, S. M. (1996). *Stochastic processes*. John Wiley & Sons.

Building a Profitable Trading Strategy with an Intelligent Price Action Bot

C. Hema and Fausto Pedro García Márquez

1 Introduction

Online automated trading bots have become increasingly popular in recent years, especially in the cryptocurrency industry. These bots are programmed to automatically execute trades based on predetermined criteria, such as market trends and indicators, without the need for human intervention. This technology has been embraced by many traders and investors in the cryptocurrency market, as it allows them to automate their trading strategies and maximize their profits.

Due to the fact that they are not governed by any one governmental body or financial institution, cryptocurrencies have grown in popularity. There are several reasons why investors may choose to invest in cryptocurrency, one such reason is cryptocurrencies have historically experienced significant growth, and many investors have made substantial profits by investing in them. Another reason to invest in cryptocurrency is diversification. Cryptocurrency is a relatively new asset class that offers potential benefits for investors. Investing in cryptocurrency can help diversify portfolios and reduce risk. One of the main reasons to invest in cryptocurrency is the potential for high returns, as cryptocurrencies can experience rapid price increases.

Another advantage is decentralization, which means that cryptocurrency operates on a decentralized network and is not subject to government or financial institution regulation, making it more resistant to inflation and market manipulation. Additionally, cryptocurrencies use blockchain technology, a secure and transparent system

C. Hema
Department of Computer Science and Engineering, B.S. Abdur Rahman Crescent Institute of Science and Technology, Chennai, Tamil Nadu, India

F. P. García Márquez (✉)
Ingenium Research Group, Universidad Castilla-La ManchaCiudad Real, Ciudad Real, Spain
e-mail: FaustoPedro.Garcia@uclm.es

F. P. García Márquez et al. (eds.), *Outsourcing*, International Series in Operations Research & Management Science 370, https://doi.org/10.1007/978-3-031-95393-4_11

that records every transaction on the network, making it difficult for hackers to manipulate the system.

The adoption of cryptocurrency by mainstream companies and financial institutions is also growing, indicating a growing acceptance and potential for wider adoption in the future.The fact that cryptocurrencies are an extremely risky and volatile investment with no assurances of returns should be noted. Therefore, it is essential to thoroughly research and understand the risks before investing any money into cryptocurrency.

Though Manual Trading is popular it can be challenging due to several factors. Emotions play a significant role, and fear, greed, and FOMO can cloud a trader's judgment, leading to impulsive decisions and potential losses. Maintaining discipline is also crucial, and traders must adhere to their strategies and rules to avoid deviation and further losses. Time management can be an issue, as constant monitoring of the market is necessary. Furthermore, the crypto market's complexity requires a thorough understanding of technical indicators and chart patterns to make informed decisions. Volatility is another significant challenge as prices can fluctuate drastically in a short period, making it difficult to predict market movements. Security is also a concern, and traders must take extra measures to ensure the security of their digital assets, such as securing private keys, using reputable exchanges, and implementing strong passwords and two-factor authentication.

Cryptocurrency offers several advantages over traditional payment methods and investment options. Decentralization, or the lack of centralized government control over cryptocurrencies, is one of their most important advantages. This makes them less susceptible to government or financial institution regulations, and can make them a more stable investment option in countries with unstable currencies. Cryptocurrencies also provide higher security than traditional payment methods, using complex algorithms and cryptography to secure and verify transactions. Transactions are irreversible, reducing the risk of fraud or chargebacks. Cryptocurrencies also offer greater privacy and anonymity, appealing to investors concerned about government surveillance or data breaches. Additionally, compared to conventional payment methods, cryptocurrencies frequently charge lower transaction fees, making them a more affordable choice for cross-border transactions. It is also a more inclusive financial system because it is available to anyone with an Internet connection, regardless of where they are located or their financial situation. Finally, the potential for high returns has historically made cryptocurrencies an attractive investment option for many.

The demand for cryptocurrency has been steadily increasing over the years due to several factors. Mainstream adoption of cryptocurrencies as a payment method by businesses and individuals has contributed to this growth. Additionally, limited supply of cryptocurrencies, such as Bitcoin, has increased demand as people strive to acquire these digital assets before they become even more scarce. The speculative nature of cryptocurrencies and their volatility have also attracted investors hoping to make a profit as their value rises. Finally, the decentralized nature of cryptocurrencies, meaning they are not controlled by any central authority, has made them an attractive alternative to traditional financial systems for many individuals seeking greater autonomy over their finances.

The implementation of cryptocurrencies faces several barriers that hinder their wider acceptance and use. The lack of clear regulations in many countries is a significant challenge, making it difficult for businesses and individuals to use cryptocurrencies in a safe and compliant manner. Scalability is another issue, with many cryptocurrencies struggling with limited processing speed and capacity resulting in slow transaction times and high fees. Security concerns such as high-profile hacks and thefts, as well as the use of cryptocurrencies for illegal activities, can erode confidence in the cryptocurrency ecosystem. Lack of understanding among the general public also creates a barrier to adoption. Moreover, the high volatility of cryptocurrencies makes them a risky investment for businesses and individuals. Addressing these challenges is critical for wider acceptance and use of cryptocurrencies as the market continues to evolve.

2 Literature Survey

Oksanen et al. (2022) add to previous research on cryptocurrency markets by examining the consequences of online crime. The study discovers that hacking incidents lessen price discovery sourced within the hacked currency and increase price volatility and cross-cryptocurrency correlations. For regulators, policy makers, and academics working on strategies to reduce cybercrime in cryptocurrency markets, these findings have significant ramifications.

Corbet et al. (2019b) investigate the impact of cybercriminal activity on cryptocurrency markets. The authors find that hacking events increase price volatility and cross-cryptocurrency correlations, and reduce price discovery. They emphasize the need to address these challenges to build trust in cryptocurrencies and exchanges.

Gradojevic et al. (2021) use technical analysis and nonlinear models to predict Bitcoin returns at hourly and daily frequencies. They find that while nonlinear forecasting models and technical analysis become statistically significant on a daily time horizon, Bitcoin prices are only marginally efficient at the hourly frequency. They conclude that the random forest model is the best at predicting Bitcoin and that, recently, trend-following has given way to excessive momentum and sentiment in the world of bitcoin investing.

Corbet et al. (2019a) analyze the effectiveness of technical trading principles, particularly moving average and trading range break-out techniques, in the high-frequency Bitcoin market. The outcomes point to the rule of the variable-length moving average as having the best performance, with buy signals yielding more returns versus buy signals. The literature review highlights previous research on cryptocurrency markets, including their pricing efficiency, market behavior, and relationship with other asset classes.

Rehman et al. (2020) discuss the issues with trust in the cryptocurrency ecosystem, with a thorough taxonomy of important aspects of trust and a comparison of the top 10 cryptocurrencies. It emphasizes the need for serious work to create a cryptocurrency ecosystem that is completely reliable. The article also briefly introduces Bitcoin as the first cryptocurrency and its evolution in the market.

Mirtaheri et al. (2021) discuss the hype surrounding cryptocurrencies has led to increased fraud, including pump and dump schemes, on social media platforms. A computational approach can be used to identify and predict pump attempts, and there has been an enormous rise in bot activity during these attempts. The allure of cryptocurrencies has also led to significant price swings and the emergence of thousands of smaller cryptocurrencies, making them prime targets for manipulation.

Cacique and Pereira (2020) propose a model called Pattern Searcher for automated trading in the stock market based on historical data using unsupervised learning and genetic algorithms. The model generated profitable trading platforms and portfolios that outperform benchmarks on the Brazilian stock market.

Frischlich et al. (2020) found that a market for social bots and infrastructure components exists on both the Clearnet and Darknet, making them easily accessible and cheap for lay users. The authors tells us that the use of social bots for political manipulation has been widely speculated since Brexit and the 2016 US election. Social bots are part of a larger infrastructure, including fake accounts and hosting services.

Daian et al. (2020) provide a literature survey of previous work on blockchain security, including research on smart contract vulnerabilities, consensus mechanisms, and transaction fees. They also discuss previous research on high-frequency trading and market manipulation in traditional financial markets. The article presents original research on the behavior of bots, including a study of their profit-making strategies. Overall, the article provides a comprehensive overview of the current state of blockchain security research and highlights the challenges posed by the evolving landscape of blockchain-based financial markets.

Basaka et al. (2019) proposed using two well-liked algorithms—random forests and gradient boosted decision trees—an experimental framework is created for the classification problem of predicting the direction of stock prices. These methods aim to capture the complex relationships and patterns in historical stock market data to make accurate predictions. While traditional methods focus on predicting stock prices, the problem is presented as a direction-predicting exercise in the current work, which forecasts whether the stock price will rise or fall in relation to the price that was in effect n days earlier. These algorithms use ensembles of decision trees to make accurate predictions. The use of technical indicators as features, which have been demonstrated to have high accuracy for medium- to long-term prediction of stock price direction, is novel in this work.

Makarova and Schoar (2020) present a systematic evaluation of cryptocurrency market efficiency and trading, focusing on the occurrence and persistence of arbitrage opportunities across exchanges. The authors Identify significant and recurring variations in Bitcoin price across exchanges using tick data from 34 exchanges across 19 countries, which often persist for several hours or even days. The fact that arbitrage spreads open and close simultaneously across national borders further demonstrates the strong co-movement in price variances between nations.

Delfabbro et al. (2021) aimed to investigate whether there is a frequency of cryptocurrency trading and gambling, including problem gambling, are related. The authors cite several studies that support the argument that day trading and other speculative pursuits may resemble gambling more. For instance, discovered that day traders had higher odds of partaking in similar gambling activities, like sports betting and poker, as well as higher odds of having gambled in general. They also shared demographic characteristics, such as being male, younger, and having higher disposable incomes.

Pelster et al. (2019) note that Increasing amounts of attention have been paid to cryptocurrencies in both academic and financial press, with criticisms that they lack fundamental value and are a type of speculation that resembles gambling, while defenders argue that they represent a new asset class that allows for increased portfolio diversification. Prior research has focused on market-level information and Bitcoin, while other cryptocurrencies have only recently been considered. The authors extend prior research by focusing on the behavior of individual traders who buy and sell cryptocurrencies, building on prior research that examined cryptocurrency traders using search and brokerage data.

Ibrahim et al. (2020): This paper aims to support traders in the best decisions by developing a model that can predict the future 5-min time frame's price movement direction. This Up/Down binary-classification problem has been subjected to testing using various machine-learning models. In this study, two cutting-edge methods for forecasting the movement of bitcoin are compared: random guessing and a momentum-based approach. ARIMA (Autoregressive Integrated Moving Average), Prophet (by Facebook), Random Forest, Random Forest Lagged-Auto-Regression, and Multi-Layer Perceptron (MLP) Neural Networks are a few of the models that were tested.

Chen et al. (2019) focused on predicting Bitcoin prices using machine learning techniques, with a focus on the viability of using various modelling techniques on samples with various data structures and dimensional characteristics. The authors use basic trading attributes for the 5-min period along with high-dimensional features like property and network, trade and market, attention and gold spot price to estimate the daily price of bitcoin. Machine learning models outperform statistical approaches in terms of accuracy when used to forecast prices for the 5-min interval.

3 Materials and Methods

3.1 Problem Definition

The cryptocurrency market is highly volatile, and prices can fluctuate rapidly and unpredictably, making it challenging to develop reliable trading strategies.

Automated trading bots can evaluate market data, spot trading opportunities, and place trades in accordance with predetermined strategies, doing the work of human traders who must act quickly in a volatile market.

3.2 Existing Work

Investors, individuals or institutions typically make trades manually based on their analysis of the fundamental factors underlying an asset's value. They tend to hold onto their investments for the long term and sell them when they've reached a target return on investment. However, when there's a lot of volatility in the market, inexperienced or retail investors can be swayed by their emotions, making risk management and ongoing monitoring important. Investors who focus solely on fundamental analysis may miss out on seasonal volatility. It's crucial to have a good understanding of the existing trading system in order to make informed decisions.

3.3 Limitations

Crypto trading can be challenging due to various factors. Emotions such as fear, greed, and FOMO can cloud a trader's judgment and lead to impulsive decisions, resulting in losses. Traders need to have discipline and stick to their strategies, but lack of discipline can lead to deviation from their rules, leading to losses. Crypto trading can also be time-consuming, requiring traders to keep a constant eye on the market, which can be challenging if they have other responsibilities. Furthermore, the crypto market is complex, requiring traders to have a good understanding of technical indicators and chart patterns to make informed decisions. Cryptocurrencies are also notoriously volatile, and their prices can fluctuate wildly in a short period, making it difficult to predict market movements and leading to unexpected losses. Therefore, traders need to be aware of these challenges and develop a solid trading plan to navigate the market successfully.

3.4 Proposed System

The proposed system is an automated cryptotrading system that utilizes various tools and technologies to execute trades on the Binance exchange. One of the main components of the system is Telegram, a popular messaging app that allows users to communicate and interact with bots. The system uses Telegram to receive signals and execute trades automatically on behalf of the user.

Additionally, the system uses Binance, a well-known cryptocurrency exchange with a large selection of trading pairs and features. By connecting to the Binance

API, the system can access real-time market data and execute trades based on predetermined criteria.

Another key technology used in the system is Docker Compose. Using Docker Compose, users can create and execute multi-container Docker applications. The system can be easily deployed and managed across various environments by using Docker Compose, which increases its scalability and resilience.

The system utilizes several technical indicators, including RSI (Relative Strength Index) and Bollinger Bands, to analyze market trends and make informed trading decisions. A momentum indicator called the RSI compares an asset's average gains to losses over a given time period to determine how strong the asset is. Bollinger Bands, on the other hand, are a type of volatility indicator that measure the standard deviation of price movements over a certain time period.

The Relative Strength Index (RSI) and Bollinger Bands are two popular technical indicators that traders use in crypto currency trading to identify potential buy and sell opportunities. Here's how a strategy based on these indicators might work.

By using Bollinger Bands the trader would start by plotting two bands around the price chart of a particular cryptocurrency, with one band above and one below the current price. These bands are usually two standard deviations away from the price of the cryptocurrency's 20-day moving average. The price is regarded as overbought when it approaches the upper band, and oversold when it approaches the lower band.

By using RSI the trader would then look at the RSI indicator, which measures the strength of a cryptocurrency's price action over a specific period, typically 14 days. The Relative Strength Index (RSI) ranges from 0 to 100; values above 70 indicate overbought conditions and below 30 indicate oversold ones.

By using the above indicators a strategy is developed that makes automated trading. The automated trading bot will use these indicators to make trading decisions based on predefined rules and parameters. For example, the bot may be programmed to buy a certain crypto asset when the RSI falls below 30 and the price touches the lower Bollinger Band. Conversely, the bot may be programmed to sell the asset when the RSI rises above 70 and the price touches the upper Bollinger Band.

The use of an automated trading bot allows traders to overcome the emotional and discipline challenges associated with manual trading. The bot can make trading decisions based on objective indicators and predefined rules, without being influenced by fear, greed, or FOMO. Additionally, the automated trading bot can monitor the market 24/7, enabling investors to benefit from potential opportunities that might emerge outside of regular trading hours. This can be especially helpful for traders with other commitments or those who cannot monitor the market constantly.

3.5 Advantages

Automated strategy-based crypto trading bots offer several advantages over manual trading. They can operate 24/7 without human intervention, allowing them to take advantage of market opportunities even when the trader is not available. These bots can execute trades at a much faster rate than human traders, providing speed and efficiency that can help to take advantage of market movements. Additionally, automated trading bots can be programmed with a predefined set of rules and parameters, reducing the impact of emotions on trading decisions. This can help to avoid impulsive trades and improve consistency in trading strategy. Overall, automated strategy-based crypto trading bots can help traders to increase efficiency, reduce emotional decision-making, and potentially improve profitability.

4 Working of Bot

The system would monitor the price of the cryptocurrency asset and calculate the RSI and Bollinger Bands indicators in real-time.

To determine whether the market is overbought or oversold, the system would use the RSI indicator. When the RSI value exceeds a certain threshold (e.g., 70 for overbought), the system would interpret this as a signal to sell the asset, and when the RSI value falls below a certain threshold (e.g., 30 for oversold), the system would interpret this as a signal to buy the asset.

The system would use the Bollinger Bands indicator to identify potential trend reversals. When price of the asset touches the upper Bollinger Band, the system would interpret this as a signal to sell the asset, and when the price touches the lower Bollinger Band, the system would interpret this as a signal to buy the asset.

The system would execute trades automatically based on these signals, using predefined rules for trade sizing and risk management.

The system would continue to monitor the market and adjust its trading decisions based on new signals from the RSI and Bollinger Bands indicators.

The system undergoes backtesting to evaluate its performance and profitability using historical data. This allows the bot to fine-tune its trading strategies and improve its accuracy.

4.1 Architecture Diagram

Figure 1 (Flow chart) illustrating a trading bot system integrated with Binance, server, and Telegram UI. The process begins with an API request to Binance, receiving a JSON response. The server runs a live market fetching script, which interacts with a configuration database containing Telegram tokens, exchange API keys, and trade type information. Price data is used for backtesting with historical data and stored in SQLiteDB. The analysis of trades is conducted, and results are communicated via Telegram and Bash. Strategies include Relative Strength and Bollinger.

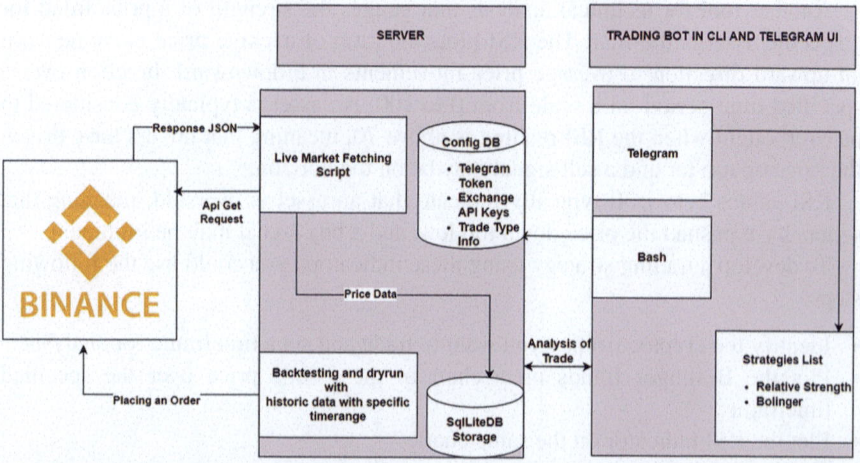

Fig. 1 Architecture diagram of the trading bot

To set up a trading bot with Binance, you need to follow these steps. Firstly, set up a Docker environment by downloading Docker from the Docker website and verifying it through the terminal. Secondly, create a Binance account by going to the Binance website, entering your email address, creating a strong password, agreeing to the terms of use and privacy policy, verifying your account, and logging in. Then, create API keys in the Binance account by going to the "API Management" section, naming the key, selecting the permissions, and getting a public and secret key. Add the API key and secret key to the config file to connect the Binance account to the bot. Download the required historical data for backtesting by specifying the time range. Lastly, use the Bot Father on Telegram to create and customize your bot by assigning it a name, username, and profile picture. Once you've set up all of these components, you can start testing and deploying your trading bot.

4.2 Developing Strategy

Developing a trading strategy using Bollinger Bands and Relative Strength Index (RSI) can be a useful approach for cryptocurrency trading. A technical analysis technique called Bollinger Bands determines the volatility of a certain asset, in this case, a cryptocurrency. They are made up of three lines, with the center band representing a moving average of the asset's rise over a certain time period and the upper and lower bands being drawn at specific distances from the moving average. When the price reaches the upper or lower band, which might signify a probable reversal in price direction, Bollinger Bands can help detect potential buy or sell signals.

Another tool for technical analysis that gauges the strength of a price trend for a specific asset is the RSI. The RSI plots the ratio of average price movements in an upward direction to average price movements in a downward direction over a specified time period on a scale from 0 to 100. An asset is typically considered to be overbought when the RSI reading is above 70, meaning that buyers have driven the price up too far and a sell signal may be on the horizon.

RSI values below 30 typically indicate that an asset is oversold, meaning that sellers have pushed the price down too low, and a buy signal may be imminent.

To develop a trading strategy using these indicators, you could use the following steps:

- Identify the cryptocurrency you want to trade and set a timeframe for analysis.
- Plot the Bollinger Bands on a chart of the asset's price over the specified timeframe.
- Plot the RSI indicator on the same chart.
- Look for instances where the price touches or crosses the upper or lower Bollinger Bands, indicating potential reversal points.
- To see if the potential reversal is confirmed, check the RSI value. The asset may be overbought and a sell signal may be on the horizon if the RSI is over 70 when the price reaches the upper Bollinger Band. The asset may be oversold and a buy signal may be approaching if the RSI is below 30 when the price reaches the lower Bollinger Band, on the other hand.
- Use these signals to place buy or sell orders, depending on your trading strategy and risk tolerance.

4.3 Backtesting

Backtesting is a critical component of any automated cryptocurrency trading strategy. It involves testing the effectiveness of the strategy on historical data to determine its potential profitability and accuracy. Backtesting is important because it allows traders to evaluate their strategies and make adjustments before committing real money to trades. Automated cryptocurrency trading strategies are based on mathematical algorithms and historical data, which are used to identify patterns and make trades. Backtesting helps traders to determine whether their strategies are profitable and to what extent. By analyzing historical data, traders can see how their strategies would have performed in the past, and can adjust their strategies to account for changing market conditions.

The ability to test trading strategies without taking any risks is one of the advantages of backtesting. Instead of risking real money, traders can use historical data to simulate trades and analyze the results. This helps them to identify weaknesses in their strategies and make changes before committing real money to trades. Figure 2 (Table) displaying trading statistics. The "Enter Tag Stats" section

ENTER TAG STATS

TAG	Entries	Avg Profit %	Cum Profit %	Tot Profit USDT	Tot Profit %	Avg Duration	Win Draw Loss Win%
TOTAL	170	0.82	139.36	1130.835	11.31	1 day, 19:09:00	118 0 52 69.4

EXIT REASON STATS

Exit Reason	Exits	Win Draws Loss Win%	Avg Profit %	Cum Profit %	Tot Profit USDT	Tot Profit %
exit_signal	126	113 0 13 89.7	4.02	507.12	4401.75	50.71
stop_loss	36	0 0 36 0	-10.17	-366.22	-3255.55	-36.62
force_exit	8	5 0 3 62.5	-0.19	-1.54	-15.365	-0.15

Fig. 2 Result of backtesting indicating the profit

includes total entries of 170, average profit of 0.82%, cumulative profit of 139.36%, total profit of 1138.835 USDT, total profit percentage of 11.31%, average duration of 1 day and 19 hours, with 118 wins, 52 draws, and a win percentage of 69.4%. The "Exit Reason Stats" section shows exit reasons: "exit_signal" with 126 exits and 89.7% win rate, "stop_loss" with 36 exits and 0% win rate, and "force_exit" with 8 exits and 62.5% win rate. It includes average profit percentages, cumulative profits, total profits in USDT, and total profit percentages for each exit reason.

4.4 *Visualization*

Visualization is an important aspect of an automated cryptocurrency trading strategy. In order to understand and analyze market data, traders use charts, graphs, and other visual aids. With the aid of visualization, traders can quickly spot trends and patterns in the data and decide when to buy or sell cryptocurrencies with knowledge. Figure 3 (Chart) showing ETC/USDT price trends from July 4 to August 29, 2021. The main graph displays price fluctuations with markers for trade entries, exist, and profit/loss points. A volume bar chart is below, indicating trading activity. An RSI line graph at the bottom highlights overbought and oversold conditions. The legend includes symbols for oversold, overbought, RSI, volume exit loss, exit profit, trade entry, middle band, Bollinger Band, exit long, entry long, and price. Figure 4 (Screenshot) of a trading bot interface showing trade details. The bot reports no closed trades with a total loss of -8.82 USDT, equating to -0.24% ROI. The bot started on April 12, 2023, with four trades executed. A section details an exit from a CFX/USDT trade on Binance, showing an unrealized profit of -0.84% and a loss of -7.58 USDT. The trade direction was long, with an amount of 2314 units. The open rate was 0.3889, and the exit rate was 0.3864, lasting 21.6 minutes. The interface includes a refresh button and timestamps.

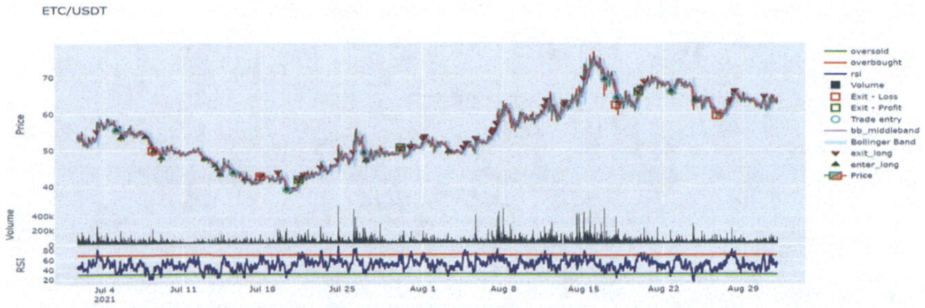

Fig. 3 Visualization of the backtested results using a candlestick plot

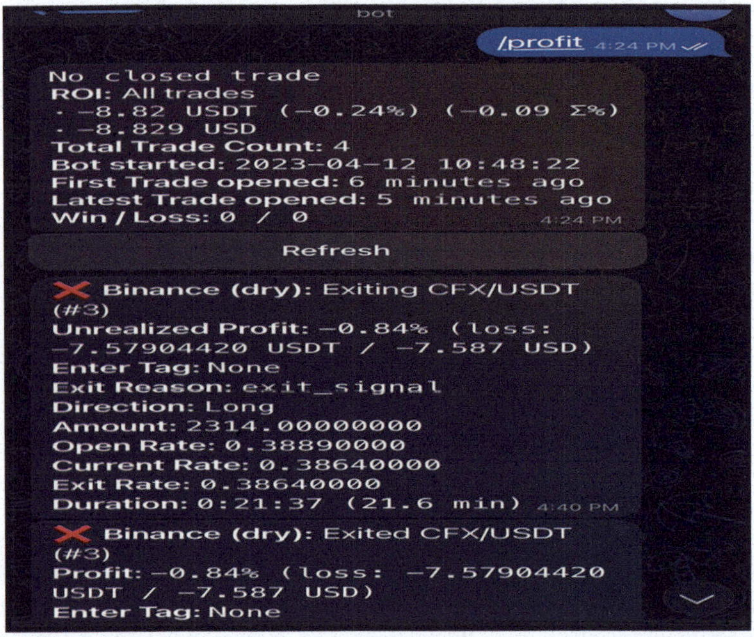

Fig. 4 Profits of the trade on telegram

5 Conclusion

By using the Bollinger Bands and Relative Strength Index indicators to create a trading strategy, the bot can make informed trading decisions based on market trends, potentially resulting in better trading outcomes. The completion of back-testing provides a way to evaluate the bot's performance under different market conditions, giving insight into its effectiveness. Additionally, data plotting can help visualize trends and patterns, which can aid in decision-making for future trades.

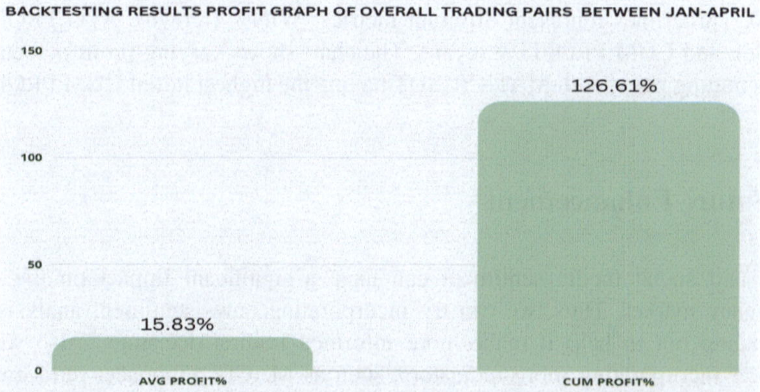

Fig. 5 Backtesting results graph of overall trading pairs between Jan and April 2023

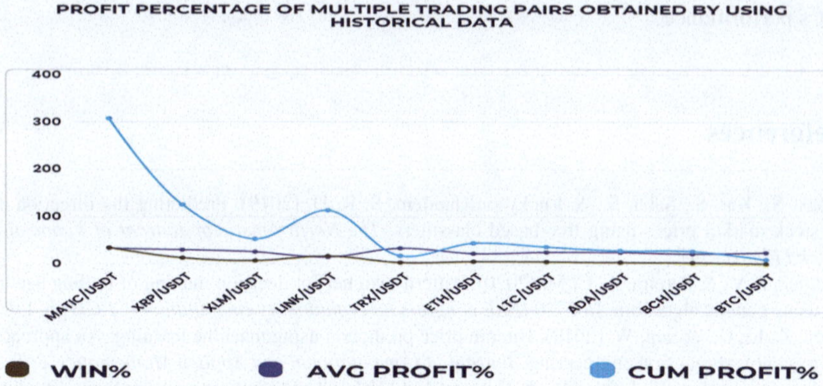

Fig. 6 Profit percentage of multiple trading pairs obtained by using historical data

Overall, the project demonstrates a strong understanding of technical analysis and the use of technology to improve trading outcomes. Figure 5 (Bar chart) titled "Backtesting results profit graph of overall trading pairs between Jan-April." It compares average profit percentage and cumulative profit percentage. The average profit is 15.83%, while the cumulative profit is 126.61%. The chart uses a green color scheme. The results were obtained using dry run. Dry runs are practice or simulation sessions used by traders or investors to test their systems or strategies without actually placing real trades or real money at risk. It is a way to evaluate a trading strategy or system's viability and effectiveness without suffering any financial losses.

Figure 6 (Line chart) titled "Profit percentage of multiple trading pairs obtained by using historical data." The x-axis lists trading pairs: MATIC/USDT, XRP/USDT, XLM/USDT, LINK/USDT, TRX/USDT, ETH/USDT, LTC/USDT, ADA/USDT,

BCH/USDT, BTC/USDT. The y-axis represents profit percentage, ranging from 0 to 400. Three lines represent different metrics: WIN% (brown), AVG PROFIT% (purple), and CUM PROFIT% (cyan). The chart shows varying profit percentages across trading pairs, with MATIC/USDT having the highest initial CUM PROFIT%

6 Future Enhancement

News and social media sentiment can have a significant impact on the cryptocurrency market. Thus, we can try incorporating news sentiment analysis into the trading bot to help it make more informed trading decisions. Also we can consider incorporating more indicators, such as MACD, Fibonacci retracements, and Stochastic Oscillators, to experiment with different combinations for the trading strategy. We can also try to integrate machine learning algorithms, like reinforcement learning or neural networks, to continuously improve the trading bot's performance.

References

Basak, S., Kar, S., Saha, S., & LuckysonKhaidem, S. R. D. (2019). Predicting the direction of stock market prices using tree-based classifiers. *The North American Journal of Economics and Finance, 47.*

Cacique, F. V., & Pereira, A. C. M. (2020). Pattern searcher for decision making of trading agents using genetic algorithm. In *2020 IEEE congress on evolutionary computation (CEC)* (pp. 1–8).

Chen, Z., Li, C., & Sun, W. (2019). Bitcoin price prediction using machine learning: An approach to sample dimension engineering. *Journal of Computational and Applied Mathematics, 365.*

Corbet, S., Eraslan, V., Lucey, B., & Sensoy, A. (2019a). The effectiveness of technical trading rules in cryptocurrency markets. *Finance Research Letters, 31.*

Corbet, S., Cumming, D. J., Lucey, B. M., Peat, M., & Vigne, S. A. (2019b). The destabilising effects of cryptocurrency cybercriminality. *Economics Letters, 191.*

Daian, P., et al. (2020). Flash boys 2.0: Frontrunning in decentralized exchanges, miner extractable value, and consensus instability. In *2020 IEEE symposium on security and privacy (SP)* (pp. 910–927).

Delfabbro, P., King, D., Williams, J., & Georgiou, N. (2021). Cryptocurrency trading, gambling and problem gambling. *Addictive Behaviors, 122.*

Frischlich, L., Mede, N. G., & Quandt, T. (2020). The Markets of Manipulation: The trading of social bots on Clearnet and Darknet markets. *Disinformation in Open Online Media, 12021.*

Gradojevic, N., Kukolj, D., Adcock, R., & Djakovic, V. (2021). Forecasting bitcoin with technical analysis: A not-so-random forest? *International Journal of Forecasting, 39.*

Ibrahim, A., Kashef, R., & Corrigan, L. (2020). Predicting market movement direction for bitcoin: A comparison of time series modeling methods. *Computers & Electrical Engineering, Volume, 89.*

Makarov, I., & Schoar, A. (2020). Trading and arbitrage in cryptocurrency markets. *Journal of Financial Economics, 135.*

Mirtaheri, M., Abu-El-Haija, S., Morstatter, F., Steeg, G. V., & Galstyan, A. (2021). Identifying and Analyzing cryptocurrency manipulations in social media. *IEEE Transactions on Computational Social Systems, 8*(3), 607–617.

Oksanen, A., Mantere, E., Vuorinen, I., Savolainen, I. (2022). Gambling and online trading: Emerging risks of real-time stock and cryptocurrency trading platforms, *Public Health 205.*

Pelster, M., Breitmayer, B., & Hasso, T. (2019). Are cryptocurrency traders pioneers or just risk-seekers? Evidence from brokerage accounts. *Economics Letters, 182.*

ur Rehman, M. H., Salah, K., Damiani, E., & Svetinovic, D. (2020). Trust in Blockchain Cryptocurrency Ecosystem. *IEEE Transactions on Engineering Management*, 1–17.

The manufacturer's authorised representative in the EU is Springer Nature Customer Service Centre GmbH, Europaplatz 3, 69115 Heidelberg, Germany. If you have any concerns regarding our products, please contact ProductSafety@springernature.com

Printed and bound by CPI Group (UK) Ltd, Croydon, CR0 4YY
30/09/2026
02225590-0006